The WHY Intersection

by

Roger Johnson

The principal characters in this novel are fictitious, i.e., the residents of and visitors to Why. Major political figures are real as is the strike that occurred at the copper mines in Arizona in the 1980s..

All rights reserved.

ISBN   979-8-9872510-3-4

Email: rogerj47@gmail.com
Website: Roger-Johnson.com

In Memoriam

Dr. Gail S. Rowe

University of Northern Colorado, History Department
The most influential teacher in my life.
Dr. Rowe taught me to revere people who try to do good in spite of their often-enormous flaws.

Acknowledgements

Julie Christensen and **Jay Johnson** for their editorial support.

Joe DesGeorges for formatting and cover design help on this and my previous novels.

Cover photograph by the author.

Books in Print

Historical Fiction

Laments for the Dead
Layers of Darkness
America's Soul
Refugees Among the Lines
The Why Intersection

Girls'/Women's Basketball Novels (Cheetah Basketball Series)

On Point
Gifts: The Return
Coach Izzy
Hoops and Seeds: A Pause in the Harvest

The WHY INTERSECTION

by
Roger Johnson

IngramSpark

2024

"We all sort of chose to live here in Why—except Cocker who was commanded here by God. Did God send you?"

Waddell Smithfield

"I'll stay until the wind changes."

P.L. Travers

Some readers may find *The Why Intersection* as the sequel to *Laments for the Dead*. Others might find it as the prequel to *Hoops and Seeds*. In one old man's head, these characters are all bumping into one another.

Roger Johnson

PLACES TO BEGIN

LONG BEFORE THE SUMMER OF 1986

A screen door bangs shut somewhere on the block, in a rural neighborhood out of time. Dog barks and children's shrieks pierce the summer air at twilight, an evanescent time of day that blurs the era, transcending the moment. It could be the Depression or the fifties or the eighties in Michigan, Colorado, or Arizona. Sprites and elves from previous times play hide and seek with the current generation. A girl—she can't be more than six or seven—sits on a porch swing bumped up to her grandfather listening to his tales. He is a wonderful storyteller with a magical voice, a voice that could be used to narrate Disney movies, Wild Kingdom, or Victory at Sea. Her lanky legs, which dangle from the swing, are long enough to touch the porch floor if she extends her bare toes.

"In my latest dream, my little treasure . . ."

The girl hears her grandfather's stories as much through her chest as through her ears. Mature and perceptive beyond her young age, she understands that these stories are parables, a word she learned in church, and that Grampa loves her beyond this day. They share secrets on his too short visits and promise to stay connected for as long as they live.

". . . you are the heroine. You meet a wounded soldier coming home from war. He returns carrying a heavy load, and you are there for him."

"I'm not big enough to carry a pack, Grampa."

"Well, in my dream you are all grown up, a woman of strength and beauty." Grampa Abbott smiles, leans in, and hugs his granddaughter.

"I'm beautiful in all your stories, Grampa. Is the soldier Johnny Malcolm? He's always playing soldiers."

"No, darling. It's none of the neighborhood boys or anyone you know now. He will be a stranger. The wind will bring him to you, just as it does in all fairy tales."

Years later, when she visits Grampa Abbott in Colorado, he will inspire her to investigate, to take risks, to write, and he will continue to tell her his stories even as he slips into dementia. When he dies, she will not attend his funeral with the rest of her family, but instead will hike into his mountains where his soul resides to remember him and vow to keep her promise to fulfill his stories.

∾

Dr. Waddell Smithfield knows every vacuum tube ever installed in the computer. He helped design and build *Whirlwind* for the military as part of the U.S. air defense system to protect America from a Soviet nuclear attack. It did not start out to be what it ended as, much like people's lives. They begin along one trail and take several turns before they find their true paths. He and his MIT colleagues started the project after World War II in 1945 for the Navy to help train pilots, but it became the vital component for America's safety in the early years of the Cold War. NORAD will base all its defense system decisions on his computer. Dr. Smithfield is proud of it, but he is also troubled. *Whirlwind* is complex, too complex for certainty. *Whirlwind* does not allow for human corrections in emergency situations, and those situations will arise. He knows, too, there is no going back; billions of dollars are being spent, and the politicians and generals will want a return on this investment. Waddell understands, but he also understands the system is... leaky. It needs constant monitoring. President Eisenhower also understands, and he will warn America about the dangers of a military/industrial complex, but his warning will mostly fall on deaf ears.

Waddell is not the first scientist with concerns about the project to be let go, but he is the first to finagle a financial settlement beyond his pension, enough to be comfortable for the rest of his life. There are concessions. He must keep the secret of *Whirlwind*, of course, but he knows eventually the Soviets will steal information and build their own, but one even more porous. What most concerns Waddell is that somewhere in the decades ahead, a young American Air Force or Navy officer might be put into an untenable situation, one not of his own choosing, and hundreds of people could die. Or thousands. The world will stand at the precipice.

Waddell Smithfield will also be monitored in some way or another for the rest of his life; he won't be able to hide, but he can accept this. He'll fade into the plains or mountains or desert somewhere where the Government won't care. He'll be off the grid to a place where little happens, left alone to study the stars, learn to play golf, and grow old. Relocation will be his new life.

∽

    Around 1970 the Lord directed Martin Lee Wagner to Why, Arizona, a town of around a hundred mostly invisible residents located on the western edge of an Indian reservation in the middle of the Sonoran Desert. In the middle of nowhere. The bus dropped him off in front of a rundown, adobe depot that featured a small waiting room and toilet. Schedules were written on a chalkboard. The ticket agent/custodian told him he might be able to rent one of the empty houses just down the dirt road if he needed a place to stay. He noticed a shuttered vegetable warehouse located at the junction of Arizona highways 85 and 86. There was a copper mine a few miles to the north in Ajo, a company town. Mexico was about 30 miles south. Martin Lee walked across the highway to the warehouse, which was locked, but since the Lord had given it to him, he broke the lock and set up house. He had work to do.

    He was to transform the abandoned warehouse into a church. His congregation would not be Pentecostals, but the Lord told Martin Lee not to worry about that. They would worship another way. As their minister he was to nurture them, provide them with the things Jesus provided his flock. He might have to minister in ways unfamiliar to him. Still, the Lord directed him. The warehouse would need alterations of course, but when Martin Lee arrived in Why, he found piles of wood and building scraps inside the warehouse as well as dozens of old folding chairs. He had laughed; he was no carpenter, he was a musician and minister, but if the Lord directed him to remodel the warehouse, he would do that. Erect a simple cross at the north end of the warehouse, build an interior passageway from the back of the building to the front, only two feet wide, and most importantly, construct a simple altar and pulpit. He didn't ask who owned the warehouse, and nobody asked him for rent or utility payments. Inside, a small room, presumably the original office, served as his temporary bedroom. He wouldn't need to rent.

Sustained by his military pension, he set out to make the warehouse into a house of worship. Martin Lee's sanctuary.

One day you're working, bringing home a paycheck, and the next day, you're walking a picket line with your union buddies with the assurance that the strike will end quickly, and life will return to normal. If your family is steeped in mining and The Union, then your whole family "goes on strike and onto a diet of beans and tortillas and honors your father." In company towns, the whole community goes on strike, but not everyone supports The Union. Relationships can get testy. Bar fights are less frequently about women and more about crossing the picket lines—and more violent.

The tall miner walks a precarious line. The Union isn't ingrained in his DNA; he married into it when he arrived in Arizona and began working at a copper mine near Clifton, on the eastern side of Arizona, to work at the Morenci mine. Still, he joined, and it worked out fine. Three years, a wife, and a steady income. Yet, he is an outsider. He isn't Chicano and he doesn't speak Spanish fluently. Frank, not Francisco or Paco. Back in Kansas he worked in law enforcement, albeit as a deputy. So, when The Strike occurs, he initially walks out with his coworkers, but he's uncomfortable and broke—and hungry. A month into The Strike, without consulting his wife, he crosses the picket line and scabs. The next day when he returns after working his shift, his wife and her family have locked him out of his house, his old sedan has been keyed, and his coworkers want to fight him—everywhere. Without notifying the new foreman or his family, he moves on, west towards California, just another Phelps Dodge miner looking for any job anywhere, desperate for a paycheck. The heaviest thing in Frank's suitcase is anger.

SPRING 1986

The elements devour him, the darkness more than the cold. His planning and practice have not prepared him for this. His body shivers as he lies against the ropes. He lifts his hand to his face, feels his forehead with his fingers to be sure, and then backs them off an inch in a vain attempt to see movement. Only gravity gives him any sense of bearing. He touches his eyes to confirm they are open. He blinks and feels his lashes flutter against his fingertips. He knows about rods and cones, the photoreceptors in his eyes, about night vision and the five-to-seven-minute gap before one's eyes adapt. But there will be no adjustment for now. He is a ghost, the shell of a dead man who will exist along the shadowy, undefined edges. The muffled shouts from above cease; the only sounds now come from water drops and the ringing in his ears.

His leap was risky, a long shot really, but a chance, a chance to end one life and begin a new one. He feels for the ribbons on the netting, indicators that will guide him off this spider's web and onto solid ground, into a drift that will take him far from the original shaft. First, he must gather up these ropes, like a spider deconstructing his web. He is counting on the authorities to be fearful of the depths and dangers of a hundred-year-old mine, hoping they will reach the obvious conclusion, that no one could survive the gunshot and subsequent fall. Make them believe he fell even further into the shaft, to depths of certain death. Months of preparation for this single act, to clear a path away from the staging area and give him one last opportunity. At the very least, it will buy him some time even though extra time is not his primary goal.

He knows small segments of the Bible. Hell is darkness and fire; so much for the bitter cold lasting. Is this his sentence for suicide? Maybe this net truly is a spider's web. What if his future existence is utter blackness, a world devoid of light? He has been in the belly of the whale before, at ocean depths unthinkable in previous times, for months on end, never seeing the sun or the stars. Jonah spent three days in his big fish, running from God. Jonah couldn't escape, but this man isn't running from God; he's running from the authorities and the little men who enforce those ultimate decrees . . . and from his former self. This great darkness is his temporary protection. But first he must survive this mine and the good man at the staging area who tried to help. That man was unexpected . . . as was the old man in town.

He finds the first ribbon, lets his hands follow the web to the second and third and fourth, pulling his body along behind his hands. Even though he has practiced this maneuver, it is much more difficult in complete blackness. He must be that spider that responds by instinct. At the edge of the web, his hands find dirt. One foot beyond is a handhold. Like an arachnid he pulls himself off the web and crawls onto solid ground. He extends his arm to the wall of the drift and feels for the lines to release the web which will allow him to collect it, leaving no trace for investigators to discover that his fall stopped here. Let them think his body lies another two hundred feet below. Or deeper. The good man at the top will investigate the shaft, will try to see into its depths, but the beam from his flashlight is weak, and the man will blame himself that he didn't do more.

His neck is wet. Sticky. The air is completely still.

He stuffs the web into a pack and slings it over his shoulder; just one more act to accomplish in this blackness, a blind man in a closet at night. Still guiding himself with his hands along the wall, he slides deeper into the drift. He finds the rope that will release the rocks to cover this drift opening. If the man above hears this, he will assume the fall caused a secondary reaction, further proof of a tragic end. He unwinds a rope from a timber releasing three dozen large rocks from a canvas on the drift's ceiling. The dust is suffocating, something he did not plan for. He spins in the dark and stumbles, crashing into a timber and falling to the ground. He now notices the tremendous ringing in his ears. The gunshot.

He lies motionless for several minutes trying to collect his thoughts. Despite the blood, there is little pain. He realizes the dust covering him will also cover footprints on the drift on the other side of the rock pile, concealing evidence of his plan to investigators. He pushes himself into a sitting position, reaches into his backpack, and finds the second, brighter flashlight. He does not shine it back on the rock pile for fear there might still be a tiny opening visible to the man above, but the reflection of the beam shows him his plan has thus far been successful. He unscrews a canteen and drinks deeply. He puts on leather gloves and stands. The dust has settled. He feared all of this could be for naught if the air in the mine was bad, but so far it has not killed him. He smiles. So far. He slips a gas mask over his face, collects his web and the canvas, takes a deep breath, and starts walking.

Thirty-five minutes later, he comes to an adit, an opening not visible to the untrained eye, sealed 70 years ago, this one far from the mine entrance. The adit has partially collapsed, and he crawls the last five yards. He waits until twilight to emerge so as not to be seen by a passerby, unlikely as that might be. From darkness into dimness. Not much, but a little lighter. He removes his mask, drinks from the canteen, and splashes water on his face. He senses the movement of air, a slight breeze. In this dim light, he has the look of a man who has lost something of great value. He walks some more, down a narrow trail to an abandoned campground where he recovers a hidden pack with a tent and a meal. Just a solitary hiker exploring the Colorado Trail. The summer night is warm, no need for the tent. He lays it on the ground, puts a foam pad on top, and covers it with his bag. There is no moon, but the stars are spectacular. He does not have the energy to reflect. The blood on his neck has dried. This has been a difficult day, and he falls asleep quickly.

Daybreak. He is awakened with a start by sounds just beyond the tree line. Seven elk have moved to within 50 feet of him, seemingly aware of his presence but not afraid. He pivots slowly on his butt to watch. Stately animals; not beasts to him. A good omen. Elk for Elkington, except Elkington is the dead man. He died in a previous life, in that mine shaft. After a few minutes, he stands and repacks his gear. His hike this morning will be longer; maybe three hours to another campground at the end of a dirt road where he parked an old car earlier. Hoisting his pack onto his back, he looks back, for the last time he hopes, hoping to heal the wound of death. A new man—maybe—but with a secret to deal with.

∽

Just minutes after scattering the soil of his passenger, a Catholic priest slows his rusty station wagon to pick up a hitchhiker. The Painted Desert in northern Arizona, millions of years in the making, at this time the result of violent forces that transformed a pine forest into stone wood and a badland of colors: reds, oranges, lavenders, and pinks. Volcanoes toppled the trees; an ocean flowed in from the west and then receded; wind and water erosion left a landscape of mesas, buttes, and layered hills, seemingly barren of life. An eon of time. Father Tellez is backtracking to a paved road that will connect with the highway returning him to his church in Hermosillo, Mexico. The phrase *off the beaten path* comes to mind as the hitchhiker lifts an empty Folger's coffee can from the seat, smells it, and settles into the passenger seat. He removes his ball cap, tousles his hair, and yawns.

"Where to?" asks the priest.

"Tuba City if you could. I can get home from there. What was in the can?" The hitchhiker has a vision of a man deep in the earth.

"A friend's dirt. Where's home?"

"Chinle for now, but I've got friends in Tuba City. I sleep in both places. Can I have the can?" The hitchhiker is dusty and disheveled. Windblown. "I appreciate the lift. Mind if I sleep while you drive?"

Forty-five minutes later, the priest pulls to a stop in front of a Mormon church in Tuba City on the Navajo reservation where two weathered old men wearing cowboy hats sit on the porch. The hitchhiker continues to sleep. Father Tellez steps out and exchanges greetings.

"Where'd you find him?" asks the older of the two men.

"I was coming off the Hopi reservation and heading back to the highway," answers Father Tellez.

"One of his favorite places to get lost."

"Lost?"

"He wanders . . . for months sometimes . . . when he's between jobs. He likes the austerity of the area. He looks for dinosaurs."

"You mean fossil bones?"

"No, real ones. Hasn't found any yet though." The man laughs.

The other old man stands. "He's a good young man. Works hard, but mostly keeps to himself. No family unless you count 10,000 years of his ancestors."

"No family," repeats Father Tellez more as a musing than a question. "What's he do?"

"Sometimes he's a delivery man, sometimes a retriever, sometimes a painter, an artist," says the sitting man. He chuckles. "Sometimes he builds roads. He's one of our nation's mythical creatures."

"We all sort of look after him. He has a gift," says the standing man. "He's preparing to look after all of us."

Father Tellez looks back at the sleeping man in his car. "He talked in his sleep about the wind tossing him around. Unintelligible mostly. Mumbled something else about family."

The standing old man steps off the porch, opens the passenger door, and shakes the sleeping passenger. "C'mon, Hector. Father here needs to get on his way. His car's not your private motel."

Hector steps out and collects his bearings before facing the priest. Something passes between them, and then Hector extends his hand and says, "Thank you, Father."

Father Tellez holds his passenger's hand and eyes, nods, and smiles. "You have an important journey coming up. God speed."

A pickle jar filled with used keys, intentionally ruined, filed down peaks, as if by compulsion. Usable once, unique, but all the same now. Useless. A son's legacy, from the time after the son saved the world from a greater war. Maybe, anyway. Another damaged key, a nickel-silver key, dangles on a gold chain around the man's neck. Walt Kramer stands motionless in his garage in Buena Vista, Colorado, searching the shelves for a spot to store the pickle jar. He ought to throw the damn things away; they were not meant to be preserved, and they will only remind him of his son's torment. But he won't. There is a secret out there and maybe these keys can unlock that secret. Broken keys to open obscure doors and shed light on his mystery. He tucks the necklace under his t-shirt, lifts the jar from the workbench to the shelf, and pushes it next to a box of old atlases and *Arizona Highways* magazines. Walt still has work to do at St. Mary, his son's church.

1

SONORAN DESERT, ARIZONA, SUMMER 1986

A Gila monster lies motionless on a newspaper on the cafe table, its guts partially exposed. An old man pokes it with a fork, while a scruffy, somewhat younger man squirms.

"Why do you shoot 'em?" asks Cocker. "This is their land, you know."

"It's a damn lizard, Cock. It was on my golf course. Besides, it reminded me of all the lizards running our country these days." He pauses. "And maybe a little of myself."

Cocker shakes his head. "Are we going there this early in the morning?"

From behind the raised counter, a tall, fit woman speaks. "Cocker's right, Smitty. Besides, you didn't go out to golf this morning. You went out to kill things, like you do every morning. Seems pretty barbaric."

"You never killed anything, Thalia?" asks Smitty, his eyes calmly studying the lizard. "Spiders? Insects? Same thing. A scorpion in your bedroom? It doesn't belong there, so you step on it or swat it with a broom." With his fork, he lifts the lizard's head to examine it closely. "This fella's sort of like us; spends most of his time hiding from the light. When he gets caught outside during the day, he's vulnerable."

"A house ain't a desert. Not the same thing," says Cocker. "In fact, it does belong. It should be safe out there." He sits up in his chair to pet the back of the lizard. "Should've left it out there instead of bringing it in here. It's not natural. People shouldn't try to tame the desert. It's Mother Nature's Garden, and She decides. The Tohono O'odham believe the Gila monster has spiritual powers, that it can bring diseases to those who harm it, so you better watch your health, Smitty." He pauses. "Can I take it?"

Smitty sets the fork down, raises his empty coffee cup to Thalia, and nods to Cocker. "Are you going to bury it?"

"No. I'll put it under a cactus and allow its soul to escape. I'll sing to it, give it a little dignity."

"Would you mind putting up the flag on your way out?" asks Thalia.

Cocker folds the newspaper around the lizard, takes Old Glory from the counter, and exits the bar, leaving the screen door ajar.

"What do you think, Thalia? Do desert creatures have souls?"

"Never gave it much thought, Mr. Smithfield," says Thalia as she refills his coffee, "but if anyone around here would know, it would be Cocker." Before she can close the screen, a husky man enters, a man obviously comfortable in the bar.

"Buenos dias, Thalia, Smitty. It's going to be another hot one. Where was Cocker heading?"

"To bury a lizard," says Smitty.

"To release its soul," corrects Thalia. She pours him a coffee as he sits at the table with Smitty. "How's your soul this morning, Alf?"

"Ah, troubled, mis amigos. Too many visitors of late to our little refuge, all asking too many questions. I might have to move back to Mexico with my wife for a little privacy."

"*Paranoia strikes deep*," sings Thalia as she turns away and resumes her station behind the bar, writing in her notebook. "They're just old hikers."

"She's a little snippy this morning," whispers Smitty. "She isn't happy about having to take Julie's shifts."

"Any word from Jack about his check-up?"

"Julie called last night, said the doctors were concerned about the pain where his prosthetic is attached. Wanted to look at it again this morning when the x-rays come back."

"You know the VA. He could be in the waiting room all day," says Alf.

"Jack'll just wheel himself out to the van and make Julie drive him back."

"Who's the new guy working on your place, Smitty?" asks Alf.

"Some Mexican. Saw him working on one of the houses along the highway on the way to Ajo a couple of weeks ago. Watched him for a few days, so I asked him if he did interior work. Seems conscientious.

Doesn't talk much. A lot of them Mexicans are good with their hands."

"Yeah, that's us. Good with our hands. We all should be named Manuel." Alf laughs. "He doesn't look like a Mexican to me, just a sun-browned dude. Does he live around here?"

"Yeah, in Benny Pacheco's house. Sort of house sitting while Pacheco works in the mines over in Morenci. Benny's a scab."

"No," says Alf, "Pacheco's a fuckin' scab!"

"Cuss jar," says Thalia without looking up. She knows not to pursue the topic of the copper mine's closing in Ajo with Alfonso. It would only lead to a hateful rant. She pulls a Steinbeck book from the shelf behind the counter, takes the pencil from behind her ear, sits on a stool at the counter's end, and begins to make notes in the margins of the book.

The two men go quiet for a time, fiddling with their cups more than drinking the coffee. This is a morning routine for them. Smitty leans over to the adjacent chair seat to retrieve a newspaper. He hands the sports section to Alf, "The Dodgers won," and folds the front section to the editorials. Smitty turns his chair sideways to cross his legs while he reads and slides reading glasses over his nose. Alf spreads his part of the paper on the table and leans in to read. Each reader makes sounds as information is gathered, different sounds, but the sounds of consideration.

Two athletic looking men in new hiking clothes enter. "Is this a café or a bar?" asks one.

"Depends on the time of day," answers Thalia. "If by café, you mean a place to get a cup of coffee, this is it. We don't usually serve alcohol in the morning. Wouldn't want to encourage bad habits. Most people get their coffee at the gas station on the highway or at the diner up the highway if it's open."

The men sit at the counter and Thalia pours them each a cup. After a few moments, the same man speaks. "We're looking for Rubicon."

Alf and Smitty share a glance. Thalia doesn't answer right away. She replaces the coffee pot on the hot plate and uses a rag to wipe up an imaginary spill. She allows the men to chew on their question, stalling for a moment to decide which pat answer she wants to give them. She looks over to Smitty and Alf, almost as if they had asked the question

The Why Intersection

before turning back to the two men with a smirk. "Rubicon doesn't really exist. It isn't labeled on any official map, although hikers camping nearby can obtain a sketch of the local trails, and it mentions a Rubicon trail that follows the wash. The wash crosses Mesquite Avenue just west of Arizona 85 and separates the most westerly neighborhood of Why from the rest of the town; really, this is just a dead-end street, the most isolated block of homes in one of the most isolated towns in America." She winks at Alf and Smitty and then turns back to the two strangers. "Are you looking for anyone in particular, or are you sniffing for drugs?"

"Do we look like narcs?"

Thalia stands in front of them behind the bar. "Yeah, you sorta do. The new clothes offer a clue."

"We're only here to do a little hiking in the Organ Pipe, but, yeah, we'd like to take some weed along. We heard we could score some here. No, we aren't narcs."

Thalia shakes her head. *Score some.* She looks to both the men. "Not here. There're lots of drugs along the border, and lots of the cars coming back from Rocky Point have some, but not here. Who told you we had drugs for sale anyhow?"

For the first time, the other man speaks. "A hippie lady in the RV park said you might."

"Oh, Doris. Why didn't you just *score some* off her?"

"We asked, but she said she was running low. Offered your place."

Thalia nods. "Sorry. Finish your coffee and head out before it gets too hot. The desert can get pretty inhospitable quickly. A little friendly advice, drugs and hiking in the desert are a deadly combination. Take lots of water, more water than you think you'll need."

The first man lays a five on the counter, and the two men leave. Thalia puts it in the cash register, removes their coffee cups, and laughs slightly. Five dollars for two cups of coffee that neither man finished. "Good thing Cocker wasn't here," she says to Smitty and Alfonso.

"What do you think, Alf," asks Smitty. "Narcs?"

"Maybe, but my guess is they aren't. Just dumb asses who've never experienced the desert, who think anyone living here is a loser. Should have asked them if they know Lizardo."

From behind the bar, Thalia adds, "They could be right."

Alf leans across the table towards Smitty. "I assume the groceries were delivered."

Smitty nods. "On schedule. Without a hitch. Should be in southern Utah now." Smitty takes a pad from his shirt pocket and flips through a few pages. "Got nothing else planned as of now."

Alf sits back and breathes in heavily. He turns his head toward where Thalia is standing. "Any word on the crawler?"

∞

Outside, sitting in a non-descript sedan parked on a nearby bluff, a man using binoculars observes the two men leave the bar. This morning, he has watched Smitty and Alf enter and Cocker leave, nothing out of the ordinary, but the two men in new boots pique his curiosity, alert his antennae. Probably nothing, but the man in the car is patient. He'll keep watching.

∞

Cocker walks the short distance to Smitty's two-hole golf course at the western edge of Why where Smitty shot the Gila monster. Cocker searches for a prickly pear or jumping cholla in the left rough to lay the lizard. Finding a full cholla cactus about 120 yards from the first tee, Cocker kneels, unwraps the newspaper carefully, and lifts the lifeless creature off the obituaries. The pink-and-black reticulated lizard goes about fifteen inches and five pounds, or it did before it lost a portion of its guts behind its right front leg. Cocker takes a loose cigarette from his breast pocket, lights it, and sucks in deeply. He lifts the lizard to his mouth and exhales the smoke across the lizard's face. He closes his eyes and softly sings the first four lines of "Amazing Grace," the cigarette still between his lips. Opening his eyes, Cocker rocks forward, slides the lizard beneath the cactus, and leaves. About 90 yards from the tee box, Cocker bends to pick up two cheap golf balls, which he inspects and puts in his pocket.

∞

The Why Intersection

Leticia is fifteen and doesn't know where to turn. She gave her baby to the nicely dressed couple who told her Fatima would be perfect for the advertising campaign. Leticia received 25 dollars and the assurance that her baby would be returned in four days and with a new set of clothes. Abortion is against God's will, against everything Leticia has been taught in church, so this advertising crusade is something she wants to support. But it's been two weeks, and her baby hasn't been returned. Leticia calls the number on the card the couple gave her, but the phone has been disconnected, and now she believes they may not have been honest with her. But they were so sincere before.

Leticia lives with her mother, three sisters, and three brothers. She is the oldest and does most of the housework while her mother works. Leticia only went to school for four years, but she had to quit when her father left for the United States to find work and her mother needed to go to work. The family lives in the Arroyo Hondo colony in Zapopan, the poorest of the poor sections in a Guadalajara, Mexico suburb, near the garbage dump. Leticia's boyfriend took the 25 dollars, telling her not to worry about Fatima anymore. Just a month earlier he bought himself a new pair of boots, not the kind you work in, but the kind you go dancing in.

At the police station, she speaks with an officer, but he doesn't write anything down. She shows him the paper the midwife gave her when Fatima was born, but he says it's not legal. The officer asks Leticia if the man who took her baby was Catholic. She says she doesn't think so, but he said he was a minister from some church. She shows the officer the Bible given to her by the woman and turns to a dog-eared page. James 1:27: *to look after orphans and widows in their distress.* The officer places his hand on her shoulder and tells her to forget about Fatima, that her daughter will not be coming home.

Leticia kneels in the Basilica and asks God what will happen to her baby, what will happen to Fatima who will grow up without her mother. Leticia prays God will not punish her for being stupid and will look over Fatima wherever she may be.

The nicely dressed couple hands an envelope stuffed with five and ten-dollar bills to the nun. "Distribute those accordingly. Baby Fatima will be delivered to a fine American couple with the means to give her a real chance in life." The nun leaves hurriedly, and the couple drives away in a white van with the name of their organization painted on the side. *Westboro Christian Services.*

"I'm not comfortable doing this in person," says the woman. "I much prefer working through the private hospitals and nurseries. I'll feel better when we're across the border."

The man slows to allow several school children in red and white uniforms to cross in front of the van. "Don't worry. The baby was exactly what the family wanted, and we had been tracking her throughout the pregnancy. It just made it difficult when the mother's family showed up at the hospital. The doctor wasn't prepared to tell the mother her baby was dead."

"Will we recover the additional expenses?"

"Completely. The market value on Fatima was high with her blue eyes. The lawyers are all on the take though. The system is based on bribery at each level, but the American family agreed to pay the extra charges. They were so desperate." He laughs.

"Will you be staying longer in Guadalajara?" asks the woman.

"I need to return to Kansas City to see my son's graduation, and then I'm meeting with an adoption foundation in Phoenix, but I'll be back later in the summer. This is an extremely profitable operation."

Baby Fatima joins three other babies for the journey up the coastal highway to the border. They cross into Arizona at the tiny checkpoint between Sonoyta-Lukeville where a small bribe to the Mexican authorities guarantees a no-questions-asked passage into the States. The nicely dressed couple will hand Fatima to a short, wiry woman just north of the border near the town of Ajo who will drive the baby to Phoenix and deliver her to a new mother and father where she will become an American child.

Thalia sits at the small table that serves as her writing desk and dinner table in the house Smitty rented to her several months ago, a house not too many steps from The Call, with a window that overlooks the dirt road that Smitty calls "Main Street." From her writing table, she can see the "outside Why" as opposed to the "inside Rubicon" at the bar. A different perspective. She arrived in Arizona three months before arriving in Why to write an expose on cross-border adoptions. Thalia is a journalist, an independent contractor, and she had become aware of the "process" when her sister adopted a child from Mexico under suspicious circumstances. How did a family from Michigan adopt a Mexican child so quickly? Her sources told her to go to Phoenix, to start there. From Phoenix her investigation sent her to Lukeville, the tiny border town not far from Ajo/Why. That was 1985 and when she met Julie.

∾

As my colleagues have shown, interracial adoptions regarding White parents adopting Black children have decreased significantly over the past decade. Nationwide, there has always been a stigma attached to such unions, but in the seventies and the first years of the eighties, opposition from Black organizations has made these adoptions even less acceptable. Adoption in America has mostly been a White, middle-class proposition, especially as a legal custodial transfer. Black and Latino communities simply take in these children as part of an extended family with no official documents involved. Here in Michigan, mores and demographic changes have led to a rejection of interracial adoptions.

Revised abortion laws, specifically Roe v Wade, *have resulted in fewer unwanted children, again specifically White children. White families wishing to adopt for a variety of reasons have found the pool of White children smaller and the wait longer, thus the search for additional pools. International conflicts in Southeast Asia are one place that has impacted this search. Adoptions by White families of Asian children have grown rapidly as orphans from Vietnam have been on the rise. The other significant pool is Mexico.*

As noted earlier in this article, the "Jones" family adopted an "orphan" from Guadalajara, Mexico, through a religious agency. This cross-border adoption was speedier with less red tape, and the Joneses were overjoyed with the opportunity to raise their new daughter in "a loving, Christian home" as the agency brochure promised. It was costly, however.

Sadly, while adoption agencies are reluctant to call this a crisis, adoption fraud seems to be on the rise. Anxious families desiring a child to complete their family have been defrauded by groups preying on this desperation. My next article will focus on these fraudulent adoptions.

T. F.

2

THE CALL

Julie London closes the door between the school and the cafe and turns the "closed" sign to "open" for morning coffee. She turns up the lights, raises the shades, turns on the jukebox, and punches C14, always the first song of the day. "You're No Good," by Linda Ronstadt. The promise of dawn is replaced by the reality of day. Depending on the situation, Julie is either the queen or the nanny of the tiny Kingdom of Rubicon. She marks an X through star date August 13, 1986, on the Star Trek calendar and writes "no rain" on it. *Yesterday,* she thinks, *always marking the past.* Julie can't be more than five-feet-four and 125 pounds, but she's strung as secure as a barbed-wire fence around a nuclear power plant that's meant to warn strangers to stay out. Even in the poorly lit bar, when The Call is a bar, patrons can see she has brown eyes surrounded by tight wrinkles, a face that has been pondering injustices all her adult life and carrying as much baggage as a Pullman porter. Fragile is not an adjective one would use to describe her. She tolerates no alcohol and certainly no drunks in the morning while summer school is in session. Thalia, "Miss Fisher," teaches seven Why students how to read, do a little useful math, and learn a nostalgic version of American history. The children of area ranchers are bused to Ajo for a more structured education, but Why's young children aren't forced to sit on a bus for extended periods each day, nor would their mothers permit them to be bused back into Ajo where their lives were undone during The Strike in '83 and '84. Neither the state of Arizona nor the Ajo school district cares about these kids.

The first person to enter The Call is not a regular, but Julie knows him. "Sheriff Harr. What brings you all the way out here this morning? Can't you find enough crime to keep you busy in Tucson?" She reaches behind her, grabs a coffee mug, and pours the sheriff a cup. Usually suspicious of law enforcement, her demeanor indicates a certain air of comfort with this one, maybe even a bit of trust.

The sheriff slides onto a stool at the bar and nods a thank you for the coffee. "Nah, I've cleaned up all the crime in Tucson, so now I have to go looking for it to keep my job." They both laugh gently. "Don't know if you heard, but the border patrol rescued a couple of hikers in the park a few days ago. Lost and baked—in more ways than one—if you get my drift. Besides their poor physical condition, they were in possession of more than a little bit of weed. The border patrol guys thought they may have gotten it across the border, but the hikers denied that."

Julie nods, sensing what's coming next. "These hikers wouldn't happen to be two men with new boots, would they?"

Harr smiles. "Ah, you remember them."

"Not me; I wasn't here that day, but they made an impression on Thalia and Smitty. They told me about them. Bar gossip for a few days. In another month, those two hikers would have been erased from our memory banks. I guess the gang teased Thalia about having a thing for one of them."

The sheriff nods his whole body. "And that's what brings me to your outpost. The hikers said they procured their stash from here, that 'the tall woman behind the bar' sold it to them."

"Oh shit!"

"Hold on, Julie. I'm not making an accusation, just following up."

"We don't do that here! We don't sell drugs here. We don't give drugs to strangers coming in to get high. That would be stupid! What? Were those two losers looking to pin their stupidity on someone else so they could get a reduced charge?"

Sheriff Harr cuts her off by holding up both hands as if a shield. "I only got involved when they told my deputies that they got the drugs here. I didn't want someone you don't know coming out here to ask these questions. I know what might happen if Jack was in on that conversation." The sheriff laughs again. "Might have a standoff with Jack exploding and pulling a weapon from the pocket of his wheelchair."

"Yeah, that could happen. Or Alf." Julie shakes her head and warms the sheriff's coffee. "I suppose you need to talk with Thalia."

"Could I? Is she available?"

Julie motions with her head that Thalia is teaching in the next room. "Those noises in the background are the sounds of young kids getting their heads filled with learning. Thalia teaches our local kids here so that they don't have to be bused back into Ajo. The strike animosity continues to rear its ugly head. We turned the old waiting room into a classroom. It works."

Harr smiles. "Only you guys." He allows that sentiment to hang over the bar.

Julie breathes out hard. "Let me go be a substitute for a few minutes. I'll send her in." She moves from behind the bar, tapping Harr on the shoulder as she walks behind him.

In a few moments, Thalia enters, taking Julie's station behind the bar. She extends her hand. "So, you want to question me about being a drug salesman. Obviously, you don't know my background." She smiles and releases the sheriff's hand.

Harr wipes his nose with the back of his hand. "Sheriff Harr. I know this group of, how shall I put it, *unique characters* from several years of minor battles. Nothing serious. They tend to be a bit protective of each other and their pasts. But that's beside the point. We arrested a couple of men on drug charges after the border patrol saved their butts in the park south of here. They claimed they bought their drugs here, and indicated that a tall, pretty women sold them the weed. Julie says that would never happen." He leaves it there, allowing Thalia to add to the story.

"I remember those two. We wondered if they were narcs initially, but decided they were just a couple of ignorant fucks. They asked for drugs; I told them we didn't have any and asked where they heard we did. They said the old hippie lady at the RV park told them. Then, they left. I did, however, warn them that drugs and the desert were kind of a bad mix. Evidently, they didn't take my advice."

"Let me tell you one detail they provided to support their allegation. They said you reached under this bar and took out a wooden cigar box and sold them a bag."

From the hall at the side of the bar, Jack responds, interrupting Thalia. His voice is both elevated and accusatory. "Fucking bullshit, Harr! Search the damn place! You don't need a warrant; I give up my rights. Get up off that stool and look under the bar. We didn't know you were coming, so we wouldn't have hidden anything, so check." Jack rolls himself into the bar area.

There's a pause for a moment, a silence. From the classroom, there is a spurt of laughter.

The sheriff lifts himself from the barstool. "If anyone asks, I checked behind the bar and found nothing but an empty beer keg and a stack of rags. Good to meet you, Ms. Fisher. Always good to see you, Jack. Give my best to Smitty." At the door the sheriff turns back. "And by the way, keep an empty chair at your table for when I retire. I think I have enough stories now to provide a little entertainment to your crew."

∽

"Pay attention. Pay close attention to the details the author adds, not just to the dialogue, or you won't understand how it happened, and then you won't know why. *Why* is really what we're trying to figure out. So, pay close attention as you read." Thalia Fisher checks for her students' assent. "The mouse. The dream farm. Curley. There are lots of characters in the book, and this may tend to confuse you, but each one is important in a small way. Just like in real life, a window will open, and you'll get a glimpse of a person's past, but then it closes, and it's confusing." Thalia could be addressing an advanced placement class in a Tucson high school, but this is a small class of displaced miners' children in an old adobe building just north of the border. At the back of the room, Julie London reads *Of Mice and Men*, glad she is not doing the teaching but enjoying the lesson. Thalia continues. "This is a short book, a hard book on one level, but it has lots of lessons about life that apply to us here in southern Arizona. You, too, are often on the other side of the fence. Outsiders." The students understand that well. Thalia speaks slowly, emphasizing each word, each concept. "Do your best and I'll talk you through it every other day. If you need to, go back and reread a passage, and, yes, you can make marks in your book if that helps." The three junior high students begin reading the Steinbeck classic, and Miss Fisher moves to the four younger children for their history lesson. "Parson Weems admired President Washington's honesty, and he wanted to promote that character trait

The Why Intersection

in our future leaders, so he wrote about the cherry tree incident. A president should be a role-model, the moral authority of our nation, honest and trustworthy."

∾

Jack London began renting his Why house in the mid-seventies, nearly a decade ago, turned it into a bar, and named it The Call of the Wild. An unwieldy name, patrons simply refer to it as The Call. At one point, it had been a bus station, a transit depot where passengers briefly sheltered to be delivered to somewhere else, but that ended several years back. Not enough traffic. Jack wheels himself around the bar to be next to the window when school is in session, and on most days, he will nurse his coffee or a beer while he pours over yesterday's Tucson or Phoenix newspaper. He's the only person allowed to drink before noon. He is older than Julie by fifteen years, but he looks even older. The Call is many things depending on the time of day: the morning coffee shop, a one-room school, a union hall, the occasional poker room, and the neighborhood news center. But mostly, The Call is a bar. A previous owner bought a single-wide trailer home and connected it to the back of the adobe bus station, which is now where Jack and Julie reside. The main structure also holds a meager stock of food, essentials, as if storing up for Armageddon or as a bodega for a cross-country journey.

It's summer in the Arizona desert which means the afternoon temperature often exceeds 110. Jack drinks beer with four friends at one of the bar's three tables at the far end of the room nearest the old window air conditioner. New window ACs are scheduled to arrive early next week. The conversation is disjointed with none of the men too passionate about any of the topics presented so far. The men discuss the past, maybe because the future frightens them, and because the future doesn't seem to hold a place for them. Cocker mentions the Messiah but gets no response. Smitty swears at President Reagan for his budget plan, and is supported by a third, but the conversation stalls, and they go quiet for a time. Julie sits on a stool behind the u-shaped bar listening to the Dodgers as presented by Vin Scully. Her drunken days are a decade in the rear-view mirror, so she sips an iced tea. From her padded stool, she can observe everything happening in the bar. She can tell if a customer or a regular wants to talk or wants to be left alone with his thoughts and a beer just by the way he sits in a chair or on a barstool.

A new man enters The Call, pausing inside the door to allow his eyes to adjust to the darker room. Julie suspects he isn't a tourist, but he does want information. She waits. He's a confident man, too formally dressed to be from a desert town, maybe from Phoenix, that city of new men, that city which has forgotten its past. Anyone from Phoenix is immediately suspect by the patrons of The Call.

In time, he sits across from her. "A cold beer, please. Preferably on tap."

"We don't have anything on tap today. She pulls a Coors bottle from the metal cooler, opens it, places it in front of him, and eases back onto her stool to listen to the ballgame.

"Will it rain today?" he asks.

"Maybe, but it's getting a little late," she answers. "The monsoon clouds look like they were steering a little south, along the border."

The man readjusts his butt and drinks the rest of his beer quickly, mostly quenching a thirst. "What do you have besides Coors?"

"Lots of Mexican beers this week. Nothing else American today. My beer guy has been back visiting his family in Chihuahua. All kinds of hard liquor though."

"Pick me a darker beer, if you could."

Julie selects a Dos Equis. Beer Guy is her usual supplier of alcohol. He buys cheap liquor where he can along the border, usually in Nogales, tries to get some Coors or Budweiser or Miller, but always has a wide variety of Mexican cervezas and tequilas. He delivered a double load a week ago because he was going on vacation to see his wife in his old hometown, but supplies are running low. A devout Catholic, Beer Guy goes across the border on Easter and Christmas and for groceries on rare occasions.

Julie pours the customer a half-shot of cheap tequila. After one swallow he asks, "Do the Dodgers have any chance of getting back into the pennant race? They're ten games back."

"Not much. Can't hit this year." Julie turns and takes a beer to one of the regulars at a table at the other end of the bar. They ask who the new guy is, and she tells them she doesn't know. They tease that he might be an old boyfriend, the standard line, and they all laugh, except Jack. When she returns, she puts a bowl of pretzels in front of the man. She has a feeling about this man.

"Interesting décor."

"I call it Alaskan Sonoran," says Julie. The man stares at a large stuffed dog of undetermined breed, and Julie answers his question before it's asked. "That's Buck."

A sketch of a scruffy hiker is taped to the mirror. "Who's that?"

"Might be Hayduke. Or it might not. Not someone a man like you would know," says Julie.

The man does know, but he lets her remark pass without comment. He senses a tension, an apprehension for him, not him personally but for a stranger in a very small town. He understands. A faded map of Alaska hangs behind the bar with the oil pipeline path marked in red ink. In front of the map hang a silver whistle and a cowbell attached to a leather string with the words "Fuck Phelps Dodge" written on the cowbell. Next to the cash register lies a tattered Bible with several sticky notes attached. In the corner nearest the five men, a stuffed grizzly bear seems to be chasing a covey of metal quail. The man nods toward a photo sharing a shelf with a dozen bottles of tequila. "President Roosevelt?"

"Teddy was a conservationist," says Julie.

"For land. Not so much for animals."

"We're none of us perfect."

"That's a true fact." He pauses. "Do the Christmas lights stay lit all year long?" It's an attempt at humor and Julie understands. "Any place around here to get a hot meal?" the man asks.

"It's Thursday so Libby will serve a pretty good Mexican dish from her food wagon. About a half-block up past the flat-roofed brick house, next to the highway."

"Spicy?"

"Oh, Libby is very spicy. Don't piss her off."

The man laughs. "I meant the food."

"I know. Just messing with you. It's spicy too. Can you handle it?"

"Probably. Guess I'll see."

Julie smiles, stands, and leans over the bar. "Who are you looking for?"

"A good friend of mine met a woman at a funeral in Colorado a while back, and since I have business in Tucson tomorrow, he wanted me to stop in and say hi while I was in the neighborhood. Patricia Frazier?" The man condenses the entire story.

Julie doesn't give away her thoughts and pretends. "Hmmm, from Why? Patricia? Can you describe her?"

"Tall. Pleasant. Attractive. Glasses. If you know her . . ." The man stops. He pretends too.

"Are you sure she said she's from here? Maybe Amado or Rio Rico? Nobody's from here, especially pretty women. Women here are a bit worn."

"No," says the man. "Pretty sure it's Why. My friend was doing some work in a church cemetery, and we'd just talked about the meaning of life, about the *why* of things. It reminded him of this town. That's when he mentioned this woman and something she said."

Julie smiles on one side of her mouth and tilts her head down, as if to question the man's story. On the radio, Vin Scully raises his voice ever so slightly and exclaims, "Forget it! She's out of here." Julie hears the homerun call and laughs. "Mister, I didn't catch your name."

"Dan."

"Well, Dan, if I remember such a woman, and if I happen to see her, and if such a woman would happen to remember being in Colorado, I'll tell her you might have stopped by." Julie picks up the beer bottle and bowl of pretzels with one hand and wipes the bar with a damp cloth. "Five dollars."

The men at the table are regulars, and they are, depending on whom one asks, either philosophers or curmudgeons. Julie knows it's the latter and teases them about their narrow views, but they are comfortable in Jack's bar. Two of the men consider themselves to be the elder statesmen of Rubicon and custodians of the neighborhood's repository. Coffee before school begins, beers in the afternoon, and more beers in the evening. Jack charges each man $50 per month for the "office space" and all his beer and pretzels. More often than not, Smitty pays more than his share. Little gets past the men's scrutiny. The Call is not a place like McDonald's or Furr's Cafeteria. The Call exists because it isn't popular, it isn't inviting, but once in and accepted at a table, it allows one to speak his mind and defend justice.

"He'll be back. He didn't come all the way out here for a brush off. I'll bet ya a half-dollar he's back after he eats."

"Sucker's bet. You can still see his car out the window."

"It won't be long. He's ponderin.'"

"Think he's the law?"

"Nah, I don't think so. Probably is looking for that woman but got bad information."

"Not a Patriot either then?"

"Fuckin' hope not."

Julie yells out, "You owe the cuss jar a quarter, Alf." The cuss jar is an old pickle jar with a huge funnel attached. The challenge is to simply flip your quarter into the funnel from wherever you are when the fee is assessed. If the cusser hits the funnel, his next swear word is exempt from the fine.

"Did ya see where the Patriots are helpin' the Border Patrol over by Douglas?"

"Just move from one muscle job to the next."

"Cause of the day. Thugs."

"Not all of them. Some of them are just scared of the Mexican invasion and really think a few armed men can secure the border. I don't think they see the scope of this illegal immigration."

"The immigrants aren't all from Mexico these days. Lots from Central America. El Salvador and Honduras and Guatemala. They're so worn out making the trip through Mexico, they can't expect to safely get through a hundred more miles of our desert."

"You're preaching to the choir; we all know that. It's about jobs. We got 'em and they want 'em."

"Shee-it. It's not just jobs; there's more to it. Trying to escape from those right-wing death squads Reagan props up."

Smitty stays quiet. The men have been over this topic before, maybe it was just yesterday; it's been personal for a few years, and they move on.

"Did you see where copper prices jumped again?"

"Too late for our mine. New Cornelia is just a graveyard now."

"The strike closed it for good, even if the price spikes back over a dollar. Maybe over in Morenci they'll keep theirs open for a few more years."

"The foreign miners get paid a tenth of what Americans get, so PD will just buy the copper in South America."

"I'm not sure PD owns those mines, but you're right about where copper will come from. The world market versus union miners. Our guys don't stand a chance."

"Little guys seldom do."

Jack London wheels himself over to the table and signals to Julie for another beer. "Not unless you've got a chain saw or a little bit of dynamite . . . and don't get careless."

Cocker rubs his whiskers and brings up his usual complaint. "It goes back to population. Too many damned people."

"Cuss jar, Cocker," yells Julie. "I know you disagree, but we decided damn was a cuss word."

"America had fewer than 110 million people when you were born, Smitty. Now we got 250 million or more. We'll have over 300 million by the turn of the century. Bound to cause more disruptions. Arizona's the same. Must have been paradise just after WWI when there were less than 400 thousand. Now we got eight times that many with no end in sight."

"So, you're saying we all gotta move out since none of us came out of our momma's womb here in Arizona?" says Jack.

"I did," says Alf. "My family pre-dates statehood by a couple of hundred years."

"No," says Cocker. "I'm just saying we look too deep for the causes of all our problems. There are just too many people in the world, and it's getting worse and worse. Take this border thing. Mexico's population is growing faster than ours, and they're mostly poor. A lot poorer than us here in America. Lot of them want a better life, so where do they go? *El Norte*, up here. Just looking for a better life, and we have

The Why Intersection

this soft border that's easy to cross. Them Mexicans will work for a lot less than us lazy Americans, so there're plenty of jobs for them. All of Mexico's agricultural jobs are drying up, so they come here."

"Lazy Americans? Present company excluded, I assume," says Alf.

"They do a public service for you. They bring you your drugs," says Jack. It's true and the others laugh. The scraggly one continues.

"And Julie her alcohol to sell to us, but that's beside the point," says Cocker. "Somebody did an experiment once about mice in a box and what happens when you add too many mice to the box. They run around and go crazy: start bumping into each other, biting at each other, running up the sides of the box, losing control. That's what's happening to humans. No space, just like the mice in the box." The others listen, but they've heard Cocker's rant before and make jokes.

"Where was the experiment? MIT? Maybe I should read up on it. I've got a few connections there still," says Smitty. "You want space? Walk to the end of the street past my place and head out into the desert on the jeep trail. There's a whole world of empty space out there completely barren of people, except maybe some of them Mexicans walking to find a job. That jeep trail can take you anywhere eventually—it's a bumpy road, sort of like life."

Cocker takes no heed. "You watch and see. Nations will be fighting over food just like Arizona and California are fighting for Colorado's water. It's why they built that nuclear power plant up the road. Too many people in Phoenix and L.A. You just wait."

"We don't need that nuclear power plant," says Jack with a bit of emotion. "It just brings more people to the Southwest. Arizona doesn't need a bigger Phoenix. Didn't you learn anything from the Chernobyl meltdown in April. Thousands will die from radiation poisoning."

"Could that experiment have been done with rats instead of mice?" asks Smitty ignoring Jack's comment.

"Maybe we could send some of our lazy workers to Mexico in exchange for all of them hard working men flooding into San Diego and Texas."

"It's happening, and you guys are just too stubborn to acknowledge it. You get old and you only see your little world; just want to drink beer and be left alone."

"Finally, you say some true shit, Cocker," says Smitty.

"Cuss jar."

∞

The burrito is spicy hot and the soda warm. Dan sits at Libby's card table under a large umbrella and watches the clouds scurry along the low mountains to the southeast. The rain will probably miss Why, like the future. He'd like to take the burrito back into the bar and wash it down with another cold beer, but he needs to give the men time. He gently spins his styrofoam cup on the table with his left hand while he repeatedly pinches his lower lip with his right.

"Would you like another one, mister?" asks Libby.

"No, ma'am. One this size will fill me up, but it sure is tasty. Thank you."

Libby wipes some hot sauce from the opposite side of the card table. "Excuse me," she says.

"Do you live here in Why?" asks Dan.

"No, mister, I live in Sells, on the reservation. I just come here a few times to sell lunch."

Dan wonders about Libby's age. She could be anywhere from 35 to 60. "Did you grow up in this part of Arizona?"

"This land is not Arizona. It is O'odham, the land of my people."

"Oh, the reservation. I didn't know it extended this far west. My map calls it Papago."

"Not Papago anymore. Tohono O'odham. The Nation."

"Are you part Apache then?"

Libby swears in her native tongue. "Not Apache. Opposite of Apache." She turns away from Dan.

Dan knows he has offended Libby. First the bartender and now the street vendor. Vin Scully would call out, "Strike two!" Dan puts his cup and paper plate into the waste basket by Libby's wagon, slips a dollar into a plastic tip jar, and walks away from the table toward what looks like an abandoned house. He feels the eyes of the bar are watching him; he's certainly an outsider. Behind the house a man works to remove nails from several planks that are lying on sawhorses. "Afternoon," says Dan. The laborer nods and grunts but

The Why Intersection

does not look up. The sun weathers the skin in the desert, whether it be human or creature.

∽

"He's about ready to come back in. Bet he comes right over and sits by us."

"Yeah, he's not trying to hide who he is, just trying not to make it obvious. He's a solver. It's not his real job, but he's done this before."

As soon as Dan walks in, he moves to the side of the bar next to the Guardians. Julie slides a Dos Equis down the bar. "Welcome back, meester." She smiles.

Dan sits on the last stool in a line of six, takes a healthy swallow of his beer, and lightly smites his chest as he burps. Sitting on the stool, Dan has a height advantage over the five men at the table. Jack London has his back to Dan. "Mind if I sit with you guys?" asks Dan.

"What exactly are you doing here, sonny?" asks Smitty, the oldest man at the table.

"Trying to return a favor; repay a debt."

Outside, a stray cloud drops a three-minute rain on Why, but it's a hard three-minute rain.

∽

Copper Joe is the youngest of the Guardians, which is what Thalia jokingly calls the five men who hold daily council at The Call. Smitty, Cocker, Alf, Jack, CJ. CJ is in his 40s and, like the others, a military veteran, his war, Vietnam. Like Cocker, CJ seldom speaks of his military service. "Maybe for you guys, war was a noble endeavor, but not for me. For me, it was pure savagery." CJ is employed outside of Why, still working part time at the old Phelps Dodge offices in Ajo. He didn't plan on becoming one of those men who sits around and complains about the world, America's problems, or local rumors all day long, but The Strike pushed men in directions they hadn't planned. His tenure as a regular in The Call is in its third summer. That first year, he drank coffee, bought beers, and sat at the bar for a few months, serving an unofficial apprenticeship, listening but not talking. The Strike gave him credibility.

Working for the corporation in '83, the year the copper miners struck against Phelps Dodge Mining Company, CJ delivered eviction notices to union families living in company houses in Ajo, Clifton, and Morenci. He supported PD as it strove to break the union, at first, but all those committed women on the picket lines! By Christmas he realized it was an unfair fight, that PD was using resources that the union, made up mostly of Chicano workers, could not marshal. When state law enforcement agencies began secretly supplying PD with information and weapons to be used against the workers, CJ turned. If Phelps Dodge had informers, so could the union. His efforts failed; the union was decertified in the age of Reaganomics, but at least on this, his conscience is clear.

It's complicated.

CJ eyes Dan, maybe less so than the others, but he's suspicious, nevertheless. CJ understands that Dan is using the regulars as a door into Rubicon, but for what purpose, he is unsure. Dan doesn't want to know about the men; he's searching for someone beyond this table, someone who most likely isn't here and never was. He isn't innocent, as if any grown man is, but Dan's been scarred, like the Guardians, and that's reason to be suspicious. When he talked with Julie at the bar earlier and she said, "We're none of us perfect," there was history behind his response; it was not just a flippant response. CJ picked it up. The others maybe didn't hear it, they're all a little deaf, but CJ heard clearly. History. Is there anything else? Future is just a concept, often just a false promise.

"So, what's the debt, Dan?" asks Cocker, his head tilted as though he has one good ear. Cocker tells people he was part of a rock-n-roll band back in the fifties and early-sixties, but drugs and alcohol ruined him for a time. His second wife pulled him out of it, but not before any musical career had passed him by. That second wife did too, when he abandoned his music. Scratchy voice. He still smokes, whereas the others have mostly given it up. "You're gonna die of lung cancer, you know," they say. He knows that's probably true. Julie questions Cocker's story. He's too old to have understood rock during that era;

The Why Intersection

maybe he played with Perry Como or Rosemary Clooney. Cocker says it was Buddy Holly, another Texan, until he died in the plane crash. Julie doesn't believe him but hasn't pried him for more; it's Cocker's fantasy to carry.

Dan moves cautiously forward. "My friend who asked me to stop by," he says smiling and nodding at Cocker, "got me out of a jam when I was a stupid, angry kid. Haven't had an opportunity to adequately pay him back so I do little favors for him." Dan senses an aura of guilt at the table, almost like a barrier to protect the men from past failures. Except from the oldest man. Dan is in Why to ask about a woman—no big deal—but the table has turned it into an issue.

"How come you stopped in at this bar instead of the little restaurant by the highway?' asks Smitty.

"I did," answers Dan, "but it's closed right now."

"I can't imagine anything worthwhile in Rubicon that could repay a debt. You musta been real bad to be sent to the desert," says Cocker. It's the first use of the term Rubicon to the stranger.

CJ extends his hand to Dan as an introduction. "Call me Joe. And this is Cocker, Jack, Waddell, and Alf. When you get to know Waddell, you can call him Smitty, or Sir, but that's a ways down the road. Jack runs this place, Jack and Julie, who you already met. Smitty owns us all. The rest of us are delinquents of a sort without many manners. We're a group of misfits who don't want inspection into our lives, especially the government or local authorities. We mind our own business, bitch about most everything, and work just enough to pay our bills. Sometimes, when outsiders come looking for answers to their own problems, they unintentionally cast a light on ours, and we don't want that. So, we're always a bit suspicious." CJ pauses. "If we have anything in common, it's we all served in the Army except Smitty. No Marines here. Certainly no Air Force. Did you serve?"

Dan nods. "Army too. Germany. No Vietnam for me. Pretty lucky."

Julie moves closer to the men, to the interrogation, something she enjoys, how it unfolds each time a stranger arrives to see what Rubicon exists for. She senses Dan knows why towns such as Why exist, as respites for the dispossessed. The Sonoran Desert in southern Arizona is littered with outposts like Why, towns for ghosts really. She wonders if Germany was Dan's respite. Not holding a seat at the table, she seldom speaks, a consideration she grants to Jack and his men's club. She absorbs information from her station behind the bar. What the Guardians want to know is if Dan poses a threat to all their secrets, whether he is a lawman or investigator of some kind—or an agent for The Government.

∾

Jack London worked on the Alaska pipeline during the mid-seventies. Attracted by the high wages and a need to flee northern California, he worked overtime in the more dangerous locations, like the Atigun Pass, as an explosives expert. For the general public's consumption, Jack lost a leg and was burned in a construction accident, forcing him to return to the lower forty-eight with Julie. He had stockpiled a nest-egg. The Call is marginally profitable, but Jack would keep it open even if it wasn't. Neither Jack nor Julie talks much about his work in Alaska or where they were before Alaska. Fairbanks is where Julie earned her degree, "Environmental studies, and leave it at that." She worked the pipeline too, also making good money.

∾

Alfonso Galvan remembers the day it started just over three years ago, the day the union walked out and shut down the copper mine at Ajo and its partner mines in eastern Arizona. He remembers a lot of days from that first year. The problems began before that, at least four years earlier when the bottom fell out of copper prices, and copper mines around the country laid off workers. A little of the strike was about copper prices, but mostly it was about unions and Chicanos and power. For Alf, it is about the loss of his mining job, his town, and his family, and it still burns. He wasn't always Alfonso Galvan; before the shooting, he was Alonso Peru from Morenci, Arizona.

Since Dan walked in for his first beer, Alf hasn't said anything. He avoids eye contact and just listens. He pretends to nap in his chair and only stirs to sip his beer or grunt in agreement with something he may or may not agree with. Or scratch his black beard that has gray flecks. Dan's demeanor reminds Alf of an undercover agent who showed up

The Why Intersection

on Alonso Peru's front door at the start of the strike and asked to help. The agent fooled Al Peru, fooled him good.

Copper prices had fallen to half their value just a handful of years earlier, and Phelps Dodge Mining was looking to cut its losses. Understandable, of course, but they had bigger plans. They weren't planning to compromise; they wanted to bust the union, and they believed they had the resources to do it. They also had Governor Babbitt and President Reagan in their pocket. Despite all that, Al Peru believed the union could win. It had won before, and it was only asking Phelps Dodge to abide by previous contracts. Al was naïve; it was a new era, an era defined by a hard recession fueling nationwide anti-unionism. President Reagan convinced America the unions caused the recession, not corporations and government policies, or new tax laws, or the rise in the cost of oil. No, unions had done America in and needed to be eliminated. Air traffic controllers, teachers, and copper miners. All Al wanted was a cost-of-living increase, and he said so in front of the Tucson newspaper, and that got him identified. And targeted. Unpopular views can be a crime!

Dan is charming and has a story. So did Carlos from Texas who said he had been laid off at his smelter near Corpus Christi and needed a job. He would start at the bottom and be a good worker. He just needed to send some money back to his family in Brownsville. *We all have been there*, thought Al Peru, miners moving away from their families to provide support. Damn if Carlos wasn't smooth. Al got him a job, and Carlos joined the union and marched on the picket lines, carried a bat, and wasn't afraid of the consequences. When some of the union members crossed the lines to sign up for a lower wage, Carlos condemned them as scabs and warned of what could happen, not just to them, but to their families. He was arrested and jailed in Tucson twice. Al warned Carlos about lowering his talk, that he was tearing the town apart making neighbors hate neighbors. Most of the violence occurred at Morenci in eastern Arizona where Al Peru lived, but the shooting happened in Ajo, at a company house, at a scab's residence, to a friend of Alonso.

Alonso Peru would never have discovered Carlos's duplicity except for the picture in a Phoenix newspaper of the governor condemning the union for escalating the violence, blaming the union for the attack on the non-union miner and his family leaving a little girl seriously wounded. Standing in the background were the undercover agents who had infiltrated the unions throughout Arizona and kept both the law enforcement agencies and Phelps Dodge aware of the union's activities. It was a fuzzy photo, one that wasn't supposed to have been taken, but Al had it. Carlos was a paid informant, a member of a covert agency within the state government calling itself the Arizona Criminal Intelligence Agency. Bullies with no sense of right and wrong, just mercenaries on the state level, complicit with inciting violence to make a case against the unions. The state could never prove who shot the little girl; it didn't need to. The newspapers wrote editorials pointing the finger at an angry, anonymous union man who shot up a scab's house and hit the little girl. Phelps Dodge broke the unions with Huey helicopters that reminded Al of Vietnam, with heavily armed state troopers and the National Guard, but mostly with public anger over the shooting of a little girl whose only crime was that her father crossed the picket line to feed her. Phelps Dodge offered a huge reward for information, and the newspapers went with that story, targeting the union. They wrote that the man who shot the little girl would most likely never be discovered, and on that they were correct. Alonso discovered Carlos's duplicity and later helped bury him in the desert south of Ajo on a knoll overlooking the New Cornelia copper mine, Carlos's final resting place, so he could overlook the mine he helped shut down. The newspapers never reported this missing man, he was simply another insignificant Chicano who left town because of the strike. Shortly thereafter, Alonso Peru sent his family back to Mexico to live with his mother-in-law, and he moved to Why and took on a new name. Alfonso Galvan still had questions.

Alf stirs and sits up. He clears his throat. "Dan is it?" he asks deliberately. "Do you know what a G-man is?" It's a rhetorical question.

Independent men. Skeptical for reasons he won't know. Dan recognizes his honeymoon window is about to close unless he can allay their initial suspicions. He steps off his stool and pulls a chair from

The Why Intersection

the adjacent table so he can sit at their eye level. He looks at Alf evenly.

"Yeah, I know, but I'm not one. I'm an architect. I live in a Denver suburb, Littleton, with my wife and two boys. Mostly I design bridges. That's what I'm doing in Tucson this week, talking to the city about building a bridge over the Santa Cruz River on the west side of town. When I was in college, I committed a felony but was never charged. The local sheriff and one of his friends found a way to hide the truth. They knew my backstory and thought I had a future, and since then, I've been trying to prove them right. I was having dinner with them earlier this summer, and the friend mentioned the lady I earlier referred to, the one I asked the bartender about. Long story short, the sheriff's friend, my friend now, witnessed a bizarre tragedy just before this and is still trying to piece things together, piece himself together. Something about this lady piqued his thoughts, and he asked me to give her a message." Dan pauses, checking for silent responses. "His wife is pregnant, and he didn't think he ought to leave just now, so here I am. When he gets an idea, he acts on it."

No one speaks for a moment; each man contemplating the conversation. Finally, Smitty stirs. "What's your friend's name, just in case someone wanted to see if he really exists?"

Dan nods. "His name is Walt. Walt Kramer."

A ditch! A piddly-ass, muddy ditch by the side of a dirt road going nowhere, and this is where he's going to die. His mother will tell her friends her son died in Korea during the summer of 1950. His squad was just north of the town of Taejon along the southern bank of the Kum River defending freedom against the godless communists. The first sergeant lies dead, shot in the neck as he raced back, retreating along the road. Walt hears the thud of the bullet even before he hears his leader crumble into the gravel. He turns and drags the body into the ditch where the rest of the squad huddles to make its last stand . . . where it hides in fear. In a roadside ditch in Korea, next to nowhere.

Private Walter Kramer did not die that day even though he was shot twice. His buddies died when they were overrun by the North Koreans and their Soviet-made T-34 tanks late in the evening. Walt survived by crawling under a prickly bush in that ditch. Hearing the cries of his fellow soldiers as the North Korean soldiers went from one body to the next shooting them and then killing them again with bayonets, he vowed not to make a sound, to even stop breathing if it meant living, and at some moment in the night, he made up his mind he was going to live. Anger at the North Koreans, anger at America, anger at his own actions, anger from a lifetime of failure—enough anger to live another day.

Years later when Walt reluctantly speaks about his experiences in Korea with other veterans, he recounts the bitter cold days up near the Chosin Reservoir and the fighting around Seoul, but never about the day in the ditch near the Kum River during the summer of 1950.

3

BEFORE DAN'S VISIT TO WHY, SUMMER 1986, CENTRAL COLORADO MOUNTAINS

Walt Kramer sits back on his haunches and wonders about this new life that now seems inevitable. His knees and back ache from an hour of gardening; not planting, but refurbishing, pulling weeds and clipping grass along the fence and headstones of the St. Mary cemetery. Using an anonymous headstone for support, he stands and stretches. This work, both in the small cemetery and inside the church, has been good therapy, but he ought to finish up and get on with that other life, that life in northern Colorado at the nuclear power plant. He walks to the cooler on the back steps for a beer and surveys the cemetery. What have I missed?

The markers are mostly old wooden crosses whose names have been erased over time. Poor people's monuments, temporary, just like the lives of the people beneath them. Men, women, children, babies: who knows? At the far end of the graveyard, away from the foot path, a common river stone marks the spot where he and Bellena and Mac scattered some of Sam's dirt. Dust to dust, or in this case, dirt to dirt. No formal headstone here; the secret secure. Yamantov. Thousands of unmarked graves. Sam carried his part in that tragedy to the mine, and now his unmarked grave is a simple stone in this cemetery. A more appropriate headstone will be set in Sam's mother's family plot in the Midwest. Bellena bought a wooden bench, a sturdy two-seater, and had her husband and father set it against the fence facing west, toward the setting sun, a place for contemplation. Walt protested at first, but Bellena ignored him. She was correct, as she usually is, and in the late afternoon, he sits on it often. So does Bellena when she visits. She is beginning to show, and her pregnancy gives her a reason to slow down, to take time away from her realty work and read. She will be an old first-time mother, in her 40s, but not as old as Walt, who is coming up on 54.

Sam did excellent work on restoring the church. Only the electrical system needed to be redone, but the woodworking is beautiful. After a 60-year hiatus, services will begin again, before the summer ends. Tourists, hikers, fishermen, local historians, and residents from nearby Buena Vista and Salida will be able to enjoy this rustic gem in a Colorado mountain setting. Bellena might even persuade Walt to attend. He laughs at the thought, but he does want his child to be baptized here. Continuation and perpetuation. Bellena once asked him when he stopped believing in God, and he told her it was when he realized he loved his country more than God. He's been rethinking that younger man's choice. Walt looks past the cemetery toward the tree line, toward the mine where several weeks earlier, he was also on his hands and knees.

    A small dust devil spins Walt back to the present. He missed a tuft of grass along one of the two marble headstones, one of the few monuments whose name can be read. Matteo Caesar Ragni, *alea iacta est*, 1832-1886. One hundred years older than Walt; 100 years ago this year. "The die is cast." Two thousand years earlier, Caesar crossed the Rubicon in northern Italy and made war on the emperor Pompey and the Roman army. A citizen of privilege attacking the government, the state. This was not a step to be taken lightly, because Caesar believed military service was the only honorable life. Walt has often wondered what Mr. Ragni was thinking to put this quote on his stone. How did he end up in Colorado? Maybe it was his wife or children who decided. Walt bends again to clip the grass on the back of the monument. It reveals another quote, one he hasn't noticed before. *"What I was and what I am are quite different, but the source is the same."* This etching looks new, as if it has been protected from weathering by the grass and shade.

    The source is the same. Walt isn't sure, but because of recent events, he hopes the final destination will be. He knows his work here at this tiny church in the central Colorado mountains is part of the healing, or at least is supposed to be, but answers have been elusive. He finishes his beer and crushes the can with one hand instinctively. Beyond the cemetery fence, beyond the stand of aspen, down the road toward the ghost town is where Walt is just now, on his hands and knees peering

The Why Intersection

into that mine shaft, searching for his son, believing the earth swallowed him up. *What am I missing?*

∾

"When's Barkley's funeral?" asks Mac.

"Saturday. Are you feeling up to going?" Walt takes the bowl of mashed potatoes from Bellena and scoops a large portion onto his plate. "Pass me a little gravy, hon, please."

"No. You and Belle go. He sure went fast after his bad fall, didn't he?" answers Mac.

"Probably a good thing. Seems his dementia had wiped out most of his memory. He couldn't place me when I was over last week. When memory goes . . ." Walt lets his last thought drift above the dining room table.

"Kind of the last link to Sam, huh," says Bellena. She reaches over and lays her hand on Walt's forearm.

"Father Tellez won't be attending. He sends his regards. I was a little surprised to hear Barkley had children; he'd never mentioned it." Walt shakes his head.

"All those other lives people have," says Mac. "Then again, maybe we can't know everything about a person."

"God, Dad, getting a little philosophical in your old age, aren't you?"

"Aw, Bellena, your dad's getting on in years too, and pretty soon he won't remember me," laughs Walt.

Mac chuckles back. "My life would have been a lot easier had I not known you. By the way, did you ever get a formal report from the Navy about Sam's death?"

Walt shakes his head before he speaks. "Nope. Don't suspect I ever will. Accident. Sam fell into the mine. Posthumous honorable discharge. Never recovered the body. Too dangerous."

Case closed, thinks Walt, but something stirs from his last visit with Barkley Abbott. A young man on the run befriends an old man whose mind is beginning to desert him. Unconditionally, they accept one another, and in the same season, they die. *What am I missing*, asks Walt to himself again? *Barkley couldn't place me, didn't cognitively recognize me, and yet we were able to carry on a conversation, mostly from an era before the young man was born. But there was a thread. Barkley said, "Go out of my mountains and take the desert trail towards the setting sun. Cross the river once and for all. The boy told me . . . he told me he'd be waiting for you." What boy*? Walt wanted to know, but the old man had moved to another subject, something about his grandchildren back east who had stopped speaking to one another, and Barkley was sad about that. Sisters.

Bellena waves her hand in front of Walt's face. "Hello. Earth to Walt. Are you in there?" He is and he returns. "Another one of your solo travels?" asks his wife.

Walt smiles. He seems to be taking these solo journeys more often these days. "No, Barkley was with me on this one. He was saying something kind of incoherent about meeting up with someone after his own death." Walt stops himself. Bellena accepts these flights, but Mac has expressed some concern about Walt lingering too long on Sam's death, that he's slipping into melancholia. Mac isn't comfortable with "dying talk," with traveling into the Great Unknown before one's time. What Walt understands is that the melancholia is Mac's fear of his own impending death. Still, tonight, over this meal, Walt wants the insights of his wife and his best friend. He turns to his father-in-law. "Bellena knows this, and I suspect you do too, but I fret over the loose ends of Sam's death. Not about all of the shaman business, that I'll never get, but about what seems to have been a plan to transfer something to someone."

"You mean besides all those souls?" says Mac with a hint of sarcasm.

"Dad . . ." cautions Bellena.

"Yeah, besides that. There was a depth to Sam in the mine that I certainly couldn't have known about before, but that he was trying to let out. He carried the Navy's secret, the nation's secret, but I felt something more, and I can't understand it."

"And you can't let it go, can you" says Bellena who knows about her husband's spirit.

Walt shakes his head in agreement with his wife. "I wish the government would accept Sam's death and let all this go."

The Why Intersection

Five days after Barkley Abbott's funeral, a funeral well attended by his colleagues, neighbors, and family members from Michigan, Walt again sits on Sam's bench and surveys the tiny cemetery. His eyes return to the words on the back of Matteo Ragni's monument. *What I was and what I am are different, but the source is the same.* What was it Barkley said? "Take the desert trail. Cross the river." What river, Barkley? Walt stands, turns toward the small stream behind the cemetery, and shakes his head. You make no sense, Barkley, but nothing else over the last few months has either. Walt's brief conversation with one of Barkley's granddaughters yielded no insight either. Walt Kramer stands motionless, like a statue, another monument on the grounds of St. Mary Church just south of Buena Vista, Colorado.

4

THE CALL, SUMMER 1986

"So here you are, *Dan*," says Jack from his wheelchair. "I'm gonna take you for your word here, that you're looking for someone for your friend. But you need to understand that we here in Why are a private bunch. Misfits. That's why we're here. The goings on over the last couple of years with the strike have made us all a little jumpy, you know, a little suspect of newcomers, so we don't give out information freely."

"Not that we have much information to give out usually," says Cocker.

Jack looks at Cocker. "I've got this, Cock." It's a mild reproach. "You're doing a favor for a friend. Good for you, but that doesn't work today. You're a proxy. What you need to do is go back to Colorado and tell your friend to come to Why himself. You might tell him it's doubtful he'll find the person he needs, but he can come and ask around." Jack stops there and holds Dan's eyes. Dan understands and nods. He stands and reaches for his wallet, but Jack waves him away. "We got this, *Dan*."

Julie slides off her stool and takes Dan's arm. "Here, let me show you out."

Just outside the door, Dan asks, "Why are you all so suspicious?"

"You're our visitor of the week. Last Tuesday, a guy just like you came looking around, maybe for a real person, maybe for a ghost. We have lots of ghosts here. He wanted information from me and the guys so he could find a missing miner. It was obvious he'd never worked at the mine up the road. He was nice too, drank a couple of beers just like you, but he had a motive. We think he belonged to a group of men who worked undercover for the state, and who broke down the union's solidarity during the miners' strike. Guys like him—and you—make us a little edgy, a little paranoid. I suspect you're here to see if that lady is around, but Rubicon isn't a neighborhood that wants to give up its secrets. On your way out, on your drive back through the Indian reservation, and when you find a high spot in the road on the east side, about twenty miles from Tucson, stop and look south. You'll see dozens of stand-alone ramshackle houses. That's where the real loners live, out among the cactus and critters, people who are truly afraid of their own shadow. Most of those people have disappeared from the world, even their own families don't know where they are and maybe never will. The desert takes them in and swallows them up." A dog wanders close to Julie, and she shoos it away with her foot. "Stray people, just like this mangy dog. It makes you think. 'How did they get that way?'."

The worker whom Dan saw an hour earlier steps into the street, picks up a box of wood strips, looks over at Julie and Dan, and returns to the cover of the building.

"What's his story?" asks Dan.

"A drifter. Pretty new. Works odd jobs, I guess. Been here just a little while. Smitty hires these rolling stones to work on the houses that he rents out so they can earn a few dollars. Keeps to himself. Doesn't live in the neighborhood, and we seldom see him. He waves when I stand out here by myself to ponder the clouds. He'll be moving on eventually. It's easy to disappear from Why since we're mostly invisible here anyway. He saw you and went back into the shadows. He fits in because he doesn't fit in. It's what losers do, you know, and mostly what we are in Why are eccentrics who don't want to give out information about how we lost. We all just bemoan the past and discuss it among ourselves. We want the government to stay out of our little corner of the country. Strangers too."

Dan narrows his eyes in a parental way. "And why are you here? What's your secret?"

Julie purses her lips, smiling with her eyes. "Speaking of moving on, Dan."

Dan nods, lifts his hand to shake Julie's, which they do, and walks to his car.

"Take care of yourself, meester." Julie smiles and waves before returning to the bar.

"Did he believe you?" asks Jack.

Smitty bobbleheads. "I don't know. I think he did, but I'm not sure. He's pretty sharp."

"Is it Thalia?" asks Cocker.

"Could be. She was in Colorado this summer. I don't know why she'd give an alias though. Patricia Frazier?" says Jack.

"Maybe Thalia is the alias," says Alf.

Smitty gives a nod to the table but conceals his concern.

The worker watches the stranger shake Julie's hand and retreat to his car. Even from the shadows of the building, the worker can make out the features of the stranger. The stranger is a confident man, but a cautious man too, a man who once struggled at a point in his life. The worker senses that he will never see the stranger again, but there is something. The worker wishes he couldn't discern these things about strangers. He shrugs. Maybe he's just taking on the habits of the suspicious loners in the bar.

The man with the binoculars has watched the morning's comings and goings from the hill across the highway, has taken notes on the individuals entering The Call. He even made a side note about the woman selling tamales. Everyone has suspicions.

When he first arrived in Why, Smitty did not like the fact he had to give the Ajo rental shop his driver's license information to get the tractor. He paid cash, a substantial amount of money to plow up a part of the desert. The store manager told him not to make a big deal of it, just show him his license info or no tractor. Told him it was a foolish thing he was planning to do anyway, building a golf course. "No, just three or four holes." There was barely enough water for the course in Why, chided the manager. "I'm 50-something years old and rich enough to do what I damn well please," replied Smitty.

That was in the seventies, and a decade later, Smitty has two holes completed: the par four dog leg that begins in his back yard and the par three that requires the golfer to hit over Rubicon Arroyo, a carry of

The Why Intersection

107 yards. Smitty lost his wife Geneva in '77, the same year he returned the rental tractor and bought one of his own, a used John Deere 3020. That's when he renamed his neighborhood Rubicon. Smitty figures at the rate he's going, he'll have three holes somewhere in the '90s. The two greens are sand, and there's no grass anywhere, but the fairways are clearly marked with white stakes, and he grades them monthly. Avoid the rough; it's filled with every variety of cactus imaginable. The numerous sahuaros that line the fairways act like spectators. He bought two golf carts after Geneva's accident, which has helped since his weight increased from what it was when he started the course, and his hips hurt when he walks. Alf said riding also lessens the chance of varmint bites. Alf holds the course record—six—but Smitty thinks that won't stand forever. Jack doesn't play but likes to ride in the cart in the evening to see the sunset. Julie brought Thalia out after she had been in Rubicon a few months, but both struggle at golf. Cocker hasn't made a par in two years but being stoned most of the time has something to do with that. It's a private course, and to this day only a dozen or so people have played it. The most famous man to play was that senator from Wyoming who was in Arizona to get the facts about immigration. Smitty is still trying to choose a name for his course. Lately, he and Alf have been going out in the evening to shoot snakes, so he's leaning toward a sophisticated name that has "Golf and Gun Club" at the end. Maybe Waddell Smithfield's Golf and Gun Club or possibly MIT West: Golf and Guns. Very elite.

Cocker starts humming, a sign he's had too much to drink. At the same time, Libby enters The Call, pours herself a small glass of mescal, and sits next to Julie. She uses a blue handkerchief to wipe her brow and the back of her neck. Her presence switches the men's attention away from the current discussion for just a moment. When Libby comes to the bar, it's usually to say something specific; she's not good at bullshitting, so she has the Guardians' attention. Libby finishes her shot of mescal, slides off the stool, walks around the table to where Cocker is sitting, and removes his baseball cap.

"Old man," she says leaning into his face, "we're done. I keep telling you to stay away, but you keep coming back. So, I'm stating this officially in front of your friends. I am not yours any longer, and you are to stay away from me. I don't want to see your drunk ass anymore." Libby kisses the top of his head, straightens, slaps Cocker's hat on crookedly, and walks out of the bar. A gust of wind sends a swirl of dust into the bar.

"How long this time?" asks Jack.

"She's pretty pissed at me. Maybe a couple of weeks," answers Cocker.

∽

Private Wagner crouches against the jeep tire, his poncho covering every part of his body except his eyes. The Chinese communists have overrun his unit on the south side of the Chosin Reservoir, and the Army is preparing to retreat south at the start of 1951. The temperature in Korea nears ten below, and the winter clothing issued by the Army is incapable of protecting him from the cold or the wind. Wind, thinks the private, the real killer. He watches a single soldier move frozen bodies off a pile to a more protected spot, a more orderly row so they can be picked up and shipped back to America. Wagner ought to help, but it's just too cold. The other soldier lifts one frozen corpse at a time, carries it ten or twelve feet across the road, and lays it under a tarp. Then he repeats the action. It doesn't appear as if he's been ordered to do this; he seems to have taken it upon himself to prepare these bodies for transfer and a flight home. Wagner can't stop shaking. The soldier tries to lift a particularly large body bag but stumbles. Unable to hoist it off the pile, the soldier kneels and drops his head, as if apologizing or praying. Private Wagner silently swears, stands, walks across the road, and helps the soldier stand. Together, the two living soldiers carry the remaining dead to the protected spot.

∽

After his discharge from the Army in 1953, after the Korean War, Wagner seemed to find every rut in the road, almost as if he intentionally steered into it. He couldn't hold a job and didn't seem to even want to work on a regular basis. He married a sixteen-year-old, had a child, and then divorced. The local police knew Wagner well. Growing up during the Depression in west Texas had set the tone; his parents operated a Standard Oil filling station in Monahans, and pumping gas and the isolation there were enough to keep him from knowing the events of the rest of the world or how to deal with the unforeseen. Without completing high school, Wagner had joined the Army in 1950 just to escape, chancing that even risking his life to fight the commies would be better than wasting his life in rural Texas. After all, Monahans wasn't Dallas or Houston; it was a stopover on the way to eastern New Mexico, itself a stopover on the way to California. He hadn't foreseen the harsh conditions of Korea and the war's brutality. When he returned stateside, Wagner took up his interest in music. After his divorce his parents kicked him out of the house, and he drifted into Lubbock with his guitar and found part time work backing up local rock and roll groups there. He wasn't Cocker back then; that moniker would come much later. Back then, he was Martin Lee Wagner.

Martin Lee was a talented musician, but his preference ran towards Gospel, the result of the fervor of his mother, a devout Pentecostal who loudly proclaimed her disdain for rock and roll, the devil's music. As Cocker would later relate, young Martin Lee was intrigued by the rising television evangelists who were springing up in the fifties. By 1960, when he failed to hook up permanently with a touring band, Martin Lee began following a charismatic evangelist by the name of Asa Allen. Martin Lee eventually joined up with Allen in southern Arizona near the copper mining town of Bisbee. Allen set up his revival tent, preached his Holy Ghost sermons, performed miracles, raised tens of thousands of dollars for his coffers, and ordained hundreds of young men into his ministry. One of those new pastors was Martin Lee Wagner, who was convinced that he had seen the Holy Ghost. Brother Allen tried to convince Martin Lee to give up alcohol and tobacco, but since Allen used both to calm himself, it was difficult for Martin Lee to abstain. The two men would drive off to Bisbee or Sierra Vista after a particularly emotional day, rent a motel room, and drink themselves into a stupor. The next day Allen would promise to beat the devil and ask Martin Lee to fight his demons too. Martin Lee had no such determination, which led to his bout with throat cancer in the late sixties, which led to a scratchy voice similar to the popular singer Joe Cocker.

Martin Lee left Brother Allen and his Miracle Revival Fellowship to preach on his own. God directed him to a town on the opposite side of Arizona near Ajo, Arizona, another isolated copper mining town, establishing his church in an abandoned warehouse just west of the intersection of Arizona Routes 85 and 86, a spot where drivers are forced to make a decision. Do they head south to Mexico, north to Gila Bend and on to Phoenix, or east through the Indian Reservation to Tucson? Martin Lee wanted to give them another choice, staying put in Why and waiting for The Rapture. He called his church Tabernacle. The temptations passing through that intersection, mostly in the form of drugs from Mexico, were too much for Martin Lee, and he failed to attract a sustaining congregation. Upon hearing of the death of Brother Allen in 1970 to alcohol poisoning, Martin Lee shuttered his church and began drawing his disability pension from the service. He withdrew from society and waited for the Messiah. A few years later, a rich mathematician from Boston bought a portion of the town, including Cocker's church.

Smitty understands why men like Cocker and Jack end up in a desolate town such as Why. He accepts that CJ and Alf and Julie will wander for some time in the desert while they figure out life's twists and turns, but Waddell Smithfield can't get a grasp on Thalia. She seems neither to be running nor hiding, confused nor questioning existence. She showed up in the middle of the street, looked around as if she was surveying a new property, gazed south for several minutes, turned back to The Call where she noticed him standing by the door, and walked directly up to him and asked him if he knew of a place she could rent. Since then, Thalia has not confided in anyone as to why Why was her destination. He knows she's a journalist, originally working out of Detroit, and in Arizona to research cross-border adoptions, information he hasn't shared with his beer buddies, but several months in Why? Another secret in a town of secrets. It's about the babies, but more. She is a delight, however, in a neighborhood that needs some positivity.

5

GROCERIES

Julie's Beer Guy carries groceries and a trunk full of alcohol when he returns to Why, driving over dirt roads through the Tohono O'odham Reservation, avoiding the border patrols who would confiscate the alcohol and return the groceries. These groceries originated in Guatemala, crossed into Mexico near Tapachula and made the 2,000-mile journey to Nogales. From there, the groceries were driven west along the border to the tiny town of La Lucita just south of the southern border of the Tohono O'odham reservation where they were picked up by Beer Guy. The groceries are unloaded at the back of the Tabernacle and stored there for two days before being taken to a Tucson church for safety as they awaited the next leg of their journey. None of the Guardians ask how the groceries make it to La Lucita; it doesn't matter. The Guardians' portion of the food chain is from the border to Tucson. In two years, all the groceries have been delivered safely to one of the churches in Tucson, by Cocker's count, 31 from Guatemala and El Salvador. Before, it was only Mexicans, and there was no real plan, just provide a cot and a meal and send them on their way. But in 1985 two refugee workers with experience working with the wars in Central America sat at The Call and asked for Smitty's help, to be a southern Arizona haven for desperate men who had nowhere else to be safe—and nowhere to call home.

The laborer observes the groceries' arrival, notices which patrons of The Call take them into the Tabernacle and who stays with them that evening. Alf speaks Spanish; Cocker knows a little, but seems to be the stocker, so to speak. It's beginning to make sense to him. There are so many people around the world on the move, trying to escape. The worker also knows that many in America simply want to return the groceries to Central America to let them spoil.

"Don't get me wrong, I know who the good guys are. We are, we certainly are, but sometimes I worry about our tactics. That's troubling to me," complains Smitty. "It's just that America always seems to be about acquisition by any means necessary. Kind of cruel, you know."

Alf grunts. "Sounds a bit like a conference meeting Phelps Dodge might have held in Phoenix. 'We're the good guys here,' they'd say. Then they used tactics to crush the union that reminded me of an assault in Vietnam to crush the VC. Helicopters, soldiers, the whole nine yards."

"There's a basic unfairness to our country these days, Alf."

"And what's that, Smitty?"

"Poverty, sort of. It's this growing disparity of wealth. It's crippling America, preventing us from fulfilling our destiny. Can't quite put my finger on the solution though."

"Tell me when you do, Smitty, so I can get in on the wealthy side."

The two men sit in one of Smitty's golf carts waiting for CJ to find his ball among the cacti. CJ is stubborn about his golf; he actually looks for his balls for the allotted five minutes. Everyone except Smitty plays cheap Top Flites, but for CJ it's the principle of the matter.

"Come on, CJ, just throw one out. We haven't got all day," yells Smitty.

"As a matter of fact, old man, we do. Hold your horses. I think I've found it." CJ bends over to identify his ball. Satisfied, he takes an awkward stance near a jumping cholla and chips his ball back into the fairway. He has escaped the desert this day unscathed. "Two." He laughs and walks back to his cart where Jack sits.

An hour later the four men sit in Smitty's dining room drinking beer and checking their scores. "I got an eleven," says Smitty. "Shit. I play this course nearly every day and rarely score par."

"Age is a terrible thing, Smitty," kids CJ. "I bogeyed number one but parred two. Eight. You guys owe me two bucks each."

"What's got a stick so far up your ass today, Smitty?" asks Alf. He finishes his beer and grabs another one from the ice bucket that sits on the table.

"Immigration reform. You'd think someone would actually come out to the border and maybe check on these people. I know, I know.

I've said this all before, but the poor guys from El Salvador and Guatemala and the other Central American countries need asylum. Shit! America funds the Contras and the right-wing thugs who don't give a shit about those poor farmers, and then when they flee to the U.S., we throw up our hands as if they're clean and send them back to be shot or tortured by the death squads. It's despicable, and we're a better country than that." Smitty gets up, goes to the liquor cabinet, and returns with a bottle of single malt scotch. He pours himself two inches in a glass and sets the bottle next to his glass without offering his guests any.

Jack, who is sitting in his wheelchair next to Smitty, picks up the bottle and examines it. "Lagavulin. Is this good stuff, Smitty? Might be nice to try it someday." Jack holds the bottle at arm's length to read the fine print.

Alf rises from his chair, walks to a cabinet next to the refrigerator, and finds shot glasses. "We'll drink in honor of CJ's impressive win today, while you rant about immigration. It's the least you can do for us." Alf sets the glasses in front of Jack, who pours a swallow into each one. The three guests raise their glasses in a silent toast to Smitty and then swig the scotch.

Jack pours another round. "You know we can't put them all up, boss."

Smitty shakes his head. "Where are the Americans who once were discoverers, who were in awe of the night skies, the unknown?" asks Smitty. "Where are the Americans who once had open minds, who hadn't been radicalized by politics? Our politicians all have the answers in their own minds, but none of them really do. I'd like one of them bastards to stand up in front of the cameras just once and say, 'I don't know.' They don't solve problems anymore; they just help create them. Our dead used to have voices. Now, we give the honored dead our words, so they say what we want them to. 'I love the Founding Fathers,' they say, and then today's politicians put their own words in the Founders' mouths. As America was becoming blind by ambition, it became righteous. As we roll on toward the 21st century, we've become creatures of the light, all but blinded to shades and nuances."

Jack looks to Alf and CJ. "Do you guys have any idea what our friend Mr. Smithfield here is saying? It's been my experience that our government has never been as pure as Smitty remembers." Alf nods in agreement.

Smitty breathes in deeply. "We want to keep communism out of our hemisphere. I get that. But the costs are greater than the reward. Do you know what we support in El Salvador? Those guys are murderous thugs. It's no wonder thousands of their people are trying to escape into the United States, and we send them back. We're not exporting democracy; we're supporting despicable dictatorships."

Jack raises his shot glass. "And fuck Ollie North too!"

Jack's statement seems to quiet Smitty for a moment. Jack pours himself, CJ, and Alf another round and taps Smitty's glass, a sign he should finish what's in his juice glass so that Jack can give him some more.

"What's this about, Smitty? Why'd you ask us out her today?" asks CJ.

∞

Smitty has driven his truck about three miles into the Organ Pipe Cactus National Monument and now sits on the tailgate watching the coming dusk. He does this frequently, always appreciating the sunset splay itself against the western sky. Until the sun sinks behind the low mountains, Smitty surveys the desert with his binoculars, hoping to catch sight of a coyote or deer or javelina. This is his alone time, his time of remembrance of all things of his wife. The desert was going to be a place of calm and solitude for him and Geneva, but it is never calm, and North America seems to be using the Arizona desert as its freeway. Then, Geneva died. Even on the stillest of days, the quietest of nights, there are air currents. And the events of the world all travel I-10 through Phoenix, the city that most exemplifies the new America, the harbinger of 21st-century America.

He spots movement behind a creosote bush 30 or 40 yards out. With his binoculars Smitty thinks it's a coyote, but he's not sure in the evening light. The animal seems to be wary, circling. Smitty lifts himself off the truck bed and gets behind the wheel. He drives up next to the bush with his lights on, scaring the coyote, which is what it turned out to be. He wants to see what the coyote was interested in. He aims his truck headlights at the bush and reaches under his seat for the high-power flashlight and his pistol before stepping out. He can't make out the type of animal, but he doesn't want to tangle with it, so he steps onto the step of his truck and fires off a shot to warn it away in case it's been injured. There is no movement, probably a dead animal. He steps down and over to the bush.

It's a small body, and the ground beneath the creosote bush is his last bed. Smitty remembers that first body he and Geneva discovered years earlier.

∾

"What did you do then, Smitty, you know, when you realized what it was?" asks CJ.

"It was pretty far under the bush, and I wasn't interested in reaching in there, especially as the light was going away. I hooked a chain to his leg and then to my bumper and dragged him out." Smitty pauses, but none of his friends speak. "He wasn't rigid yet; must have just died. Burned almost black. I picked him up and put him in the back of my truck and drove to the Border Patrol shack. Corey and Louie were working there, just by chance, but I was happy it was them. They treated the body with a good deal of respect."

The men are quiet for a time. Finally, CJ ponders, "I wonder why he came through the desert and not San Diego or Las Cruces?"

Alf knows. "Because maybe he's not a Mexican. He didn't know the procedure. Probably from Central America running for his life. He was dropped off after paying some coyote and left on his own. Crossing through the desert is a killer."

Jack pours each man another shot; this time it's tequila. They all know what Alf is saying, they've seen it before. The standard punch line is that living in Why doesn't make sense—unless one is a loser. But today, away from The Call, living in Why does make sense.

Alf raises his glass and glances at CJ. The others raise theirs. "To all those other dead bodies in the desert."

Smitty drinks and then proposes a second toast. "To this new America, the one where a person can't hide or run away, even in the middle of a God-forsaken desert. Where the government sticks its nose in everywhere." It's a sarcastic toast, tinged with anger.

∾

It wasn't always CJ. It started as a derisive accusation in late '83 as Copper Joe, much like Yankee Doodle Dandy. Alfonso, Al Peru then, confronted Joe in the street in front of Al's house in Morenci; warned him that if he delivered an eviction notice to him, he would kick his ass all the way back to the Phelps Dodge offices in Phoenix; cautioned him about working alone. It was in the fall. The union was beginning to doubt its infallibility. Al's wife seemed desperate, asking him what they were going to do if the strike wasn't successful. Al couldn't answer her question, so he went outside to let off steam, and that's when he encountered Joe. Joe and Al. Two working American's who should have been on the same side.

"Your union demands will destroy PD. You guys don't get it; they're losing money."

"Tell me your stockholders aren't still getting paid, motherfucker, and then we'll talk about losing money." Al steps toward Joe and slaps at his papers. He misses, but as Joe moves them away, he loses his grip, and the stack falls to the street.

"What the fuck do you guys want? Why can't you just take what's being offered and go back to work?" entreats Joe.

"What do we want? What do we fuckin' what? We want dignity. We've been after it since my grandfather started working for PD. Each step along the way has been a struggle. He couldn't even take a shower after work with the white guys, because he was a Mexican. We didn't have health coverage. Now we only ask for our cost-of-living guarantee, and you fucks think we're going to bankrupt you. Have you even thought about us as people?" Al stops because he fears he will slug Joe. "Pick up your papers and get the hell out of here. You don't know."

Joe stoops to retrieve his notices. As he stands, he notices the curtain in Al's small house drawn aside and Al's family watching. Then he makes a strange request. "I'd like a cup of coffee. Do you have any inside?"

Moments later, Al introduces Joe to his family. "This is my wife,

The Why Intersection

Elva, and my boys, Charlie and Leroy." Joe shakes the hand of each family member and gives a slight bow. "Honey, if you would pour a cup of coffee for our guest and then take the boys into the living room, I would appreciate it." Al offers a kitchen chair to Joe.

In time Joe speaks. "Just as you've been doing your job, I've been doing mine. The thing is . . . I think I'm on the wrong side of this conflict. Anyone on the other side is thought to be the enemy, and I don't want that to be the way of things. Before the strike we were all on the same side, working for the same company, trying to get on with our everyday lives." Joe realizes he's skirting the margins. "What I mean is we shouldn't be enemies. I'm not a muckety-muck, higher up guy, just a guy who never gave much thought to you guys who go down in the ground every day." Joe pauses again. "That's not quite right. I guess I have thought about you miners, but not deeply. These weeks didn't change my mind much about you and your fellows, but it made me see behind that curtain where your wife and kids were hiding when we were in the street. They feel the same passion in all of this that you do. I've never experienced that. When I got my job with PD and was assigned to Arizona, my wife left me. I'm on the far side of 40 and live by myself; work for a paycheck. What I've seen here in Morenci and Clifton and in Ajo are families working the mines. The union is family and family history. You struck not for a wage, but for something bigger. Until this moment, I never understood." Joe looks into his coffee and wonders why he's baring his soul to a stranger. Fifteen minutes ago, he thought he was going to fight Al.

Al fidgets in his chair. "Am I supposed to say something here, cause if I am, I don't know what it should be."

"No, not yet. Guess I'm just trying to work this out myself. I know a couple of things. One, if things keep going the way they are now, you're going to lose. PD doesn't care about your cola or health insurance or anything. They want the union gone. Second, they've hired some assholes to infiltrate your ranks. PD knows pretty much what you plan to do before you do it. These men were in place before you guys walked out. I don't know who they are, but I will. They go to your meetings and report back to PD." Joe takes a deep breath. "It isn't fair; this fight never has been."

"Fuck!" Al stands and turns around. "Fuck! We wondered how they could know." He walks to the doorway leading to the living room where his family sits obediently. "Sorry about my language. It won't happen again." He turns back to Joe and stares. He takes two steps and grabs the back of his chair, turns it backwards, and sits down. "Tell me. What do you propose?"

Joe leans across the table and speaks in a whisper. "If PD can have spies, the union ought to have one too."

∽

"Miss Fisher." Josie, the oldest girl in Thalia's class, has a puzzled look on her face.

"Yes, dear, what is it?"

"All these people at the ranch. I'm getting confused. Why does Mr. Steinbeck need so many? The story's just about George and Lennie, isn't it?"

Thalia sits on a stool near Josie. "You're correct, it is, but they don't live in a vacuum. George is sort of like Lennie's guardian, and if they were alone and free to live on their own ranch, everything might be okay, but it would be an even shorter book without many lessons for us. All those other characters muddy up the waters, just like life is complicated and . . . muddy." She pauses to let Josie comprehend her words.

Josie smiles. "Will they all be on the test?"

"Not all of them, but some of them will be."

"Also, Miss Fisher, I don't know who the bad guy is."

It's Thalia's turn to smile. "Start with Curley. He's a privileged bully, isn't he, who can't distinguish right from wrong."

Josie looks at her notes for a moment before responding. She flips back a page and nods slowly. "George sees through him, doesn't he."

6
WHY

Why, Arizona. Why Arizona?

"It's the convergence of two Arizona highways in the Sonoran Desert. You'll fly to Phoenix where there'll be a car for you. Drive west on I-10 about 30 miles, then turn south on State Route 85. Eighty miles down the road, you'll pull into Ajo, a quaint little mining town, a copper mine whose workers are on strike and maybe a little out of sorts. Keep going ten more miles and you'll come to the junction of 85 and 86. That's Why. Maybe a hundred people plus the RV park where you might be staying for a short time. From Why it's 28 miles to Sonoyta, Mexico, through the Organ Pipe Cactus National Monument. That's the portal. If you head east toward Tucson, you pass through an Indian Reservation. They won't be any help. There's a bounty hunter who works the area, kind of a shady character himself, but seems to be carrying a grudge. Good instincts, but, as I said, not one to trust." The anonymous voice provides no other information, he is simply relaying information that was given to him by higher ups.

The Navy officer nods. He knows this is most likely another false tip, but all of them need to be checked out. The web of secrecy so carefully constructed about Yamantov is unraveling. The last thing the military wants is for amateur sleuths to get involved in this case. Too sensitive. Cooley hangs up the phone. He rocks his empty coffee cup as he ponders the tip. The last tip sent him to Rolla, Missouri, and it proved to be simply an AWOL soldier stationed at Ft. Leonard Wood who knew a little history and liked conspiracy theories. The nation will learn about Yamantov eventually, but Cooley's job is to delay that knowledge by three decades. Even then, certain material about that Soviet city north of the Arctic Circle will remain classified.

∽

Alf and Cocker sit with a man of indeterminate age in the hallway of the Tabernacle while he eats one of Libby's tamales. Alf picked him up at the border on the Tohono O'odham reservation earlier in the evening, collecting him from a Mexican driving a dusty Oldsmobile. They wait for Smitty who had a dinner appointment with a deputy sheriff in Ajo.

Segundo Vasquez is exhausted from his three-week trek from El Salvador along dirt roads, sleeping in safe houses until his savings ran out. Then, he was on his own. When he crossed the border, he hadn't eaten in three days. Segundo told Alf that his sister had been picked up at a market in his small village, accused of being a communist because she was wearing jeans. Two days later, her body was dumped in the town square for all to see as an example, as a warning. She was no longer wearing her jeans. The Death Squads need examples. Once a Salvadoran is labeled a communist, his or her life is in peril. At least, Segundo told Alf, his sister didn't just disappear; the family was able to give her a decent burial. The Death Squads gave Segundo a choice. Join the unit or die. Segundo joined the murderous thugs but deserted after three days. His escape took him across mountains to Honduras, then to Guatemala, across the border into Mexico in the state of Chiapas where he posed as a seasonal laborer. His real occupation was as a journalist, which was the reason his sister was murdered. He was covering her activities to unionize the local mine. That warning.

Smitty arrives around 10:00. He speaks little Spanish, so his conversation with Segundo is translated by Alf. "You will hide under the back seat of my car, and I will drive you to Tucson, an hour trip, where you will be given over to a priest. There, you will be safe, and in time join a secret population of Salvadorans living in Los Angeles." Segundo shakes Smitty's hand and thanks him profusely. He tells the three men that he wants to return to his village, to his country when it is safe.

༄

Thalia watches the latest temporary worker, inspects him, studies the newest man in Why. She heard from the Guardians that he was here; now that rumor is fact. He's not a young man, as they suggested, but he's far from an old man. Late 20s, early 30s maybe. Already the men at The Call have given him a past, one that has no

The Why Intersection

basis in evidence, but one that will suffice until the new man tells them otherwise. Smitty hired him as another carpenter to repair one of his numerous properties, the second worker hired by Smitty this season. Smitty says he might be a student minister who's out here in the desert looking for the real God, like Cocker. *Aren't they all*, thinks Thalia. Maybe he's a new guest, one who's hiding in the open. This new man doesn't live on a Smithfield property but is staying in a small house over by the oil tanks nearer the highway, a house hidden from Rubicon.

The new man peruses the used books on the top shelf and takes a half-dozen. He places them on the counter and smiles at Thalia but says nothing. *A man who reads*, she thinks. He moves along the food aisle, stocked with items donated by the Guardians after their infrequent trips to Ajo's supermarket—to be shared. He selects a few cans and jars, mostly soups and peanut butter, puts them on the counter as he did the books, and walks back to the food aisle. He takes coffee, sugar, bread, and cereal this time, walks back to the counter and puts them next to the soup.

"I can give you a sack to put that all in," says Thalia.

The man nods. "Thanks," he answers in English. "I'm almost done." He turns around searching for something but doesn't seem to locate it. Turning back to Thalia, he asks, "Milk?"

She points him to the cooler. He could be a minister, soft spoken and polite, but something in her skin tells her he isn't. There's something translucent about him, a word that just pops into her head, and one she can never recall using before. But there is. In the dim light of Cocker's Tabernacle, his features are muted, and what he really looks like is difficult to identify. His edges are not clearly defined.

Placing the milk carton on the counter, he reaches into his front pocket for cash. No billfold. Thalia enters the various items' cost into the manual cash register, simultaneously placing the items in a used brown grocery sack. Normally she makes small talk with familiar customers, locals, but she waits.

"Eleven eighty-nine," she says.

"Hector." He holds out twelve dollars. "It's Hector."

Thalia smiles and nods. She smooths the bills with the counter's edge before putting them in the drawer and gives him a dime and a penny, slightly touching her fingers to his palm. She looks up and finds Hector staring intently into her face.

"I have this image of you ... or a memory of some kind. You were with a handful of kids and holding a baby. Who lives here?" he asks.

Thalia doesn't answer the question seriously. "Ghosts mostly. Maybe Libby's not a ghost; sometimes CJ regains his form, but, yeah, the rest are ghosts."

"You too?"

"I don't know. Can you see me?"

"Yeah, but that doesn't prove anything. I've seen ghosts before." He nods, turns, and leaves.

Thalia is confused. She thinks she would have remembered him, but maybe she didn't see him. That would make sense in Rubicon. Unconsciously, she places her fingertips on her lips, and her body shudders slightly.

∽

Rubicon, Arizona. It's not shown on the State Farm travel atlas. The laborer knew it wouldn't be. One block of houses in various states of repair intentionally avoided by the rest of a forgettable roadside town. He laughs when he considers why anyone would seek sanctuary here. Had he crossed the border at a different location, at Sasabe or Nacho or Douglas, a different turn in the road ... but he was directed here. It sits on the southwest corner of the unincorporated town of Why, a group of houses and one tavern that showed up for sale in several national newspapers for next to nothing. Waddell Smithfield bought them all, plus an old vegetable warehouse across the highway. The laborer wonders about Mr. Smithfield's motivation. If things go well, maybe he'll have a chance to ask him someday.

The laborer finds an international atlas left by a previous tenant. He flips to the maps of Europe. He finds Italy and begins to search for the Rubicon River. He could use the index to locate it more quickly, but he has always enjoyed the search. He knows its general location in Northeast Italy. Starting in the Apennine Mountains, the Rubicon flows mostly east into the Adriatic Sea, a short distance for such a famous river. He notices the Arno River originates nearby in the Apennines but flows west into the Tyrrhenian Sea. Raindrops from the same storm, from the same cloud, could end up in different seas. The laborer ponders the ramifications of this for himself.

Further north, he traces the Po River's course. A greater river flowing from the Southern Alps in France to join the Rubicon in the Adriatic. He remembers reading about recent flooding in Northern Italy and wonders which rivers were involved. Why did a dozen houses at the end of a dirt road gain the name of this river on the other side of the world? He knows enough history to recall when over 2,000 years ago, Caesar crossed the Rubicon and started a civil war within the Roman Empire, but beyond this he is unsure. He wonders if there is a library in Ajo.

∽

The encyclopedia states the Rubicon changed its course frequently since Caesar crossed it in 49 B.C., especially in the thousand years leading up to the Middle Ages. Only two places remain constant: its source in the Apennine Mountains and its mouth into the Adriatic Sea. Several paths to take one from where he starts to where he ends. Caesar committed everything when he led his army across this small stream, and Europe was forever changed.

The laborer wonders if there are catchable trout in the Rubicon River of Italy. He also has a strange feeling about the new worker who is working at one of the other vacant houses Mr. Smithfield owns. It isn't trepidation, more just curiosity.

∽

Cocker watches Hector paint the bedroom wall. He doesn't speak, he just watches. Hector senses Cocker's presence, the most ragged of the ragged men of Why, but he will wait until Cocker chooses to speak, if indeed he does. Cocker is intrigued by the handyman's method. Hector covers the edges of the wall with careful attention not to get paint on the ceiling, floor, and other two walls. Then, Hector outlines a square in the center of the wall and begins to paint the remainder of the surface, leaving that square bare.

Cocker seems uncomfortable with this.

"Why?" asks Cocker.

Except for Mr. Smithfield who just this week hired him for odd jobs, Hector has not formally met any of the men who hang out at The Call, and this is the first word any of them have spoken to him. He turns to Cocker and nods, sets his brush on the lid of the paint can, wipes his hands on his jeans, and smiles. "I heard you come in. Just waited for you to say something. Figured you would eventually." He extends his hand to Cocker, who reaches out to shake. "Why what?" asks Hector.

"Why did you make that square so deliberately?"

Hector turns back to the wall and studies it for a moment. Without turning to Cocker, he says, "I don't remember." He shakes his head slightly and then faces Cocker. "I get these things in my head when I'm doing menial tasks, and I guess I'm responding to those thoughts, but I don't remember what this one was now. Hmm."

"People in your head too?"

"Running around like crazy."

"So, you're here in the desert now?"

"This desert for now," says Hector. "I'm from another desert." There is a short pause between the two men before Hector asks, "You and your pals don't mind, do you?"

"Nah, not really. A couple of them are always suspicious, but you seem to be harmless."

Hector nods, but he says the word to himself. *Harmless.*

Cocker walks to the wall and puts his palm in the unpainted square. "I guess some jobs allow a person to be aimless at times. Others require some attention. We here in Rubicon are in the desert for now too. Just a collection of damaged souls passing time, together by chance, I suppose." With his index finger, he traces the outline of the square.

"Careful. That's not dry yet."

"Not all of us are permanents here. Me and Smitty, maybe. Maybe Jack. That's all though." Cocker leans in and smells the wall. "Musty. A fellow could walk in here and look at your wall and say, 'You missed a spot.'" He turns to Hector. "That's a joke, young fella."

Hector laughs. "That fellow could say lots of things about my wall."

The Why Intersection

Cocker picks up the paint brush, dips it into the can, but hesitates. Then, he draws a butterfly in the square. He studies it for a moment and then bends over and wipes the paint from the brush. "A soul needs a goal, a focus. It can't be in hiding forever; it has to explore." He sets the brush back on the can. "Butterflies are silent except for the flit of their wings. They often migrate for thousands of miles, but they're quiet. No harm to nothing. Just simple beauty. Would you be willing to paint some walls with me over at the warehouse across the highway? I can't pay you."

∽

Lizardo is back. His presence unnerves the Guardians because he's a bounty hunter and persistent at his job. He works out of Phoenix, although he once said he came from Wichita, Kansas. "More fugitives in Arizona. High bails. I guess it has something to do with the proximity to the border." Lizardo is licensed to carry a weapon, and he makes no bones that he does. He wanted to earn a few extra dollars, and he discovered he liked the adrenaline rush of the chase and the capture. Tall, wiry, and a bit bow-legged, he looks like he could have been a Wild West cowboy from the previous century, and he dresses the part, bolo tie and Stetson. His wide-set eyes take in everything, and when something catches his attention, he blinks rapidly.

Lizardo patrols State Route 85 from Buckeye to Lukeville at the Mexico border and I-10 from Tucson through Phoenix and I-8 to Yuma. He knows every bar along the way. Hundreds of square miles of desert in southwestern Arizona. Occasionally, he will veer off towards Nogales on I-19, but the Border Patrol usually controls that. He refers to Why as "Onionville. Peel back the layers one by one to see what you find. Such a pathetic little town, it makes me want to cry." Then he laughs. Lizardo frequents the small towns listening to rumors. He checks court and police records and consults with bail bondsmen. For Lizardo, everyone in these hovels is a suspect, and that unnerves the Guardians. And there's usually someone who can't keep a secret, doesn't want to keep a secret, and can be bribed or extorted. Today at The Call, Lizardo orders a shot of tequila and a beer, sits with his back to the wall, wraps his long fingers around his drinks, and surveys the bar.

"Who are you looking for this time? More smugglers?" asks Jack, the only Guardian in the bar. Three Why men sit at another table but say nothing. When Julie places Lizardo's drinks on the table, she stares at him and pauses. Lizardo reminds her of another reckless man from another decade.

"White guy, medium height, a little chubby, brown hair. Skipped bail in Phoenix a couple of days ago. The police think he's headed north, but he has family in Tucson, so I'm taking a shot here."

"What crime?" asks Jack.

"Embezzling his bank. White collar."

"So, your fee will be pretty lucrative."

"Yeah, but I gotta get him before my competitors do," answers Lizardo. He swallows half the shot of tequila. "Don't suppose you've seen him around here."

Julie laughs. "We don't get bankers in here."

"Never trusted a banker," drones Jack.

"Never underestimate a bail jumper," replies Lizardo. "They're always desperate. Stupid usually, especially if this is their first time breaking the law, but desperate. This one will know to avoid big cities, plus he has a kid in Phoenix too. Won't go too far."

"You talk like you know him," says Jack.

"Not him, just his kind. He's from privilege and thinks he can get away or finagle his way out of this. I'll just be patient and he'll mess up." Lizardo finishes his beer and then swigs the rest of his tequila.

"Why'd you show up here today, Lizardo?" asks Julie.

"Thirsty."

"You make me nervous."

"I shouldn't, unless you've got something to hide."

"Everybody's got something to hide. You know that, Lizardo. Even you probably."

The bounty hunter smiles. "I just stopped in to say hi and to let you know I'm still working. Never know what might turn up at The Call."

"You've got a skewed picture of Why, Lizardo," says Julie.

Lizardo nods. "My job gives me a skewed picture of the whole country. I like to stop in here just to get a reality check." He stands and leaves a quarter tip. "Tell your loser friends I said hello. Remind them that some son-of-a-bitch needs to do this kind of work. I'm that son-of-a-bitch."

"And what kind of work is that?" asks Julie.

"Rounding up the bad guys."

∽

"So Lizardo's on the prowl again," muses Alf that evening as the Guardians sit with their usual late beers. More than any other Guardian, Alf seems to hate the bounty hunter the most. "Did he ask about any of us?"

Jack shakes his head. "We live in a strange time when a low life like that can move freely, and others have to hide in the shadows."

Smitty stands, walks to the wall, and flips the switch to the bar's overhead lights. "Does that help rid us of our shadows tonight?" He moves behind the bar and takes a bottle of beer from the cooler before returning to his seat. "We Americans are a peculiar lot."

"More than that," spits Jack. "Angry, divided, contentious, fucked up."

"Did Julie get the groceries delivered?" asks CJ.

"Yeah. She's on her way back. Smitty shouldn't have to get his own beer much longer tonight." Jack spins his wheelchair toward Smitty. "Still have that one guest out at your place?"

Smitty nods. "I'll move him later tonight."

The table goes quiet for a time. Lizardo's aura remains. Cocker gets up and leaves.

Jack breathes in heavily. "Should you warn the two recent laborers about Lizardo?"

"I already talked to them. Neither seemed worried. The Hector fellow is Indian and laid back."

"T-O?" asks Alf.

"No. Navajo from the rez up near the northwest corner. Said he was just bored up there. I laughed that he would come here for excitement. Said he might go to Mexico, so he's picking up a few dollars from me. That, and the wind. Interesting guy."

"And the other guy?" asks Alf. "Does he have a name?"

Smitty nods again. "Told me to call him Joe when he first started earlier in the summer, but I told him we already had a Joe in town, so he said to just pick a name. I suggested Diego, thinking at the time he was half-Mexican, what with his behavior. So, he's Diego now."

Alf sneers and shakes his head at Smitty.

Jack looks at Alf. "Those two do look a little alike, Hector and Diego. Ever notice?"

Smitty hadn't noticed. Maybe it was how one is so comfortable with tools and is bent over with a task while the other seems to be just interested in earning a few dollars. Diego might stick around Why for months, could fit in with The Call crew over time, while Hector seems to be a rolling stone. Smitty imagines Hector making a few dollars, saying, "Thanks, Mr. Smithfield," on payday and heading out again, the direction not making a difference, probably back to the rez. Smitty does see the similarity now as he drinks his beer, and the table is again quiet.

Smitty finds Diego at the third house he looks, one of his houses that is still unoccupied because of its rundown condition. Also, no one is looking to move into Why. Technically, it's not in Rubicon but closer to the oil tanks a block away. Diego is rebuilding the wall between the kitchen and small bedroom, a wall that looked like an angry miner had taken a sledgehammer to it out of frustration. Payday. Smitty trips over a piece of gypsum board by the door, catching his balance before he falls, which gets Diego's attention.

"Sorry about that, Mr. Smithfield. I shouldn't have left those scraps by the door."

"No, not your fault. I'm just a clumsy old man."

"Are you okay?"

Smitty swivels his body in an effort to realign his skeletal structure. "Yeah, at least from this incident." He places his hand against the wall for stability and steps over the pile of refuse. "Your beard's getting pretty scruffy. You're hardly recognizable compared to when you first arrived." Diego offers his hand but waits for his boss to speak, which he does. "Looks like you're making some progress. Is the structure sound?"

Diego nods. "Yes, sir. I took down the brace a few days ago after I tore out the wall to inspect it, but it's okay. Whoever went after it missed the support beams."

"Do you have what you need to make all the repairs?"

Diego smiles. "Yeah. I send Hector over to Ajo when I need something, and he just charges it to your account."

"You don't go?"

"No, it takes too much time out of my job, and Hector enjoys being useful. He's kind of a people person, a bit more gregarious than me."

Smitty nods too thinking neither of his two current workers are what one might call people persons. "He is that. Nice young man. Think he'll stay around long?"

"I have no idea. He hasn't indicated one way or the other."

"What about you, Diego? You've got a real skill with this house repair thing, and

I've got plenty of work for you, as you've seen."

The worker turns and lifts a two-by-four from the floor as an act of deflection. "I haven't given it much thought, sir. You've kept me so busy; I just work and sleep."

Smitty knows this isn't true. He's watched this man, had a few conversations with him, and thought about why a skilled craftsman might have wandered into this part of the desert. "I came over to pay you. I think it's been two weeks since I last gave you a wad of cash." Smitty takes an envelope from his hip pocket and hands it to Diego.

"From the feel of this, you've overpaid me again but thank you."

"I'm curious, Diego. How'd you find Why? This isn't exactly the intersection of choices, and the tourist bureau here doesn't advertise that I pay well. The amenities for a single man are sparse." Smitty smiles at his last remark. "We all sort of chose to live here—except Cocker who was commanded here by God. Did God send you?"

Diego recognizes the probe in the form of a joke but doesn't sense danger. It's something else. "Well, as you've seen, I kind of like working and being by myself. I grew up small town, a metropolis compared to this, but when I was looking for my next stopover, I saw the name Why and thought it might be interesting to see. With a name like

Why, how can a person not spend a little time on contemplation here." He pauses. "Besides, from all appearances this is a town one settles in when all the good choices have been exhausted."

Smitty remembers from a time a decade back. "Sounds familiar. Why," he says not as a question but as the town's name. "What do you have to contemplate?"

"I don't know . . . borders, boundaries, frontiers, the horizon. Just the things that give men pause early in life, I guess. I couldn't do that if I was raising a family with a nine-to-five job. Time enough for that later, maybe?"

"Old men ponder those same things. And you couldn't do that in Tucson or Phoenix?"

Diego shakes his head. "I've got too many questions bouncing around in my head. Don't need others demanding my time, asking me to explain myself too. Sort of like you, Mr. Smithfield. You know a lot, but it's nobody's business but your own."

Smitty realizes that he's been reprimanded gently but continues anyway. "I noticed the tattoo. Nautical star. Navy?"

Diego glances at his own arm and nods. "Once."

"I did some work for the Navy a long time ago too. Not really in the Navy but connected. Maybe that's how I ended up here, in a very roundabout way." Smitty lets that statement hang in the air, and Diego doesn't respond. The old man walks past his employee into the kitchen area where he inspects the cabinets and counter. "Lots of rumors about you around the bar."

"Lots of rumors about any stranger that walks into The Call. I suspect when each of the guys came to Why there were rumors about you. What about your past, sir?"

Smitty turns back to Diego to answer. "It wasn't Rubicon until I got here." The old man pauses and then smirks. "One rumor is that I'm a mad scientist who built a rocket to the moon, part of the NASA program that sent Armstrong up there. Another rumor is that I built computers for a defense system for America that was stolen by the Soviets after the war, giving rise to James Bond movies. Those are the old rumors. The latest is that I built a computer small enough to fit in a briefcase. You know, wild stuff, unbelievable stuff that the boys at the

The Why Intersection

bar run with after a few too many beers."

A wind blows through Diego's body. He lets it pass as a deep breath that he expels through his mouth. "But you're here now. Are you planning to live out your days here drinking beer and golfing?"

Smitty turns away from Diego and looks out the window that faces west toward the uninhabited desert. "We all face choices at various times in our lives that seem innocuous at that moment, but in reality, are life altering. Sort of like Robert Frost's poem—which road do you choose—or like coming to Why." Smitty turns back to Diego. "Which highway do you take from here? 85 or 86? Seems like you've already made a few hard choices, and here you are, son, at another intersection. Back to your question. I guess as long as I'm allowed, and trouble doesn't find me, I'll remain here off the beaten path. And you? I can't imagine a young man with your skills settling in this desolate edge of the world forever."

Diego rolls his tongue in his mouth and shakes his head. "I haven't settled anywhere my whole life. I don't know what that would be like. Anyway, my skills are useful nearly everywhere."

Smitty runs his hand along a countertop. "Well, if this is an example of the work you do, I could have you working for me for a long time. I have a room over at my place that needs a little work."

7

SHADOWS

Smitty has tentacles. He knows people. Old people. What that means keeps his friends in Rubicon guessing. He is the most even tempered of the men who frequent the bar, the rest of whom seem to have embers that flare weekly, especially Jack and Alf. He and Jack read newspapers, Jack looking for articles to stoke his long-smoldering anger, especially articles about the Palo Verde nuclear power plant, the dragon he'd like to slay. Smitty searches like an archeologist at times, interested in the articles within the articles. He enjoys discussing nuclear power with Jack, about its feasibility for the future, about its inherent dangers. Smitty's 66 and looks it. He's been retired forever unless one counts his real estate enterprise. Rubicon.

When new people come to Why, the first person they seem to meet is Smitty. Those tentacles. When Smitty first met them, Alf and CJ were Al and Joe. Cocker predates Smitty. As far as any of them know, Smitty has no children, but, according to Thalia, he would have made a wonderful grampa. During the frequent evening gripe sessions, Smitty pokes Cocker, because he's generally a puppy dog, and Jack, because it's necessary as a pressure release. Occasionally, he will gently cajole Julie, especially when she gets frustrated with her role in Rubicon. He monitors his words with Alf, not wanting to ignite Alf's smoldering demon. CJ is so even tempered that sarcasm only makes him smile. CJ seems to be growing into a role similar to Smitty's, although that is quite a ways down the road. Smitty likes these Rubiconers. Like him, they've lived through personal crises and reinvented themselves.

Smitty's house sits at the western boundary of Why, of Rubicon. Three bedrooms, two baths. It's the nicest house in Why, although the exterior looks much like the rest of the town. Wouldn't want to attract attention to it. It's a private house, and guests are only entertained in the kitchen and living room. His patio takes the full heat of the summer sun and heat, but for the cooler months of each year, it's where he finishes most days, watching the sunset with two fingers of a fine scotch. And his thoughts. Talking with his ever silent but ever-present Geneva. When the sun finally goes out, he will read or return to The Call to be with his friends.

Why has no Sunday church, no minister unless one allows Cocker to continue his ministry. Whyans who wish to observe the Sabbath travel to Ajo on Sunday mornings. Most of the Guardians just pray to the God of Nature if they pray at all. Smitty frequently discusses faith with Cocker, challenging his beliefs, often over a beer. Still, Smitty will drive to Tucson every month or so to meet with ministers and priests of various Christian churches, not to attend an organized service, but to discuss faith and the practice thereof. Frequently, Smitty will take another with him, but he always drives home alone.

∾

It's Saturday morning at The Call. By his appearance Cocker looks like he slept there, sleeping off a long evening, now nursing a strong coffee. Julie sits at the bar reading her Bible, also drinking coffee. Smitty enters the otherwise empty space, turns on one of the new window ACs, pours himself a coffee, kisses Julie on her forehead, and sits with Cocker.

"Mornin'," one of the men offers. The other nods. Smitty takes a pocket-sized spiral notebook from his shirt and begins to make a list. After a few minutes of silence, Cocker asks Smitty what time he returned from Tucson.

"Late." He smiles and nods his head. "Or early depending on one's point of view."

"Everything okay?" asks Cocker.

"On our end. Father John's probation isn't slowing him down. The courts know he's doing the right thing with the illegals, but the law says something else. A good man."

Cocker sits up straighter. "See, there are real Christians in America." He presents this statement like it's the closing argument for a previous discussion.

Smitty writes something on his notepad. "A few, Cock, a few."

"I was born on this path, you know that. I don't apologize."

"And you shouldn't, Cock. You've a good Christian." There is only

Julie in the audience for this discussion, so Smitty isn't pushing for a laugh at Cocker's expense. When Smitty returns from Tucson after delivering groceries, he's often saddened. "A minister who tries to save immigrant lives gets convicted of a crime. The government that abets in killing innocents..." Smitty goes quiet.

Julie puts a marker in her Bible and moves to the table with her coffee. "I think you're a Buddhist, Smitty." She smiles.

Smitty tilts his head, his expression asking her to explain.

"The core of your faith is behavior. Ethics. The core of my faith, Cocker's faith, Christianity, is salvation. At least it is for today's modern American Christianity for most people. 'Jesus is the Way.' You probably don't even believe in a personal God who makes you rich." Julie says this with a lilt that only slightly masks her seriousness.

"Father John warned me about spies; told me to be careful. We've been doing this chapter for three years. We've been lucky. We keep our numbers small."

"Spies?" asks Cocker.

"Not exactly. More like suspicious people who resent our private little world here," answers Smitty.

Later that morning, pulling a wagon with food supplies for the pantry, Cocker goes to the warehouse, his Tabernacle of years past, restocks the shelf and cleans. He wishes this warehouse had a shower to supplement the small sink. When he finishes, he returns to The Call. He leaves Julie and Thalia a list of what he has before returning to the warehouse.

∾

Do I start at the top or the bottom? Hector holds a crowbar in his left hand and a cup of weak coffee in his right. The carpet pieces will need to be removed to see what type of wood lies beneath, but he shakes his head trying to imagine what the original owner of the house was thinking when he laid the carpet in the first place. The second floor is a single room, an add-on built as an afterthought, and the only area in the entire house with carpet, along with this stairway. Remnants. This job should be easy, a day and a half at most if the wood doesn't need much sanding, but it's a gateway job since the house is in need of several other repairs, and the owner doesn't want to do the work himself; it might interfere with his time with the guys down at The Call. Hector asked about what tools were available. Mr. Smithfield told Hector he had them all, but they were scattered in different parts of the shed or loaned out to friends, so Hector would have to look for them. He found the belt sander, the most important tool for this job, and before Diego left for his job, he replaced the sandpaper for Hector. Not for precision work, however, not for wood for display or ornate exposure. Something in Hector stirs.

The temperature hits 100 just after noon, and Hector's body glistens. If he were outdoors, he would cover his body with clothing and rags to battle the sun, but here inside, he works only in his cutoffs and work boots. Gloves, of course. This is what he was wearing the first time Thalia came by with a sack of food that she apologized for not having when he first came to the pantry. On this day, the supplies are just a prop. He slips on a tee-shirt while she opens two beers.

"We don't carry much food, just the essentials. When people want a lot, they drive to Ajo or maybe Gila Bend and stock up for a month or more," says Thalia.

"I don't eat much. Lots of sandwiches and canned chili," says Hector.

"I noticed you took several jars of peanut butter. You'll need a better diet if you're going to work this hard."

"Thanks, Mom." Hector understands Thalia's reprimand is not serious. He wants to fit into this small town for the time he's here, so he's going slowly, a word or two to the men at The Call, a brief introduction to Julie and Thalia, a handshake to an Indian cowboy on a dirt road east of Why. "I've been skinny before."

"So, you're living out in the old Pacheco place, I hear. How'd you hook up with that?" asks Thalia.

"Diego asked me if I needed a more comfortable place instead of the old trailer. He said he had room. Lots of empty places since the mine closed, but that trailer had no air conditioning. I'm used to that, but still. Diego said he got his place cheap so I wouldn't have to pay rent. The guy who owns it is working in Morenci, at the copper mine there. Diego worked out a decent price he could afford. Basically, next to nothing if he would just take care of it and see to it the illegals or drug mules didn't move in, or the unemployed union miners didn't bust it up out of spite. It was the longest conversation we've had."

"Diego keeps to himself, hasn't engaged anyone here to any extent except maybe Smitty. He just works." Thalia drinks her beer and surveys the room. "That's sort of how I got mine, another empty house. It's next to the bar, which is how I found work so easily. It was once a miner's place too, until Waddell bought it." Thalia still uses Smitty's given name at times.

"Which one is CJ?" asks Hector.

"The one who doesn't wear a hat. Early 40s maybe. A decade older than me. He's seldom there in the morning, works in Ajo at the mine somehow. We've never understood how since it's closed now, but he knows what's going on with the Phelps Dodge soap opera and keeps us informed." She smiles as she speaks and her eyes sparkle. There is energy in her body language.

"That's quite the crew. They looked me up and down the first day I went to the bar. They didn't say much, but I know they have questions." Hector remembers that first day. The crew was suspicious of him, it seemed, not because of his color, but because he was new.

Thalia smiles and raises her beer bottle in agreement. "We all do, but we have the manners not to ask. Sort of our code. We bite around the edges and try to piece stories together. None of us are very interesting, but the secrecy adds a little . . ." She pauses and considers her next word. ". . . mystery."

"This beer is good. Thank you."

"Can I get you another?"

"Thanks, but I probably ought to get back to work. I'm trying to demonstrate my worthiness to Mr. Smithfield and Diego, and you're already trying to sidetrack me."

"You'd fit right in with our reputation if you didn't complete this job on time, you know."

Hector rises, offers a hand to Thalia to help her get up, and then dusts off his pants. He hasn't touched a woman in a meaningful way in months, since long before arriving in Rubicon. "I promised Mr. Smithfield."

"Okay." She turns to go but wants to find out about the other thing. "Why don't you take the rest of the beer home with you? Maybe your roommate would like one." *One step at a time*, she thinks as she leaves.

Hector laughs when he thinks about this roommate. It would be nice if this roommate talked more, but he's almost mute and spends most of his alone time in his bedroom with a notebook. In the evenings he'll sit on the flat part of the roof and gaze at the stars. He just seems to hide out. Hector gathers up the stained carpet and takes it out back.

∾

Sitting at their table in The Call, Cocker can't control himself. Try as he might to stifle his giggles, he just can't, and when he starts, a grin spreads across Smitty's face. Then CJ and even Jack. Alf shakes his head and says, "Fuck you guys!" It's almost 3:00 a.m., and the Guardians are drunk. Really drunk.

Earlier that night, Alf had driven over to Ajo to meet and share beers with some union friends, friends who didn't cross the picket lines, who didn't scab. Unemployed men. When a handful of scabs showed up in the bar, a fight broke out, something about one scab's ugly girlfriend with loose morals. Out in the street, the fight turned vicious, and Alf was cut across the neck by a broken beer bottle. Lots of blood, but no arteries were severed. His union pals rushed him to the hospital to get sewn up, nearly 50 stitches in all. Someone called CJ about the incident, to come and drive Alf home when the doctors were done with him. CJ brought Cocker and Smitty.

Standing by the table in the emergency room where Alf had been repaired, waiting for Alf to sober up from both the beer and the anesthesia, after the medical personal had moved to treat another patient, Cocker tied Alf's bootlaces together, unbeknownst to the others. An hour later, when the nurse released Alf, he was helped from the table by CJ and Smitty, only to fall flat on his face. More blood. More stitches.

Cocker just can't stop laughing. Neither can the others, and finally, Alf does too.

8

PERSPECTIVES. LATE SEPTEMBER 1986

Captain Cooley, "Cool Breeze" to many of his Navy buddies and fellow officers, knows the legal names of the residents of Rubicon. He doesn't care that they have aliases, in fact, he really doesn't care about them much at all. In his investigation, these people are a sidebar. If Cooley had time to ponder them, he might admire what they do, even though it is illegal. He can't remember ever shaking his head at the misadventures of a cast of characters like these who are assembled in Why: a computer genius who built a two-hole golf course in the middle of the desert, a minister with no congregation who was once a bar singer, a half-brother, a couple with a history of minor acts of sabotage in California and Alaska, an angry miner fired from Phelps Dodge for union activity, a Phelps Dodge employee who shouldn't fit in but somehow does. The attractive divorcee from Michigan is an independent journalist whose original assignment seems to have petered out. People generally move because of an itch, or they're forced out of somewhere or attracted to another, but why they stay involves several factors. The randomness of settlement. Cooley laughed aloud when he discovered that a beaten-down border town of fewer than a hundred souls had a suburb. Rubicon. It couldn't be because the grass was greener.

Cooley's assignment is to follow another tip, since a body was irretrievable, that loose end that tugs at one of America's secrets, so Cooley follows even the strangest leads. An architect from Colorado who goes to a remote town in southwestern Arizona is the strangest so far. That secret could be the subject of a Tom Clancy novel, and it is Cooley's orders to see that such a novelist never gets his hands on the secret—or at least the truth. Rumors are out there, but rumors always surround such events. Let Clancy write about those, because America loves conspiracy theories, the odder, more unbelievable the better, like Three Mile Island was insider sabotage or the Kennedy assassination was CIA directed.

The Why Intersection

∾

"Am I going to have to check on Diego's green card now?" asks Smitty. He knows he won't, but he's curious about the responses his friends will give him. Always entertaining.

"Diego ain't no Mexican," says Alf. "He's American, maybe Italian."

Cocker raises his bottle. "To Italians!"

Copper Joe laughs. "Nobody's sure what Diego is, unlike Hector. That boy's Navajo."

Jack lowers a book into his lap, spins his wheelchair away from the window, and comes closer to the Guardian's table. "Unless you're hiring three or more Mexicans, you don't need to check."

"Are you sure?" asks Cocker.

"Yep."

"And Reagan signed this law?" asks Cocker again. "I can't believe that."

"It's only three months until Christmas, Cocker. Maybe he's playing Santa Claus." Alf may not be a Democrat, but he's certainly anti-Republican. "What's this law called, Smitty?"

"The Immigration Act or something like that."

Jack knows. "It came out of the Congress as the Simpson-Mazzoli Act. The President just signed it."

"I knew him way back when," says CJ.

"Who? The President? Bullshit, CJ," says Cocker.

"No, Senator Simpson. He attended the same junior high school I did in Wyoming, a few years ahead of me. Pretty much of a hell-raiser along with a bunch of his friends. He's living proof a man doesn't have to be what he once was; he can change. You especially don't have to be what you were as a kid." CJ nods his head to Cocker, but it's as if he has enlightened the table.

"Shit, CJ, none of us is what we once were. That's why we live in Rubicon," says Jack.

"Even Rubicon isn't what it once was. It even changed its name along the way," says Smitty. "Maybe I should have named our little haven Purgatory, a temporary stopping place for our previous sins, a place to atone for our youthful behavior." He looks at Jack. "You and I might have to be here a bit longer than the others." He laughs and Jack smiles back.

"Is this law gonna make it harder for me to cross the border and get my drugs?" asks Cocker.

"Probably, but not right away. The government doesn't do anything right away except make war. The President and Congress want the border secured, but my guess is they'll worry more about California and Texas and not our little section by the reservation," says Jack. "Once the government starts tightening the border, it'll pinch traffic toward the middle, and we're the middle. Illegals, drugs, pretty much everything coming across will start flowing through here."

Cocker is scheming. "Maybe we ought to buy up some real estate for the boom?"

"Jeez, Cocker! All this isn't happening overnight," says Alf.

"All I know is buy low and sell high. It all goes back to my theory. Too many people. We've passed the point of no return. Too many people on this planet," says Cocker.

Julie shakes her head, amazed at the men's charade. Even among themselves they pretend.

"Aren't you working in the national park today, Alf?" asks Cocker.

"No, tomorrow. A couple of their trucks are down. Those rangers treat them like shit. Desert sands are hard on the engines. I did get a call from the RV park manager. One of his guest's motorhomes has broken down, so I'll go over and see what I can do." He pauses. "After coffee. Shouldn't take too long."

"If you have a few extra hours sometime this week, could you look at mine, especially the jeep?" asks Smitty. "I know, I know, the desert sand is hard on engines."

※

The next morning, Louie Ordonez and Corey Davis sit in their large Dodge truck waiting for The Call to open. Already the desert is getting warm, even for October. The wind is up with the sun and promises to remain strong all day. Julie unlocks the front door, which opens to the inside, pushes on the café doors, and waves for the two border agents to come in. Jack already has his coffee when Louie and Corey join him.

The Why Intersection

"I still can't pronounce the Papago's new name correctly," says Louie, the shorter, stouter agent. "Ta-ha-na Autumn, or something like that. It's not a new name; they're just reclaiming their old name, rejecting the name the military gave them which was always demeaning."

"None of us can. They're good with it though," replies Jack.

"Still," says Louie, "it's a sign of respect, and I'd like to offer it to them. Their tough life is getting a whole lot tougher these days."

"You're right about that," says Jack.

Jack London likes the two young border agents who come in for coffee several mornings each month. It's taken awhile for the suspicions to ebb and the trust to follow. Louie and Corey are two of the half-dozen additional agents assigned to the area surrounding the Tohono O'odham Reservation, a border corridor extending roughly from the Organ Pipe Cactus National Monument on the west to Nogales, about 90 miles worth of serious desert. Those who live on or near the reservation don't warm to authority of any kind; it's the historic nature of the area.

"The problem is they live on both sides of the border and the new immigration law will try to restrict their movements," says Corey. "It's an odd situation for them; the U.S. recognizes their reservation, but there's no such designation in Mexico. We're gearing up for the new law. The bosses talk about it all the time. It's a soft border and won't be tolerated." Corey looks the part. He stands about six-three and is strong as an ox.

"Pandora's Box," says Jack.

Julie joins the three men at the table. It's an hour before school starts, and then children will rule The Call for four hours. "What's Pandora's Box?" she asks.

Louie scoots his chair forward and leans into his coffee. "The reservation. The T.O.s are the lowest rung on the ladder, but up to now, they've been left alone by the Border Patrol, by the Arizona authorities, and by the drug gangs. But things are ramping up."

"*La Migra* won't be able to turn a blind eye as much," adds Corey. "Too much political pressure from Washington, from people who have never seen the border, but don't want Mexicans coming into the country. Sadly, the Indians are illegal in most people's mind when they really aren't."

"Hell," snaps Jack. "It's fuckin' Phoenix!"

"Cuss jar," says Julie.

"Nope. Fuckin' is part of Phoenix's official name. It isn't real Arizona anymore; just a bunch of people with no allegiance to anything except the gawdamn dollar. They leave almost as quickly as they come because it's too hot for them. No respect for the local cultures."

"I grew up there," says Corey. "It's my hometown, and you're right. It's lost its roots. All the surrounding towns are melding into one big cement city. You can't even smell the oranges most of the time."

"Where were you two working during the copper strike?" asks Julie.

"We were both in Texas, where I grew up. We got transferred together out here in April of '85, about a year-and-a-half ago," says Louie. "We started at the checkpoint near Tucson, but Corey and I have been migrating south and west with the birds." It's the first time the two agents have shared this information with anyone in Rubicon.

"Louie volunteered us," says Corey with a grin.

The table goes quiet for a moment before Julie asks, "Volunteered?"

"Yeah, we're on the front line now. We're *Migra*, but being young and observant, they want us to look out not just for Mexicans, but for drug smugglers and the wanted union members from the strike," says Corey.

"Don't forget the eco-terrorists and the anti-cruise missile protesters," laughs Louie. "We don't even know what any of the bad guys look like, except maybe the white college students from the U of A who show up near missile silos. Seriously, our bosses warn us to be on the lookout for all these guys. Seems like every new face is suspect."

Jack throws a glance to Julie who sees it but ignores it. "So, the Indians get hassled," says Jack. He rubs his thigh above the prosthesis and shakes his head.

"We gotta go," says Louie. "Thanks for the coffee." Always respectful, they don't don their hats until they are outside the swinging doors.

Julie rises and slides her chair under the table, picks up the coffee cups, and sets them on the bar. She takes the handles on Jack's

The Why Intersection

wheelchair and pushes him into the light by the window. "What are you thinking, Jack?"

"I'm thinking if the Palo Verde nuclear plant was shut down, Phoenix would quit growing. Maybe not wither and die, but level off. Without the extra energy, it couldn't control the desert like it's been doing. That damn city slurps up the water, lights up the night sky, and invites people to Arizona who have no regard for nature."

Julie lights a cigarette, probably her only one for the day, and pours herself a cup of coffee. "I just read where Phoenix will be the fifth or sixth largest city in America early in the next century it's growing so fast. Imagine that."

"I have," says Jack, 'I certainly have."

Diego is a cereal guy; wakes early, eats, packs a sandwich, and then heads out to work on Smitty's latest project before Hector crawls out of bed. Today, Hector will wash his clothes at the local laundromat on AZ 85. He doesn't have a job today, so he'll sit on a plastic chair along the highway and watch the traffic pass through Why. The *drugstore Injun*. He learns a lot about a town and its citizens by watching, or feeling, waving occasionally. A while back, he was in Chinle; now he is in Why. At lunch, Hector will walk to where Diego is working and sit with him while he takes a short break. They don't talk much, but it's company of a sort. Diego arrived in Why months before Hector but hasn't sat at a table in The Call. Or at the bar. Hector doesn't like to sit with his back to people, so he finds an empty table when he goes for an afternoon soda. On this day, sitting with Diego while Diego eats his peanut butter sandwich, Hector sings a Beatle song, skipping half the words. It's not polite to ask questions when your company is eating. Diego finishes and takes a drink from his canteen.

"Have you ever been to Mexico, Diego?"

Diego ponders, sloshing water in his cheeks. "Maybe in another life. Why?"

"I was thinking about going down for a while. Thought you might have a suggestion or two."

"Nah. As I said, a lifetime ago." They go quiet for a moment. "Anyway, you don't impress me as a person who needs a schedule much."

Hector smiles at that, nods gently, and goes quiet. Diego waits, believing his new friend has more to say.

"A lifetime ago, huh? I guess we all have other lives. I sure do. Sometimes they don't even seem connected, like I was a different person altogether, but I know that's not the case. Different, but the same. I understand that I'm never out searching for myself, just trying to create a bigger me. Knowing that tends to remind me that all these other lives are really just one. Me." Why is the furthest he's traveled from the Navajo reservation in his life, and he's not sure why he came. It doesn't bother him though.

Diego asks, "Aren't you hungry?"

"Hadn't thought about it. I will be when I do though. Haven't eaten since yesterday when you shared your sandwich with me."

To Diego, at least what he's observed, nothing seems to bother Hector. Diego has never known a man who seems more into observation and contemplation than Hector, unless he counts himself over the past few years.

Hector reaches down for a stick and draws something in the dirt. "I like drawing in the dirt." He pauses. "If I like my picture, I leave it. If not, I just scratch it away with my boot. I don't have to please anyone but myself." He hands the stick to Diego. "If I go to Mexico, want to come along?"

Diego laughs aloud. "What would you want me for, to work a little to get a few dollars so you can sit on a street corner and analyze the people?" He laughs again.

Hector laughs now. "Haven't thought of that angle, but I wouldn't object if you felt like doing that."

They go quiet again. In time, Diego leans over and draws his picture in the dirt, a building of some kind. When he finishes, he studies it. He rubs part of it out with his boot and draws again.

"I like it," says Hector. "Don't know quite what it is, but I like it."

Diego hands the stick back to Hector, rolls up his empty lunch sack, stands, and takes one last look at his drawing. "Neither do I, so you can add to it or scratch it out as you please. I've got to get back to work."

The Why Intersection

Hector doesn't watch Diego leave. Instead, he studies the drawing for several minutes. He slides over to where Diego was sitting to change his perspective. With the stick, he adds a garden next to the structure, then adds a cross to the top of the building. After a few minutes, Hector scratches out the cross and redraws it in the garden.

9

THE NOTAJO AUXILIARY

Ruby Mendez inspects the small house thoroughly, while Smitty sits on the front porch patiently. She walks from room to room tapping the floors and walls with her cane. She opens doors and windows, runs the tap in the kitchen, flushes the toilet, and measures closets. Even though it's a small structure, less than 600 square feet, it is more house than she can afford on her strike pay, more house than her old company home, but she dreams. Ruby will return to Ajo, return to her shared apartment with another laid-off miner and continue to make do, extended families eating lots of beans and tortillas until the strike is settled. Maybe she could have kept her company-owned house if she hadn't stood the picket lines, but then she would have dishonored her father. He worked the copper mines for over 30 years and was union to the core. Crossing the picket line would be worse than going hungry for a time. Her kids understand; they support her decision not to scab.

"Thank you, Mr. Smithfield, but this is too much for me to afford at this time."

Smitty stands, stuffs his magazine into his back pocket, and extends his hand. "I don't remember giving you a price. What can you afford?"

"If the strike had a timetable, maybe I could use some of my savings and go as high as 40 a month, but if Phelps Dodge won't settle, my little nest egg will get used up. No, I just need to keep my head and quit dreaming the impossible. I sure would like to get out of Ajo for a while though, get back into a place of my own so the kids could have a room of their own." She pauses. "And I could have a kitchen of my own again."

Smitty points to the house next door and one across the street. "I own those places and a few others nearby, and they aren't doing me any good sitting empty. Could you afford maybe eight each week?" He turns away and smiles.

Ruby does a quick calculation. "That would be 32 each month." Before she can continue, Smitty interrupts.

The Why Intersection

"Okay, you drive a hard bargain. Three dollars a week paid on Sunday evening, but you have to promise you'll mention to a few of your union sisters I have two other houses in need of renters."

That was how Ruby, Crystal Gonzales, and Jade Moreno moved to Rubicon back in '84. All three women lost their husbands due to strike pressures, and all three said good riddance when the men were out of the house. Phelps Dodge was never into negotiating honestly with the union, but wanted to break the union, much like PATCO, the air-traffic controllers union, had been dispatched by President Reagan or the airline workers by Continental. The copper mine at Ajo was shut down for good in '84, but the strike continued, since the mines in eastern Arizona were operating with replacement workers. Scabs! The most vile creatures in the desert, more loathsome than the sidewinder or scorpion.

Ruby had been roughed up by the state troopers in '83 for cussing out the men who crossed the picket lines. She simply could not control her mouth. She insisted to the authorities that the baseball bat she was holding was a prop, and she never intended to do violence. What? Her puny Louisville Slugger against their M-16s? All she had was her attitude, her mouth, and her middle finger—which she used often. Her husband didn't think it was proper for the women to be picketing; hell, he had been against her even taking a job in the mine, but he didn't object to the paycheck she brought home each week. When he left to work in Morenci at the PD copper mine there, to scab, she divorced him. She couldn't live with a man who had no principles. "The union protected us, had given us dignity when no one else would, and PD and the law broke us. Now, we are vulnerable, but it's no excuse to go scab. Poor people know how to experience hunger for a few months. Rich people never go hungry; they don't understand what a generational home is. When my husband forgot his roots, I couldn't live with him any longer."

Jade Moreno had been arrested for fighting. Both sides, union and scabs. At the American Legion Hall, she punched the wife of a union man for saying the union might need to give in. There was no argument to precede her action; she just moved her skinny, six-foot body over next to the husband and asked him if he agreed with his wife.

When he said she might be right, Jade turned and dropped the lady with a right hook to the nose. Then she slugged the husband. Blood everywhere. A short time later, she fought with a scab in an Ajo bar. One minute she would be smiling, and the next she would be fighting. Her husband was intimidated, and just before Christmas in '83, he took off for Montana.

Jade is White and never worked in the mine. Her family owned a small diner, and she hoped to leave Ajo after her high school graduation, flee to Tucson to attend college, to see what life beyond the restrictions of an isolated mining town could be like. But a pregnancy ended her dream. Being Catholic, she married her older boyfriend who already worked in the mine, moved into a company house, and quietly fumed at the prejudices that came with a White girl marrying a Chicano man. By the age of 22, with three children, Jade was angry and surly. She worked as a secretary for the union when the strike began, and this changed her outlook and social life. Working for the union introduced her to Ruby and Crystal.

Crystal Gonzales was the organizer. When the men left to find work elsewhere or were let go for being union and turned to drinking even more than miners already did, she began to use her high school math skills to allot weekly payments to the families. She showed up at the union hall dressed to the nines with her hair done up and her face painted, demanding to see the books. Union families would come to her pleading their cases for additional money for a special situation, but she would have none of it. Gently, she would tap her foofed hair, look over the top of her bejeweled glasses, and deny most of their requests. She lost some friends but gained respect.

Like Ruby, Crystal had lived in Ajo nearly all her life. Born in Mexico she arrived in Ajo before she could walk, and her family lived in the same house ever since. Her father was a union miner, her husband was a union miner, her brothers were union miners, and they all worked for PD. When she married, she and her husband moved into the company house next door. When her husband was injured in the mine, the union's earlier efforts to secure insurance helped ease the physical and financial strain. However, when the union struck in '83, PD refused to continue their health insurance and eventually evicted

The Why Intersection

Crystal and her family from their homes. "They stole my home and gave it to scab men. They had rules about single men living together, but when we went on strike, they ignored those rules." Crystal's husband returned to Mexico to live with his parents, to let them care for him, but Crystal stayed. "I won't let PD win."

The three women did not know each other well before the strike even though they all worked in Ajo, but the strike brought them together. Now, they live in the last three houses at the end of the block in Rubicon. They continue to drive to Ajo once or twice each week to picket, even though the mine has been shuttered for over two years. They took new jobs around Why doing menial labor, but they have homes again. Dignity once again. They even gave themselves a name: The Notajo Auxiliary, and they meet once each week at The Call to drink and raise their voices about the injustices occurring in the Sonoran Desert, at the intersection of two Arizona highways posing the question, "Why?".

Thalia suggested the school. Listening to Crystal, Ruby, and Jade complain about sending their kids to Ajo where they were taunted by the children of the scabs and non-miners, about the long and irregular bus rides each morning and afternoon, and about the deterioration of Ajo in general, Thalia offered an alternative. Sitting on the opposite side of the bar, she casually said, "Why not educate them here?"

"Where? In Why?" asked Crystal.

"Sort of. In the kitchens of your homes."

"Who would be their teacher?" asked Ruby.

"Me," answered Thalia. "It's what I was educated to be. Well, it was my minor. Double majored in English and journalism."

The union women thought about it. They sipped their beers and went silent. Finally, Jade spoke up. "No. The kids need a real school, not a kitchen or coffee table. Formal. Desks. Discipline. They need to wear clean shirts every day. They need to say The Pledge of Allegiance each morning."

Thalia rose off her stool and walked to the entrance to the bar where the unused bus waiting room was. She raised her right hand

and with her finger counted silently. She turned and nodded. "We'll hold it here. We'll clean it up and make a one-room school out of it. Your kids can walk here each morning."

"In a bar?"

"Yes, but it won't be a bar during school hours. Rubicon Escuela, *a safe place to learn and grow*."

The Call became one more thing.

It's the first of October and Libby is trying to convince Crystal to walk the last five miles of the pilgrimage to Magdalena, Sonora, Mexico, for the Fiesta of St. Francis. Crystal remains adamant, if there is any walking, she's not going. "I'm overweight, Libby, and my feet wouldn't take it. I'd be down for months, and I need good feet for my job. You're Indian; it's in your blood."

Libby has walked this pilgrimage before, walked even further, and for her and the Catholics of southern Arizona and northern Mexico, the pilgrimage is sacred to their culture. "You were a Mexican before you became an American, Crystal. You're part Indian too. We can pray to the statue of St. Francis for your feet as well as for the babies." Libby often stays with Crystal and her children when she is in Why selling from her food truck when she isn't with Cocker.

Crystal answers the knock at her door and is surprised to see Cocker standing on her porch clean-shaven and combed. "I hardly recognize you, Cocker. Have you seen Jesus?"

"That's nothing to joke about, Crystal. May I come in and speak with you and Libby for a moment?" Crystal nods, does a low bow, and sweeps her arm around indicating for Cocker to enter.

"Hi, Libby," says Cocker. "I've missed you." Libby smiles gently but doesn't speak. "Libby, I would like to attend the pilgrimage with you and Crystal. In fact, I would like to offer to drive you there and bring you back at your convenience."

Before Cocker can continue, Crystal pushes him toward the kitchen, just a few steps away in the small house. "Let me get you lemonade, Cocker, while Libby and I discuss your offer." At the other side of the room, Libby turns and seats herself on the worn fabric

The Why Intersection

couch. Crystal hands Cocker a glass and pours it full of lemonade. "You see, this is more of a religious mission and not just a fun trip to Mexico. It's the biggest event of the year for us, besides Christmas and Easter, so I'm not sure it would really interest you once you got to Magdalena."

Cocker raises his glass slightly, a sign of appreciation for her hospitality. "That's exactly why I would be going. Do you think I'm not a religious man, Crystal?"

From across the room, Libby speaks. "Your faith is of a different kind, Martin Lee. I've been aware of your deep spirituality for all these years. I've listened to your incomprehensible mumbles and tried to make sense of them. You have a good heart, but this pilgrimage to Magdalena is not about the Holy Spirit and your Pentecostalism. It's Mexican Catholicism. We won't be expecting the return of Christ; we'll be praying in gratitude for things He has done for us, for answering our prayers over the past year."

Crystal feels Cocker's disappointment and takes his arm. "Come and sit with us."

Libby leans into Cocker and kisses him on the cheek. "We're going to pray to a life-sized statue lying in the local church. Then, we'll see our families and celebrate. You wouldn't be comfortable, I don't think."

"Are you afraid I'll get drunk or high?" asks Cocker.

"It's a real possibility. It's what drives me away from you, you know."

Crystal admires Libby's dual personality. From grumpy food server to gentle consoler. Crystal raises her hand slightly, "Maybe there's a compromise." She looks to both of her guests to get their consent to continue. "How about it you drive us to Nogales, and we'll walk in from there? You can pick us up again when we're done. We can call you."

Cocker sips his lemonade and then holds it with both hands between his legs. "If it's what you both want, then it's settled, but let me tell you both something. Crystal, Libby knows some of this. Back in the 1960s, I was living down near Sierra Vista at a religious camp. Pretty gone. I was made an apostle, ordained by the evangelist who ran the place. Miracle Valley. After he drank himself to death in

California, I moved here and set up my own church. I succumbed to the sins of alcohol and lost it all. Seems that's where I've continued to worship all these years. Anyway, you're right about my faith not being your faith. I do hear voices and still believe in the Second Coming of Christ sometime soon."

Libby takes his hand understanding that some of his recollections are confused. "You know I've forgiven you for that, you old fool. It isn't happening in this lifetime for any of us. We make the best of it we can and ask forgiveness from our Maker for our mistakes."

Libby and Crystal hold hands as they watch Cocker return to The Call. A small whirlwind blows past him and musses his hair, returning it to its natural state. The women giggle as does Elder Brother, the spirit of another religion. Another ghost.

"How did he know about your trip?" asks Crystal.

"These things just come to him. I didn't tell him. Maybe it was part of the bigger plan to convince you to join me," answers Libby.

10

HUNCHES

Cool Breeze smiles. How a first-generation Italian American by the name of Fulvio Fano became Waddell Smithfield tells him a great deal about the march of culture in 20th century America. *Inferior stock, my ass*, thinks Captain Cooley. Smithfield's parents were Italian immigrants just prior to World War I, The Great War. Non-Whites at the time, and unskilled Catholics to boot. Their son Fulvio was a genius who became a star at MIT. Top-security clearance for government work. Then, abruptly, he's off for a decade of cross-country wandering, but seemingly with a purpose. Liberal causes, mostly civil rights. A few years in Rolla, Missouri where he married. More travel and a real estate career. Labels change just like names. Aliases. Smithfield seems to be the leader of Rubicon, which makes sense given his educational background and wealth, so Cooley moves his photo to the center of his schematic. Smithfield's arms reach out to every other resident in Rubicon. Captain Cooley swivels his chair back to his desk looking for the report on Walt Kramer. *What is his special interest in this group? Did Kramer have a previous connection to Smithfield?* Cooley takes out each man's dossier to look for any connection.

The lines on Cooley's schematic connecting the residents to Smithfield are solid and intertwined, except Kramer's. It's a dotted line.

∞

Jack mumbles and occasionally swears when he reads the newspaper. Usually, he sits by himself, while Thalia holds school, but this morning, he is having coffee with Smitty. This morning, he is particularly upset with an article about President Reagan's Strategic Defense Initiative.

"Shit!" he mutters.

"I can tell already this is going to be an expensive day for you at the cuss jar," says Smitty. "What you got?"

"Damn Star Wars project. More dollars down the military money hole for something that will never work. A false promise for America's safety."

Smitty doesn't look up from the sports page. "What if it would work?"

"Is that how the military works these days, on 'what ifs'? Pretty expensive plan."

"Sadly," says Smitty, "that's how it does operate. I'm sure SDI was presented to the President in just that way. 'What if, Mr. President, we could build a defense system that could protect America from incoming ICBMs from the Soviet Union? Wouldn't it be great? It'll only cost a bazillion dollars, but it's for the military and will protect us.'"

Jack lowers his paper. "Is this another one of those topics you have intimate information about, Smitty?"

Smitty smiles from behind his pages. *Yes, Jack,* he thinks, *as a matter of fact, I do have intimate information about this topic, but I can only give you bits having very little to do with the essentials.* "Did you ever see the movies 'Dr. Strangelove' or 'Fail Safe,' Jack?" Smitty lowers his paper and picks up his coffee.

"Yeah. Fail Safe is a great name for all this bullshit. There are no guarantees for safety. What are you driving at?"

"Can you recall the rooms full of computers in those movies? Entire rooms housing computers designed to protect America." Smitty leans forward just a bit.

"Vaguely. Why?" asks Jack.

"Well, when I was young, . . . "

"Can you remember that far back, Smitty?"

"It was a while back, for sure. Anyway, back after the war, I helped build those computers, and I know a little about what your concerns are. No matter how good they are, they can't protect us in all situations. It's a lie we tell ourselves. We always will."

"Smitty, is there anything you don't know something about?"

Smitty laughs slightly allowing for Jack's frustration to dissolve. "I don't think so, Jack, but I'll think about it and get back to you."

The Why Intersection

The winds rise with the temperature, and by the early afternoon, into the mid-30s. The desert, according to Libby, comes alive with the winds, when the sands are tossed skyward, and the landscape forever altered. Like people. Cocker will always add that the Tohono O'odham people think like that, giving people characteristics like the desert flora and fauna. "In the time before America," that's how Libby begins when she has her mescal, "the wind breathed life into the desert, relentlessly pursuing a goal we cannot understand. The desert is never still, even on the calmest of days. Sit on a bluff and watch the dust devils perform their dances in the valleys and you will see. The wind is a messenger and a deliverer, much like a shaman. It brings us our souls ... or takes them from us," Libby will go on to tell whoever is close by. With another shot of mescal, Libby will begin to chant and her body transforms. Cocker believes this is when the Holy Spirit is over her, brought in on those winds she talks about. Powerful.

Until she became comfortable with the trails, Thalia kept to the easy hikes originating from the visitors' center in the Organ Pipe monument. Her first week in Why, she drove south, and the unique cactus piqued her curiosity. She had always found that the wilderness eased her soul, her respite, but was concerned the desert would not do what the lakes and forests of northern Michigan near the Canadian border did. Different, but soothing still. More difficult, and she was warned about others who might be passing through the isolated trails. Within a few months, she was wandering even the most difficult trails, camping overnight, learning about an environment completely different from her home. Except for the deer, the wildlife was not at all like Mackinac Island, Michigan.

Julie hiked with Thalia once but refused to go again. "You walk too fast, with those long legs of yours. I can't keep up." The Guardians cautioned Thalia to hike with a group, with the park rangers, with someone familiar, but Thalia just smiled and told them she would be fine, which she always was. By November, she wonders if she might like to share this solitude with Hector, the visible ghost, and his unique aura.

Roger Johnson

∽

If Bellena Kramer feels any pain, she conceals it from the nurses. Despite her age the pregnancy has been without incident, except for *the song*. When the obstetrician finally decides the baby is ready, he pops a tape into a portable cassette deck, which begins an hour long "Stairway to Heaven" marathon. With Baby Babette still holding on to the insides of mommy's womb, Bellena yells, "Would someone turn that damn song off!" Walt, who has been standing by her side throughout the birthing process, reenforces her request with a stronger adjective, and with only the sounds of the medical staff working and Bellena's breathing, Babette releases her grip and enters the world. Small, at an ounce under five pounds, she is in all other ways healthy. A Thanksgiving baby.

An hour after the birth and still wearing his hospital gown, Walt holds his little princess. Behind the glass, Grampa Mac beams with pride. Walt wonders what it would have been like to hold his first child at birth, a son born 36 years earlier in 1950, a son who grew up without his father, lived a solid life, but died before Walt could reestablish the bond. Babette will not suffer for attention. Walt promises to be there for every step of her childhood. Thirty-six years from now will be 2022, and by then Walt will probably be gone.

Autumn in the Collegiate Peaks range in central Colorado has been mild, so the drive to St. Mary Church at the base of Mt. Princeton is easy. In some years snow would have made this drive impossible. Father Spreewell, even though he is Catholic and not of Bellena's faith, will baptize Babette in the church Walt's son restored. The priest was a friend of Walt's son at a time when he needed one, a minister of God in the truest sense. Walt did not attend church as an adult, but since the birth of his daughter, he accompanies her and Bellena each Sunday and reconsiders his faithless past.

"Babette Princecella Kramer, I baptize you in the name of the Father, and of the Son, and of the Holy Spirit." It is Sunday, December 1, 1986, and Walt Kramer wonders what his son would have thought about his baby sister.

∽

The Why Intersection

Hector notices a shiver in Diego's persona. They are working together on the roof of a house on the east side of the highway, a house not in Rubicon, a house that sits on the bluff overlooking the warehouse that was once Tabernacle. Hector asks Diego if he's cold, but Diego waves that notion away.

"Just a strange feeling. It's gone now," answers Diego.

※

A few days later, Diego leaves the rental house. He doesn't tell Hector where he's going or for how long. Hector senses his new friend is going to a lodge, maybe doing some work there. The Navajo man doesn't know if his new friend will be returning.

11

THE CODE

Walt Kramer watches. He is most interested in the two women, the man in the wheelchair, and the old man who owns the neighborhood. The entire cast is an interesting lot, but their secrets are their own and not related to his search, his investigation. His sources provided detailed information about Waddell Smithfield and Jack London, a little about the two women, but nothing out of the ordinary. Walt speaks with the manager of the RV park, a secretary at the Ajo community building, and the clerk at the Why convenience store, an aging hippie with missing teeth who is glad to relate local gossip. "Watch out for the Gatekeeper, he has a violent temper. A couple of the border guards drink coffee there a couple of times each week and may know more. A few of the area ranchers come in on the weekends for a beer, and old campers from the RV park wander in because they don't know any better. Most of Why avoids The Call; they ain't too friendly towards us. But, yeah, watch out for the Gatekeeper."

Walt's drive through Why on its dirt roads takes him back in time, to the year he spent in northern Georgia. "Jesus Saves" signs adorn three fences, citrus trees are numerous, nearly every yard is fenced and has a barking dog, and plaster animals stand guard in many yards. The houses are small, and several trailer homes are permanently parked in these fenced yards. Across the highway where the two Arizona routes join, there is a volunteer fire department garage, the gas station/convenience store, and a warehouse, plus a handful of larger brick homes of varying styles. None of these homes seem to be occupied. The largest building, yet still small, is the warehouse with faded lettering on the side, and it looks unused. Why has one restaurant, The Kitchen, not counting The Call. Walt assumes that if residents, border guards, national parks agents, or tourists want a meal away from their home or RV, they head for The Kitchen. To the north looms the rim of the New Cornelia Copper Mine in Ajo, now shut down to break the strike and destroy the union, to put American workers in their place.

The Why Intersection

A neighborhood populated by nearly a dozen adults on the losing side of life and seven children who seem destined for better. Walt rented a fifth wheel in Phoenix and camps in the RV park on the north side of Why. He acts like a stereotypical photographer and hiker, snapping photos while trekking the nearby desert trail. He eats at Libby's truck when she has it parked near the convenience store, purchases various gems at a curio shop, and pretends to find Why worthy of a few pictures during his evening strolls. He sees nothing leading him to believe the answers he seeks will be found in this desert outpost. What he does find are men and women so suspicious of strangers that figures such as Mother Teresa, Atticus Finch, or Santiago from *The Old Man and the Sea* wouldn't be trusted. Only three women and their children acknowledge him when he waves. He also learns the residents of Why are suspicious of those in Rubicon, confirming what Dan reported after his visit and have concocted various stories about who these misfits are. Walt feels that while he is observing, he is also being watched, probably by the people he is watching. The desert is a new experience for him. When he returns to Buena Vista, he laughs as he relates to his wife and father-in-law about Why. Walt didn't see anything that makes Dan's report more than a curiosity account, and Walt didn't see the woman he asked Dan to find.

"Maybe I'll go back again after I consider what I saw," says Walt.

Mac sets a cup of coffee in front of his son-in-law and sits at the kitchen table with him. "Will you talk with them directly next time?"

"Yeah, eventually. I'm hoping what I bring them might soften them up a little. I've been able to get a little information on some of them, but it's all speculation since they hide their true identities. The old guy who owns most of the properties is Waddell Smithfield. He's probably a genius. He has degrees from both Harvard and MIT and was working on a top-secret computer for the military when he up and left the Boston area back 30-plus years ago. A couple of my contacts are still trying to find out why, but now it seems he's a bit of an eccentric. Built himself a small golf course and writes papers on the desert flora and fauna for the Tucson newspaper. The other guys are harder to pin down. The owner of the Why convenience store thinks they're all ex-convicts and part of the drug running that goes on across the border. He also warned me about one of the people in Rubicon called the Gatekeeper by the residents of Why. Alfonso Galvan. Evidently, he has a pretty nasty temper. Ex-union copper miner who lost his job with Phelps Dodge and has scores to settle and goes to Ajo frequently to fight. His real name is Peru. Seems to be hiding out in Why for some reason I haven't determined yet, but then, everybody there seems to be hiding out. My guess is that anyone who wants to find Peru would have little trouble locating him."

"Is this convenience store guy's information reliable?" asks Mac.

"Probably not much. Old hippie with long hair who took too many drugs to remember clearly. He did say the Border Patrol guys sometimes go into Rubicon for their morning coffee or a beer later. They might know some more." Walt jots a note on his legal pad and then takes a drink of coffee.

"You still don't know what you're looking for, do you?"

"Mac, you've known me all my adult life. You know I don't like to go on hunches, but that's all I've got here. I make myself uncomfortable with this shit. Bellena thinks it's almost comical, although she's a little pissed I'm leaving so soon after Babette has come to us. I promised her it would only be a couple of days. I'm not going to miss her first Christmas. Just another couple of days; blow in and blow out."

Hector steadies his right hand with his left as it glides along the junction of the wall with the ceiling. A yellow-gold paint covers the light green that is at least 20 years old in a house three times as old as the paint. Waddell Smithfield's house. Thalia leans against the wall near an east-facing window reading loose, type-written pages. Her pages. Her first attempt at a novel, she says, to accent her journalism. She met an older gentleman in Tucson who wrote novels and who told her just to fill up her pages and see where that might lead her. Then he laughed and said, "Just like life." She has put her other hobbies on hold. "Lots of material here in Rubicon; lots of sad sacks to make interesting characters." Since early November, she and Hector have

The Why Intersection

been meeting in the afternoons after school, wherever Hector is working. Also, a few early-evening hikes. The Guardians and the Notajo Auxiliary talk, but it's small-town gossip.

Smitty wants two colors in the room but said he would accept whatever is available. Hector is amazed at the dozens of gallon paint cans in Smitty's garage, no two of which are the same color. Hector thinks he can do that and make the room light and cheerful. Painting is a mind-freeing job for Hector, and he likes the end results, as if he's accomplished something. Thalia walks over and shakes the ladder. "Get down from there and let's talk." Thalia amazes Hector with her optimism in the face of difficulties. In Rubicon it's not a common occurrence.

"How's the book coming?" asks Hector.

"Slow. I thought romantics were doomed lovers, but romance novels have to end up optimistic and leave the reader satisfied," answers Thalia.

"Not always like real life, huh?"

"Not my experience, and yet . . ." she pauses, wondering if she can trust Hector with this part of her past life. "Tell me something about yourself you haven't shared with anyone else, Hector. Tell me something we can share as a secret."

Hector lays his paint brush on the can and steps off the ladder. "Let's get something to drink and sit where it's not so messy."

At the kitchen table, Thalia sips a coffee and holds it to her lips, a full lower lip that seems ready to pucker like Marilyn Monroe's once did. She stares at Hector as he stirs milk into his coffee, now more milk than coffee, but his eyes are down as he wonders what of his life is worth sharing. He decides to wing it, smiles to himself, and begins.

"There's a certain, how shall I say, randomness to bad luck. Each of us has experienced it, some more than others here in Why, but everywhere really. Most people don't believe it, especially rich or fortunate people. They have this deep-seated belief they control their own destiny." Hector finally looks up at Thalia who hasn't moved since she took her first sip. "You are really a beautiful woman, you know. It disarms men."

"Quit stalling. I need a secret." She gives him a faux-demanding look. "Why needs another secret."

Hector nods. He unfolds his words, his secrets, like a hungry man unwrapping his monthly allotment of chocolate. "Okay, without specific details, a few years ago, I became depressed about my life of little achievement, and I couldn't get over it. Suicide even crossed my mind. Suicide rates on my reservation, among the Navajo young adults, are pretty high. Then . . ." Hector pauses and looks away from Thalia, out the window toward the lone saguaro cactus in Smitty's back yard. The cactus has two perfectly formed arms, and it reminds Hector of a man trying to surrender. "Then, I ran away. Problem is I didn't have a place to run to." Hector turns back to Thalia, looking not for understanding, but for simple confirmation. "Seems like any place would be acceptable. Went to lots of places to figure things out. My people began calling me a medicine man, but I don't know about that. Now, I walk or hitchhike all over, like to here, almost as if I was drawn here. Maybe Why is where desperate people run away to when there's no place else, but I'm no longer running away. Now, I just go where the wind blows me."

Thalia wants to reach across the table and take Hector's hand. She remembers Libby telling her about the loneliness of the young saguaros, of the decades it takes for them to grow arms in order to hug. Instead, Thalia moves her coffee away from her mouth and breathes out heavily. "Okay, well, my turn. You don't strike me as the suicide type, but then, I don't know anyone who has committed suicide. What you just said about running away when there's no place else. Maybe this can be a new start, Hector," Thalia smiles, "or whatever your real name is. I grew up in a sort of blended family, so I always tried so hard to please. My father left before I turned four. I never knew him. I went off to college, but it took me seven years to graduate, to get my degree. Long story. A person can wander through lots of elective courses trying to discover the right path. Art, literature, philosophy, anthropology, journalism, theology, and some business courses. I did meet some wonderful people though. Got married young, but it didn't pan out, but I tried hard to make it work. I overlooked a lot of his affairs. Crazy ex wanted to control my life. I imagine somewhere, he's still plotting, but that's over. Rubicon's anonymity protects me, I suppose."

The Why Intersection

"You don't need to tell me anything to balance things out."

"I know, but here, no one tells anyone about their past and it gets lonesome, at least for me much of the time."

They go silent for a while, a time uncomfortable for some, but for Hector and Thalia, they understand how important their next words are in the land of forgetting, in the last neighborhood of Why. Thalia once remarked to Hector that one of the reasons she felt so comfortable with him was that they could be quiet in each other's company. That observation is being tested at this moment.

Hector starts. "You were abused by your husband, weren't you?"

"Yes," Thalia answers. "How did you know?"

Hector leans forward and takes her right hand with his left. He turns it palm side up, and with his right hand, he mimics a seamstress pushing a needle through a thick blanket from below. With his left hand, he carefully receives the needle emerging in her palm with his fingertips. He holds them there long enough to look up into her eyes, and then he takes his fingertips and touches them to his lips. "Remember?"

"You can't have known. You were out the door before I did that," answers Thalia.

Hector curls his lips inward and bites down, preventing his mouth from speaking, almost as if he's reluctant to answer. "I think I'm a little messed up. I don't know how, but it happens to me sometimes." His eyes hold Thalia's. "The elders up on the reservation call me a channeler, but they believe in lots of goofy explanations. This usually only happens with people who have experienced a similar phenomenon." Again, he waits. "Tell me."

"I fought back... finally. Gave as good as I got, but the second and third black eyes are difficult to explain to co-workers and family. I left because I hated what I was becoming, a violent, angry person, and that's not who I am. I don't ever want to be that again."

"You're a strong woman, Thalia," says Hector. "It's a quality that could serve you well in the days ahead."

They go quiet again, this time for longer.

"Tell me about your roommate, Diego, the hermit."

"He's a real ghost. Not sure he really exists." Hector laughs at that.

"I'll keep his secrets for now, not that I know any. He comes and goes. He works hard and seems to be really good at fixing Mr. Smithfield's houses. They seem to have formed a quiet friendship beyond just an employer-employee relationship. He likes the night sky. I keep waiting for him to start baying at the moon. Maybe I'll call him 'Coyote' if he does." Hector smiles. "Do you want to meet him?"

Thalia almost says yes, but she catches herself. "Not until he's ready, not until you're ready to share him."

"You've been very patient." They are still holding hands and their stares remain unbroken. "Interesting you say, 'when I'm ready.'" A moment passes before Hector continues. "Where were you born?"

"Bay City, Michigan, up on Lake Huron. Cold place. Nice, but really cold. This is much nicer." Thalia mimics hugging herself and then returns her hands to Hector's.

"So, you came for the weather, huh?" He knows she didn't. "My recollections of childhood are sketchy; a lot of it has just evaporated. These days it seems like my memories are fused with stories of other persons' childhoods. I grew up alone though, I remember that. No father either. He and my mother were together for only a short time. He's a ghost to me." Hector squeezes Thalia's hand. "You hold hands well."

"With you I do. It's not all I do well."

Hector smiles. "You may not accept this, but I want to as much as you do. I'm just not sure of what I'd be getting you into. If it was just a broken heart, I think I'd risk it for both of us, but there's more. I think one day we'll decide, but I haven't crossed that bridge yet."

"Or that river."

Hector's eyes reflect a question about her response, but he allows it to pass. "This is a crazy bunch."

Thalia whisks away a housefly. "You can say that again! They just sit at The Call all day and drink. They bad-mouth America and politics. They all had their day, I guess, but none of them are particularly forward thinking. The Notajo women are only slightly better. If it weren't for the copper strike, they'd have nothing to talk about. They discuss the strike more than they talk about their kids. I fear Why is a harbinger of the new America, an America in various stages of anxiety.

Look at the people here. They fear the foreigners coming across the border, they fear a big government, they're afraid of Phoenix, of corporations, that the Japanese economy will conquer ours, the decline of Christianity, and even their own shadows. When you showed up, and before that Diego, I thought Jack and Alf might have heart attacks. Anything or anyone new, they fear. America is changing—fast—it always has, but this anxiety seems to be based on anger and irrational fear rather than logic or evidence. Each day, another panic attack. The patrons at The Call are so filled with self-doubt."

Hector nods. "Each one here has something going on that extends beyond Rubicon. This is a beehive of activity," says Hector. They go quiet again.

Thalia stands without releasing Hector's hand, which forces him to stand too, to face her at an intimate distance. She doesn't know what to make of Hector at times. What was the word she used in the store at The Call? Translucent. Fuzzy edges for sure, but it's his inner core that intrigues and perplexes her.

"You left out a step in telling me your journey to Why," says Hector.

Thalia shakes her head softly. "Yeah, I did. You're pretty perceptive, Hector Jego." They go quiet and try to see beneath the skin of the other. Finally, Thalia speaks, "There's the babies. I'm a journalist." She looks for a response, but Hector conceals any emotion. Thalia turns her back to him, holds a fist to her lips, and remembers the first Mexican baby she held, that first stolen baby.

"I never told you my last name," says Hector.

"I know. I just gave you one."

"What's it mean?" Hector's voice is almost a whisper.

"It's the desert wind that stirs up the dust before a summer rain, before the monsoon. It's from the Tohono O'odham. It's often a warning of a bigger storm."

"Hmm. So that's who I am, huh? Hector Jego." Behind Thalia's back, unseen to her, he bows his head as if to acknowledge a baptism, maybe his own. He steps forward and puts his arms around Thalia's shoulders, simultaneously allowing his forehead to touch the back of her head. She reaches up with her hands and takes hold of his forearms. She slides her head off to the side, allowing it to fall back onto his shoulder.

Thalia wants to remain in this position; she feels warm and secure. Is this what trust feels like? "Groceries sometimes refer to the babies, stolen babies from Mexico who are delivered to Christian couples here in America; sometimes they go as far as Europe. The babies are also called crawlers, and the people who deliver them are mailmen. A lot of money changes hands for this type of adoption." Thalia lets out a short grunt. "Adoption. It is, but it isn't. Most of those involved are good people who think they're doing what's right for the baby, but it's illegal, and I think it's immoral."

Hector tightens his hug on Thalia. "Julie is a mailman, isn't she?"

"Yeah. That's what makes it so hard; she's a good person who believes what she's doing is for the best. As far as I've been able to ascertain, she doesn't take a cent for her part."

"Black market babies and the baby brokers. A lot of Mexicans don't think these people are doing good." Hector says this with contempt. The Navajo have a dark past with stolen children. "Are the others involved?" he asks.

"No. They know, but it's the Rubicon Code. Occasionally, Cocker will drive a crawler from Mexico up here. He'll pick the crawler up at the church in Sonoyta or Nogales. They move other people."

"Authorities?"

"No. I spoke with them for my article when I was gathering information. It was just going to be a few months. I've done my job and should leave, but I've grown attached, and I want to see how it plays out, I guess. The authorities don't seem to be interested any longer. And there's the other thing."

"You couldn't have come here out of the blue?"

Thalia hesitates, but she trusts the man who is holding her. "My sister adopted one." She turns to face him. "And then you came along." Her eyes tell him she accepts the complications. Life has its risks.

As my colleagues have shown, interracial adoptions in regard to White parents adopting Black children have decreased significantly over the past decade. Nationwide, there has always been a stigma attached to such unions, but in the seventies and the first years of the eighties, opposition

The Why Intersection

from Black organizations has made these adoptions even less acceptable. Adoption in America has mostly been a White, middle-class proposition, especially as a legal custodial transfer. Black and Latino communities simply take in these children as part of an extended family with no official documents involved. Here in Michigan, mores and demographic changes have led to a rejection of interracial adoptions.

Revised abortion laws, specifically Roe v Wade, *have resulted in fewer unwanted children, again specifically White children. White families wishing to adopt for a variety of reasons have found the pool of White children smaller and the wait longer, thus the search for additional pools. International conflicts in Southeast Asia are one place that has impacted this search. Adoptions by White families of Asian children have grown rapidly as orphans from Vietnam have been on the rise. The other significant pool is Mexico.*

As noted earlier in this article, the "Jones" family adopted an "orphan" from Guadalajara, Mexico, through a religious agency. This cross-border adoption was speedier with less red tape, and the Joneses were overjoyed with the opportunity to raise their new daughter in "a loving, Christian home" as the agency brochure promised.

Sadly, while adoption agencies are reluctant to call this a crisis, adoption fraud seems to be on the rise. Anxious families desiring a child to complete their family have been defrauded by groups preying on this desperation. My next article will focus on these fraudulent adoptions.

T. F.

12

CHRISTMAS 1986

Bellena Kramer puts her foot down, "Two days," so Walt flies to Phoenix a week before Christmas with a return ticket for the next evening. He drives a rental car to Ajo and meets there with just two of the Rubicon residents, Waddell Smithfield and Thalia Fisher. When Walt called the "leader of the contingent," Smitty had offered to pick him up in Tucson, but Walt declined. He didn't want to have an uncomfortable return drive if their conversation became sensitive. Dan warned him about the possible volatility of the group. Smitty also offered his guest bedroom, but again Walt said no. At a truck-stop diner on the north edge of Ajo, Walt explains his reasons for intruding on the lives of the Whyans.

"I guess you noticed me when I visited earlier."

"We notice everyone who walks around Why, especially anyone with a camera taking pictures. There ain't anything worth a photo. The Organ Pipe, yes, but not our dusty old neighborhood." Smitty goes on to tell Walt that they were on the lookout for him after Dan visited and told them about him. "Your young friend was a nice fella."

"Dan is a good man. He certainly had a few laughs at your crew's expense. He warned me." Walt squirts ketchup on his fries and puts one in his mouth. "I wasn't a good father. Ran out on my son's mother when I came home from Korea, which was probably a good decision since I held a lot of anger from my time there." Smitty interrupts to make sure Dan isn't Walt's son. Walt clears that up. "I got over my anger mostly but never reconnected with his mother or my son. She did a great job raising him though. Anyway, Sam, that was his name, became friends a few years back with an old man in southwestern Colorado, but this past year, my son died in a fall while he was on leave from the Navy. I won't give the details because it's still pretty raw. Anyway, at Sam's funeral, I got to meet this old man. Barkley Abbott." Walt starts to go inside himself like he does with Bellena but catches himself. Smitty notices.

The Why Intersection

"You don't have to give me all the details. From what I remember, you were looking for this Abbott fella's granddaughter that you met at the old man's funeral?" Smitty stops there to take a bite of his chicken-fried steak.

Walt scratches his nose and nods. "Yes and no. Barkley was losing his memory, dementia, but said some weird things just before he died. I guess I was grasping for straws to find a connection to my son, maybe out of guilt. I kind of have a reputation for being detail oriented in my work, but I screwed up with the granddaughter's location. I only shook her hand in the reception line at Barkley's funeral, but I could easily have located her. My wife showed me the funeral program and it listed her. I must have heard wrong when I spoke with the old man the last time I spoke with him."

"Understandable." Now, Smitty nods in a gesture of empathy for Walt. "You could have saved Jack from a lot of stress had your friend Dan explained it this way." Smitty smiles. "Well, maybe not Jack, he worries about everything, but the rest of my crew."

"Sorry about that. My wife tells me I'm not quite myself since my son died, tells me she'll be glad when I come to grips with my guilt. Tells me I need to get back to my regular work."

"And what kind of work is that?" Smitty knows this already.

"I supervise the nuclear power plant in northern Colorado, the never-up-to-speed plant that the electric company wants to retool."

"Nuclear power plant. Jack would love to give you his thoughts on nuclear power."

Walt tilts his head as if to ask why.

Smitty waves his hand over his face. "Another life, one of those other lives we all have, one of those chapters that closed years ago. He just blames our local plant up the road for the growth of all things bad in Arizona."

Walt nods. "I thought it was the warm weather that brought everyone here." Both men laugh, and Walt continues. "Dan gave me a rundown on everyone who was at the bar when he visited. 'Suspicious' was the word he used to describe his greeting."

"As I said, Walt, all visitors are suspect."

"What about you? What brought you to this outpost?' asks Walt.

Smitty lays his fork alongside his plate and wipes his mouth with his napkin. "Maybe it was that weather you referred to. When my wife and I were looking for a retirement place, we thought Phoenix might be it, but it didn't have the right feel. Geneva, my wife, did connect with this desert though. She particularly liked the night sky in the Organ Pipe Park just south of here and the seasonal bird migrations. All sorts of birds and butterflies pass through my little part of Arizona, so we took a chance. Didn't like this town much, too much of a company town, and that big mine is pretty ugly, so we took a look down the road. Found a house and bought it. In case you didn't notice, real estate in Why is dirt cheap, so we could afford it even before we sold our other one. Thought maybe we'd be snowbirds at the time, but after the first year, we sold the snow house and moved here permanently."

"Snow house?" asks Walt.

Smitty smiles in a way to end this line of questioning. "The other house that wasn't in Arizona. You said your son was Navy?"

"Sorry, none of my business. Yeah, Navy. Honorable discharge. Posthumus."

"Walt," Smitty looks at the man across the table seriously but not confrontationally. "The biggest reason we don't want scrutiny in my neighborhood is not because of what we all did, what we were, but because of what we do now. All that previous baggage has been discarded, so I'm going to let you in on our secret. I trust that you'll keep it to yourself when you leave tomorrow. Thalia tells me you contacted her and will have this little apology talk with her in the morning." Smitty pauses again, this time a little more forcefully. When he gets a silent promise from Walt, Smitty continues. "We move people." Another pause. "Mostly from Central America who have been targeted. Men who need protection from the right-wing governments that have labeled them as communists. You know we can't have them dirty commies acting like journalists or teachers in Guatemala or El Salvador. Everyone we move fled to America once before but was rejected, turned away, sent back." Smitty clenches his jaw and gnashes his teeth. "What we do is illegal, and you don't need the details, and none of it has anything to do with whatever you're looking for down here."

The Why Intersection

❧

The next morning at the same diner, Walt waits for Thalia Fisher. He knows what she does—or at least did—for a living. She was a freelance journalist, a very good one too. He wonders if she's writing about this people-moving venture in Why. He stirs his coffee and waits. She arrives ten minutes late, and he rises from his chair.

"Sorry I'm late. Traffic on the interstate was horrible."

Walt laughs, then responds in kind. "Those ladies with their picket lines and baseball bats can back up the cars, can't they."

The waitress walks over with a cup of coffee for Thalia and takes their orders.

Thalia speaks first. "Smitty briefed me on your reasons for visiting. Sorry we can't help you. Sorry about your son."

"I'm sorry I caused such a stir. That was never my intention. I was just looking for closure, I guess."

"Smitty said you have a thousand questions, and that he didn't answer many. Let me answer your first one. I came here for a story about cross-border adoptions. I got it—and more. I discovered many, if not most, are illegal. Still working on it in a larger context. I got to know three women whose husbands were miners and are now trying to survive since the mine closed. Tough women. I met an Indian who walks all over the state trying to understand deserts, especially this one. Why is a cornucopia of stories. Who'd of guessed?"

Walt smiles. "Good thing our eggs haven't been delivered or this conversation might be over."

Thalia relaxes a little. "Smitty says you work at a nuclear power plant in Colorado. Any good gossip I should be aware of if I ever happen to finish the stories down here?"

"Nothing that hasn't already been written about nuclear energy. My wife kids me that being around the plant has radiated my brain. I just tell her that my brain operates weirdly from birth."

"New baby, huh?"

"Yeah. Little girl. My Princess."

The waitress returns with their orders and one plate of toast. She tops off their coffee cups and leaves.

Thalia breaks her egg yolks and stirs them into her hashbrowns.

"When I arrived that first day, Julie commented, 'Look what the wind blew in.' You know which one is Julie?"

"Yeah, the tight woman who runs the bar."

"You are a perceptive one, just like Smitty warned. I need to be careful what I tell you, except he already spilled the beans on Rubicon's illegal enterprise. The wind truly does bring all sorts of people here. The wind . . ." Thalia's voice trails off.

Walt's face doesn't show how perceptive he really is, and he allows Thalia to continue.

"It's really an amazing story. I'm still working on it, but the gang doesn't want me to write it, at least they don't want me to publish it. Maybe after they're all dead. With their lifestyles, that may not be long. Drinking is the main activity." She shakes her head about the habits of the Guardians. "If you have time, you might stop by The Call and say hi to everyone, let them see you up close, shake hands and all."

Walt concedes that he has lots of time before his late-afternoon flight, several hours in fact. They talk about Why's residents as they eat, but Thalia is cautious about her revelations, and Walt doesn't probe. He agrees that Thalia's friends are paranoid, and that they really do want to be left alone. When they finish their meals, he thanks her for driving over from Why to meet with him, asks where he can get a hold of any of her articles, and pays the bill. They walk out together, exchange pleasantries, and drive off towards Why separately. This morning, two pairs of eyes watch them.

༄

Julie has the Christmas lights on in the bar all month, Advent. But for Ruby and Crystal, Christmas Eve is the ninth day of Las Posadas, and they are preparing a Mexican feast for the residents of Rubicon to be served in the school section of The Call. December 24 represents the end of Joseph's and Mary's journey to Bethlehem to find lodging, and also the ninth month of Mary's pregnancy. Chiles rellenos, tamales, two kinds of soup—Smitty informed Crystal and Ruby he won't eat the menudo—and lots of breads and candies. After dinner, the seven children will perform the procession where they go to each of the houses on the block and ask for lodging, but at each they will be

The Why Intersection

turned away. Only upon returning to The Call will they be received, welcomed. As Ruby says, "The Posadas has a happy ending; Jesus will be welcomed into our little world."

Rose and Thalia decorate the tables with colorful plates and napkins. Candles burn and glittering confetti has been strewn; a nativity scene sits on a windowsill. The Christmas tree and the blow-up Santa are out of sight in the bar, and no presents, most of them compliments of the Notajo Auxiliary, are visible. Jack is perturbed by it all. This is to be a religious celebration. Hector returned from wherever he went nine days ago and sits with Thalia. Cocker and Libby are together and monitoring the children. The kids behave out of respect for Libby and apprehension of Cocker. The older children help their mothers serve the dinner. Jade arrives on the arm of CJ, knowing he will be interrogated at length later. In four-inch-high heels, she towers over her date. The four oldest children, two of Jade's and one each from Crystal and Ruby, are relegated to a card table at the back of the room near the blackboard. None of the men wear a tie, although Smitty has on a bolo, but all are bathed and shaven. The women, however, are dressed to the nines, fitting for such a formal dinner.

When the food is placed on the table and the glasses of chimayo and apple cider are refilled, everyone stands and holds hands—as Ruby has demanded. Crystal bows her head.

"Let us pray. Bless us, dear Lord, who are gathered at these tables. Bless the food we are about to eat. Bless this building which shelters us tonight and all the year as it serves as the school for our children. Bless especially our children as they grow in Your eyes and give us the wisdom to raise them right. Bless our little neighborhood and our country. Bless our guests and care for them as they move down the highway. Bless Mr. Smithfield for his generosity in providing us with houses, without which we would all be scattered with the winds. And finally, we thank You for sending Jesus into our lives, to give us hope and to forgive us our sins. We are poor and needy, and He gives us comfort." Crystal pauses for a moment. "Amen."

As the crew begins to sit, Libby speaks. "May I say something?" The neighborhood resumes their respectful stance, and Libby speaks. "Thank you for including me tonight and all the other days. I am an outsider and your acknowledgement of me is appreciated. If I may, I would like to say this evening feels like the evening after a rain on my land, and that is good."

"Hell, Libby," says Smitty, "you've been here on this land longer than any of us. We're the outsiders."

"Thank you, Libby. We are honored to have you join us," says Ruby. She smiles. "While we're standing, is there anyone else who has something to say?" No one speaks, so Ruby says, "Well, then, let's sit down and dig in." She looks at Smitty. "And there will be no more swearing on this night."

༄

Forty-five minutes later, Cocker stands and taps his knife against his glass. He waits until everyone is quiet, and he has their attention. "Ruby and Crystal, this was a mighty fine dinner." He claps and is immediately joined by the others. "We each have our unique views about this night; they are not the same by any means. As some of you know, I believe the re-arrival of Jesus is imminent, and each day He doesn't show is a disappointment to me. I know I should be patient, that He will come when He is ready and not on my time, but that's beside the point. What I want to do is sing a Christmas song for you all, since the spirit moves me tonight. I'll do *Silent Night*, just the first verse, and you all can join me if you please."

Cocker's voice is gentle and melodic, and no one interrupts or joins him. His eyes are closed as he sings, as if he is alone. When he finishes, the tables remain silent out of respect. Finally, when Cocker opens his eyes, CJ speaks. "If you would, could you sing the second verse, Martin Lee?"

༄

After dessert Ruby, Crystal, and their children excuse themselves to prepare for the procession. Jade, Julie, Libby, and Thalia bus the tables and do the dishes, the "women's work," while the men retreat to the bar for more tequila.

"Whoa, CJ. Jade looked mighty fine tonight. When did this happen?"

"She's always looked fine," answers CJ avoiding the real question.

"I didn't think there were any secrets in Rubicon."

"This one isn't any longer, but all Rubicon is is secrets." CJ knows there will be more questions down the road.

"This was one hell of a dinner," says Smitty. He finishes his glass of tequila, stands, and begins to examine the shelf of liquor behind the bar. "What's the correct one for Christmas?" He grabs an opened bottle of Jim Beam and returns to the table.

"What did you find out about Walt Kramer, Smitty?" asks Jack. "I'd like to know more about that sombitch; he could be dangerous."

Smitty pulls his feet back under his chair and leans into the table. Only Hector is standing, but he is completely tuned in to what Waddell is about to say. "Kramer lives in Colorado all right, like he said. Buena Vista, a mountain community. Has a wife and new baby. Kind of old to be starting a new family, but his wife is pretty young. She's a hotshot realtor there. He lives in his father-in-law's house. Dean McElroy. McElroy used to be a small-town sheriff but had to retire when he got cancer. I guess the old guy is pretty sick. Kramer has been the supervisor at a nuclear power plant in northern Colorado, Fort St. Vrain, but his role there isn't clear anymore. The plant has had some problems getting up to full power, and there's some talk it will be shut down or converted to regular energy. Regardless, he knows his stuff. Whenever there's a problem at any nuke plant in the country, he evidently gets called in." Smitty looks to Jack. "You ever heard of him, Jack?"

Jack shakes his head no.

Smitty continues. "I don't think his visit had anything to do with his work, though. It just didn't have that feel. No, I think his visit to our little neighborhood was personal. I don't think he's concerned about our groceries."

Alf finishes his drink, and Hector laughs silently to himself. Is it required at this table that a person finish his drink before he can speak, and then, when he's finished talking, he can refill his glass? "What about the first fella, Smitty?" asks Alf. "The Dan guy?"

"He is who he said he was, an architect from Denver. I couldn't find what crime he was supposed to have committed," answers Smitty. "Maybe Kramer did take care of it. Anyway, there's more about

Kramer. He's an Army vet. Served in Korea like you, Cocker. Nothing out of the ordinary that my friends were able to find. Returned to Colorado after the war and lost a decade like a lot of men just trying to figure out who he was."

"So, he could have lived in Rubicon during those years," jokes Cocker. The men laugh.

Jack rolls his wheelchair over to the bottle of Jim Beam. "He knows about us."

Alf nods his head in agreement. "He wasn't bluffing. He's an important guy with sources, maybe better sources than you, Smitty. I got the feeling he liked us, but I don't trust him at all."

Cocker polishes off his third glass of tequila. "Did any of you get the feeling he still doesn't know what he's looking for? He wanted to find the woman his friend asked about, but when I asked him what he wanted to ask her, he gave us a nonsensical answer about chasing some little boy over the mountains and through the woods."

"To grandma's house, huh?" Alf smiles. "It wasn't over the mountains, Cock, it was over the river, but you're right, it made no sense."

CJ lays a hand on Jack's shoulder but comments to the entire table. "Just a friendly visit, my ass."

"I'm not convinced," says Smitty. "There was a measure of sadness to him." Smitty pauses to allow some consideration time.

Thalia enters the bar first, followed by Jade and Julie. "Mind if we join you," asks Jade.

"Not at all," answers Smitty. "We were just doing what we do best."

"And what's that?" asks Jade as she sidles up to CJ and puts an arm around his shoulders.

"Bullshitting," says Julie. "Bullshitting and complaining about America." Everyone laughs.

"Where's Libby?" asks Cocker.

"She said she was bushed and was heading back to the rez to be with her family on Christmas," says Julie. "I think she was a little miffed about how much you were drinking."

"It's a holiday," says Cocker. "A man ought to be able to have a few drinks on a holiday."

"Oh, you can, Cocker, and such a privilege will allow you to sleep

The Why Intersection

alone." Julie steps to Cocker and kisses him on the head. "You never learn, do you?"

"We need to go out to our houses," says Jade. "The kids will be starting their procession soon. This is their last house, and Julie and Jack need to welcome them."

Julie pushes Jack's wheelchair out first and the rest follow into the school part of the building before heading to their own houses. Hector and Thalia are the last to leave. Thalia asks, "What are you thinking? You've been so quiet."

"Ironic, isn't it? We're the innkeepers on this night. The Call is the stable." A hundred thoughts race through Hector's mind. Walt Kramer is a dangerous man to Rubicon, maybe not intentionally, but dangerous, nevertheless. Hector senses a connection between Kramer and Thalia, and yet, neither of them seems aware of it.

"The stable, huh? The Call is many things," says Thalia.

"I wonder how many infants have spent the night here?" asks Hector.

"More than you might guess, my dear." She hugs Hector, hiding her face from his view. "What else?"

"The guys are all in a stew about Rubicon's latest visitor, this Walt Kramer. They really see him as a threat, don't they?" says Hector. "Maybe he's not the only one."

Thalia nods and pulls back from Hector. "I don't think I told you, since you left so suddenly for a few days, but while you were away, I met him. Very nice and polite. Julie told me he was looking for me, wanting to talk with me about meeting him briefly at a funeral in Colorado, but when we met, he said he didn't recognize me, and I certainly had never seen him."

"What was it all about?"

"I'm not sure. It was as if he knew I wasn't who he was looking for, so he didn't elaborate. Mistaken identity, but when we parted, he paused for a moment and then looked back at me, sort of like he had another question, but he never asked it." Thalia looks into Hector's eyes for understanding.

"If Kramer is all Smitty says he is, then I would imagine he always has another question. Men like him always do." Hector purses his lips like he often does. "A lot like you; you always have another question. Your mind is seldom still." He kisses Thalia. "I like that."

"You like what, that I kiss you well or that I ask lots of questions?"

"Both. Maybe someday I'll get to meet this guy."

∽

About two in the morning, CJ leaves Jade's house to walk home. He hears a familiar sound, the sad sound of a drunken man crying. CJ knows because he's seen it before. He watches Cocker throw stones at the only streetlight in Rubicon, a light located at the end of the block nearest to the highway. His tosses miss by a mile, and after each miss, Cocker loses his balance, falls, and swears. CJ reaches down and pulls a revolver from his boot, aims, and shoots out the light. He walks over to his half-brother, lifts him from the street, and supports him so he doesn't fall.

"Come on, Martin Lee, let me take you home. That was some beautiful singing after dinner."

∽

Diego returns two days after Christmas, but he stays quiet about his trip. When Hector asks about it, Diego only says that didn't go too far, that he just needed a break from the work routine. It's Hector who talks about the season.

"For me, Christmas tends to throw me into sadness. I don't have family anymore. A car accident, a suicide, usual rez stuff. My tribe is my family, but I didn't feel like I needed to be on the rez this year. Needed to be here for someone." Hector smiles.

Diego wants to tell him that he once had a girlfriend who was part Navajo but withholds that information. "Did Rubicon live up to your Christmas traditions?"

Hector nods. "Yeah, it was cool, lots of food and presents, a tree, and some kind of Baby Jesus celebration for the kids. I didn't dance though, and that's sort of a major thing for my people at Christmas. I spent a lot of time with Thalia."

"She digs you, you know."

"Can't last. Different life paths."

13

PASSENGERS

Jack London makes one New Year's resolution; to find out what Walt Kramer knows. Jack has been snapping at Smitty frequently, "You need to get more information on him," believing Smitty can call up his previous life contacts and discover Walt's entire resume. Waddell sits across from Jack in The Call drinking coffee and reading an old newspaper, the only Guardians in the bar this morning.

"It doesn't work that way, Jack. If I had top level security, do you think I'd be living out here with you derelicts? I know some guys from when I worked at MIT, but they're old and washed up too." Smitty laughs. "You're taking this a bit personal, aren't you, Jack?"

"Fuck you, Smitty."

From behind the bar, Julie asks, "Where's my Alaska map?"

"You have too many gawdamn trinkets from Alaska on the walls. We left there a long time ago. We need to move on?" says Jack.

"Where's my map, old man?"

"I burned it, okay. It's gone."

"How many sticks of dynamite did you use, Jack?"

"Shut up, Julie! Just shut up!"

Smitty slides his chair back and stands. "This sounds like a domestic dispute, so I think I'll leave and go shoot snakes on my golf course. "You young-uns have a good day. If I were you, Jack, I might remember where I hid Julie's map."

Julie waits until Smitty is out the front door to the school section before she continues. "Get it out, Jack, so we can get on with this next year of our *so happy lives*, but first tell me where my map is."

Jack reaches across the table for Smitty's coffee mug and slides it next to his. "It's under my bed, but gawdamn it, you're keeping too many clues around here."

"What's gotten into you? That misadventure is ten years in the past," says Julie.

"Walt Kramer knows."

Julie scrunches her entire face. "You're paranoid delusional. Nobody knows about Alaska. You blew off your leg in our garage tinkering with explosives. End of story. I could stand on the bar and tell all of Rubicon, and none of them would believe such a story. We're not that important. Jesus, Jack! Kramer couldn't possibly know."

"Unless you told him something about it."

"You've got this wonderful talent for annoying me, you know, and it's getting worse. Have you ever thought of leaving Rubicon?"

"This is my bar, not yours. I ain't going anywhere."

"Actually, it's Smitty's bar. We just rent it." Julie walks around the bar and retrieves Smitty's mug. She stands facing Jack defiantly. "I have options, unlike you. You keep planning the next great act of terrorism, but never acting on it. Palo Verde will send nuclear power to Phoenix and the rest of the southwest, just like the Alaska pipeline never got blown up and sends oil to the Lower 48." She turns to retrieve her map.

"You stay out of my room, you hear!"

"I'll get my map and stay clear."

"Don't you go talking to Kramer, either!" he yells.

The next day Julie picks up a crawler from a mailman at a Baptist church along Arizona's southern border. She examines the baby for any signs of abuse, for any signs it might not be entirely healthy. A young minister stands a pace away and watches, unsure of the procedure. Thalia guards the door, taking mental notes of the entire proceedings. Julie unwraps the infant's clothing like she would unwrap an expensive porcelain vase for a museum. The baby squeezes Julie's finger and coos, unaware she will be delivered to new parents far away from her birth mother. Satisfied, Julie buttons up the sweater and hands the baby to Thalia. Julie takes the minister by the arm to a corner of the church where they exchange a few words and an envelope. The mailman leaves when Julie okays the condition of the groceries, and now it is time for Julie and Thalia to deliver the baby to another mailman in Phoenix, the next address along the route.

The Why Intersection

∽

The highway patrolman clocks Julie at 72 on Interstate-10 west of Phoenix, pulling her '67 rusted Malibu over near Buckeye, about thirty miles from Phoenix. Thalia thinks of the old term, "courtesy patrol," but is nervous about a law enforcement officer checking Julie's license and registration. He's formal at first, asks if Julie knows how fast she was going and what the speed limit is on this stretch of highway, but when the baby lets out a soft cry, the officer puts his book away.

"So, Mrs. Simpson, all the more reason to obey the posted limit. What do we have here, a little boy or little girl?" asks the patrolman.

"A little girl," says Thalia, who reaches back to the rear seat to comfort the infant. "My daughter is just a month old. We're headed up to Phoenix to see my sister who hasn't seen her yet."

"Cute little bugger. Well, Mrs. Simpson, I'll let you off with a warning today but keep it under the speed limit. We all disagree with the double-nickels limit, but it's the law. Your passenger is too valuable to be driving carelessly." The patrolman tips his hat and returns to his car. Julie puts her license and registration back into her wallet and slowly pulls back onto the freeway. There is a moment of awkward silence as the women understand that one secret has been uncovered.

"It's Katherine Simpson. Kate for short, but I haven't used that name in over a decade. Julie London is my latest and most long-lasting alias. I couldn't get a driver's license under my current name. When I renewed it the last time, I was really nervous, but it turned out to be no big deal. I guess they don't have much history in their data banks."

Out of the corner of her eye, Thalia watches Julie as she drives, trying to discern whether or not she wants to open up. Thalia told Hector a few weeks earlier she wanted to talk with Julie about ending her role in the baby trade, and Thalia considers this opening. "Do you ever second guess what you're doing here? You know, delivering someone else's baby to a couple thousands of miles away?"

"It obviously bothers you, Thalia, so tell me your concerns."

Thalia wasn't anticipating Julie turning the question back on her, so she stays silent for a few minutes. Julie waits. Finally, Thalia answers. "I get that these babies will most likely have better lives, and if everything was done on the up-and-up, then maybe I could go along with it." She pauses. "What am I saying? I'm already going along with it. It's just at the end of the day, these babies were taken from their mothers, and people are making lots of money for doing this."

Julie interrupts. "I don't take a dime for any of this or the others."

"I know, but thousands of dollars are changing hands for each baby, and almost none of it goes to the birth mother, the poorest and most vulnerable person in the process."

Julie sets her jaw for a moment, and Thalia can hear Julie's teeth gnashing. Then Julie speaks. "The babies can't be returned. There's no record of the mother after she gets her twenty dollars. If I didn't do this, they would just find someone else, someone who wouldn't care, who would just take the money."

Another pause before Thalia responds. "Maybe not. If someone broke the chain and alerted the authorities."

As they enter Phoenix, Julie slows the car again to the new speed limit. "Don't need to be stopped again." She looks to her left to change lanes. "Tee, honey, that little girl in the back seat has no chance for a life in the slums of Mexico. The conditions down there are desperate, and life is a daily struggle. Up here, we're giving her to a family who will love her and give her the opportunities to fulfill her destiny. I know all this sounds corny, but it's true. It's not the first time in history this kind of a decision has been made."

Again, Thalia considers Julie's argument. Julie stays quiet and drives. Her ultimate destination is Scottsdale. "Jack isn't your lover anymore, is he?" asks Thalia, more of a statement than a question.

"Nope, hasn't been since Alaska."

"But still you stay and take care of him."

"For now. Old habits are hard to give up."

"Jack's an old habit?"

"Twenty or so years ago, when I was an impressionable kid in my twenties, Jack seemed like such a visionary. Jack." Julie laughs loudly. "Do you want to know what his real name is? Fallon. Fallon Andrews. That's a bleeding-heart liberal name if you ever heard one. All the right causes and sex appeal flowing out of his pores." Julie goes quiet, and Thalia waits. A dozen more interstate miles are covered before Julie speaks again. "Tee, is it possible to really get redemption?"

"That might be better asked of Cocker or Libby."

∽

Smitty told Diego he didn't have to work today; it would be too cold to get anything done productively. Diego is beginning to believe the boss was right. "It's just a garage, son. It'll keep until the weather changes." Diego stands in the street facing the southwest, the direction of the wind. It's the wind making the 38-degree temperature seem even colder, but if the rain holds out until the afternoon, maybe he can get the roof covered in plywood, and he'll be able to work inside, away from the wind. He rummages through a box of old clothes in the corner of the garage for a jacket or sweatshirt. Finding a tattered yellow sweatshirt, he slips it over his head and pulls on his gloves. He steps outside to the stack of four-by-eight sheets of plywood, lifts the first one, and wedges it up to the roof. Diego waves to Libby, who seems to be getting enjoyment watching the only person in Rubicon who works harder than she does.

"I know, I know," he yells to her, "this could probably wait." He rubs his hand over a tickle under his arm. "I'll be ready for a burrito at noon, so don't leave." Suddenly, Diego lets out a yowl and grabs the flesh where the tickle was. He twists violently and continues to howl, noises which have now become curses. "Help me, Libby, something's biting the hell out of me!" He pulls the sweatshirt over his head, taking his two undershirts with it. "Shit!"

Libby runs to Diego, and using a dishrag, she removes the scorpion from his armpit. "Nasty critters! Hold still. Let me see how many times he stung you."

"Fuck, that burns."

"Hush, Diego. There's no reason to be swearing around me." Libby pokes her finger at two spots. She pulls the half-naked Diego by the arm to her truck. "I'm going to wash them and fix you up." She points to the customer table. "Sit there and try not to squirm." She vanishes into her truck and returns with a pan of soapy water, which she uses to wash Diego's stings. "Hold this cloth over the bites," she orders. Again, she goes into her truck, this time for ice. Libby places a plastic bag holding the ice over the stings. "Hold this on them for ten minutes. I'll be right back."

Diego's pain shows on his face, but he sits and does as he's instructed. He is unconcerned about the temperature and wind, as if the scorpion stings removed them as factors in his comfort zone. The ice pack seems to be numbing his chest enough to lessen the pain, but the stings still burn. Libby returns from Cocker's house carrying a house plant. She sets it on the table next to Diego, pulls out a pocketknife and cuts off a stem.

"Aloe. Indian medicine. The bark scorpion is poisonous, but it won't kill you." Libby uses the juices from the aloe stem to blot the sting.

"I thought scorpion bites were deadly."

"Can be for kids and old men, but not for you."

"Could have fooled me. These hurt like hell."

Libby walks to the garage and picks up the sweatshirt. Carefully, she turns it inside out. Three more scorpions scurry off the fabric. "Looks like they were nesting in here. You're lucky only one got to your skin. I can only imagine the dance you'd have performed if all of them had stung you." Libby laughs. Back in her truck, she finds a cook shirt and wraps it around Diego. "When you live in the desert, you need to watch for unseen dangers. Something's always ready to jump up and bite you."

Diego nods. He presses the ice pack against the stings. The rain dodges Rubicon, passing well to the east on the Tohono O'odham reservation.

The flash flood temporarily isolates Rubicon from Why. Geneva's Arroyo, renamed by Smitty for his wife when she died, is Brawley Wash on local topo maps. A rare heavy rain for this time of year fell five miles east of Why, but the waters rushed down the dry creek bed. The wall of water measured only about five inches, smaller than many in the past, but enough to scare the campers in the RV park, and enough to uproot a few bushes along Smitty's golf course. After all his years in Rubicon, Smitty has never seen a river of water in January.

The Why Intersection

∾

"I haven't uttered the name Fallon Andrews in nine or ten years, not since we left Alaska. I loved Alaska. I finally understood nature and preservation and ecosystems and the need to take care of it all. I didn't think I would like the cold and the isolation, but I did. In northern California I was role-playing. It was exciting and adventurous. Our groups disrupted industries and businesses, made it difficult for them. Spiking trees, arson of equipment, cutting power lines, and downing billboards. For the first anniversary of our relationship, Jack bought, well, stole a chain saw and gave it to me all wrapped up. I think he's still committed, but he's in that damned wheelchair." Julie doesn't make the turn at Buckeye that would return them to Why. Instead, she continues along I-10 west. "Let me show you something." She drives another twenty minutes before turning off at Tonopah. She drives through "town" and continues for a few miles where the Palo Verde towers are clearly visible. "America's largest nuclear power plant; the crown jewel. Jack wants to shut it down, but it's a pipe dream. He's part of a team planning to do something spectacular. They talk on the phone, even though he worries his calls are being recorded."

Thalia finally responds. "Why did you leave Alaska if you loved it so much?"

Julie takes her eyes from Palo Verde, starts the car, and heads back toward Tonopah to get on the interstate. "Jack wanted to go. After the explosion he was housebound. There was some concern he could die. You can't blow your leg off and expect to carry on as normal. There were other serious injuries. The authorities were suspicious. 'Why were we making explosives in our garage?' Jack worked on the pipeline, and everyone was guarded, so he decided we had to go. I felt responsible for him then." She pauses while she checks traffic, but Thalia senses it's something else too.

When they passed the baby over to the couple in Scottsdale, Thalia knew Julie was having second thoughts. Julie and Thalia were not told where the baby was going next; they were simply thanked and handed the envelope. Impersonal. Thalia did not ask how much money was inside, but she was convinced Julie would not keep it for herself. Where would it go?

"Jack blamed me for the explosion. It's silly because I took no part in making the damn thing. I happened to walk in and startled him. Something touched something else and the whole garage was destroyed. Both of us lost some hearing. I had a broken arm. It's a blur now. The good part is we lived with some others who were able to give us help immediately and get us to the aid station."

"When did your religion begin?" asks Thalia. It's a jump from the revelation about the explosion, but Julie has avoided talking about it during casual conversations. Cocker brings it up frequently, asking the others what they believe, but nobody gets serious. Julie, though, doesn't ever participate.

"There were lots of small religious communities in Alaska, people from the Lower-48 who were ex-hippies and disgusted with capitalism or whatever. I guess they weren't ex-hippies, but real hippies, wanting to live in peace and harmony, wanting to be self-sufficient and independent. When Jack was seriously injured and I thought he might die, I talked with some people at one of these communities near us, just trying to understand. About a week later, my mother died. I wasn't there and hadn't spoken with her in years, but it just crushed me. Everything I had been doing for all those years seemed meaningless. The members of End Time, the religious community, basically confirmed my new beliefs. While Jack was in the hospital, I lived with them. I might have stayed, but Jack said we were going back. I thought he meant California, but we ended up here." There's a pause. "Why. Running a bar slash safe house. Plotting to shut down Palo Verde. And I deliver babies to Christian parents who can't have one of their own. Just a link in a long chain."

"What kind of work did you do while you and Jack were in Alaska?"

"I was a part-time prostitute, if a girl can be part time."

༄

As Julie and Thalia drive through Ajo in the evening, they notice Jade and CJ standing together in front of a bar. Jade's arms are flailing, and her head has lurched forward. Fifteen minutes later, Julie pulls up at Libby's food truck, gets out and hugs Libby, exchanges a few words, and then hands her the envelope.

The Why Intersection

∾

Diego meets Mr. Smithfield outside the warehouse just as darkness is settling over the desert. Smitty is driving his station wagon, the one with the false backseat. He gets out and shakes Diego's hand but says nothing. The old man puts his hand on Diego's shoulder and leads him across the intersection to the convenience store which is closed. Smitty pulls a ring of keys from his trousers and unlocks the front door. Inside, Smitty pours himself a coffee from the day's pot and warms it in the microwave. He asks Diego if he would like something, insisting that it's okay and the night will be long. Diego takes a soda from the cooler, and they walk back to the car.

"We need to drive around to the back to pick up another passenger." Smitty pauses. "You understand?"

Diego nods.

Six hours later, on the return trip from Tucson, Smitty pulls off the nearly deserted highway just west of Sells to relieve himself. Diego does the same, and the two men lean against the hood of the car and study Baboquivari, that magnificent mountain that the Tohono O'odham believe is the center of the universe.

"You don't say much, do you?"

Diego makes a noise almost like a sarcastic laugh but stays mum.

"Our passenger was Salvadoran. The ones who come through Rubicon are not quite like the others who mostly pass through Nogales and head up to Tucson. Ours generally are in dire need of immediate protection. Lots of reasons. Almost all our groceries are men who their government wants dead." Smitty allows that thought to hover over Diego before continuing. "Half-dozen years ago, a couple about your age and a Tucson minister approached me about being part of this, of being a station in this, for lack of a better word, human smuggling operation. The couple worked for an international refugee organization and the minister was just following his conscience. These people from Central America are pawns in the Cold War, and the United States is supporting non-communist dictators who kill non-cooperative citizens in their countries. America has been abetting those dictators. The bigger picture, we say. As such, Reagan's people refuse to grant these refugees asylum. Send them back to be killed."

The two men continue to look at Baboquivari.

"My name's not Diego, as you're well aware. I appreciate that you've never pressed for more information." He goes quiet for a moment. "That minister, Father John, and the others . . . what are they like?"

"Most in my neighborhood use different names. No big deal about what you call yourself. Most of us have these other lives that we've run away from or at least moved away from. Sometimes, moving away is the only way to discover the truth." Smitty pauses. "And to gain a bit of peace. Father John and the others? Gentle souls, but tough and fierce about the refugees. No compromise." He goes quiet again. "I have a feeling you know a little something about this Kramer fellow, but I don't need you to tell me what. That's your backstory. What I surmise is that you're a grocery too, just from a different aisle."

Diego turns slightly. "I know what Rubicon does, and I respect that. I won't tell anyone, but I think you know that. Your neighborhood is sort of like my Tucson, a temporary destination on my journey. What made you get into the grocery business?"

Smitty turns to face Diego. "It didn't happen overnight. Back in the fifties when I left my first job, I traveled around the country quite a bit. I saw things; met some people. That's when I first met Jack. He wasn't Jack back then, and he was whole. We reconnected after his accident. He lost much of his energy. Understandable." Smitty pauses with an image of years past before continuing. "Fell in love with a woman a dozen years older than me. She showed me that I lacked purpose, and a person needs purpose. I lost her a while back, but we still talk. She's very patient with my old age eccentricities and the company I keep. Golf isn't purpose, so I move groceries. I know that doesn't answer your question, but it's all I've got. Anyway, getting back to the situation at hand, just want you to know that beyond that great investigator, there are all kinds of little men who might want to do you harm. Don't get careless."

"Do I bring unwanted attention to what you do? If I do, I'll leave."

The old man waves off the younger man's offer. "We're not helpless, son. Hell, we put up with Alf; he's been unwanted attention ever since he showed up." He puts his hand on Digo's shoulder. "Load up."

14

ANOTHER VISIT

"Walt Kramer's coming back," Smitty adds casually. It's a full house at The Call: the Guardians, the Auxiliary, a half-dozen ranchers, and Hector and Thalia. Julie stays behind the bar on her stool with Hector and Thalia at the bar, while the others drink, gender segregated at two tables.

"Did your sources alert you, Smitty?" asks Jack.

"No, actually, he called me. I'm sure he just missed us all, since we're such a hospitable group. Asked me if I'd drive over to Tucson to pick him up from the airport. Said he was tired of pretending to be a tourist."

"Sounds like a man-crush," says Crystal.

"Whoa. The accountant makes her first comment of the new year, and a snide remark it is." says Jade. She reaches over and high fives her friend.

"When are you going to get him?" asks Alf.

"He's coming in, what's today? Saturday? He'll be in on Tuesday, the 20th."

"Did he give you any hint of what he wants?" asks CJ.

"Nope. As we've all seen, he doesn't really know. Even though we're all suspicious and can be a bit abrupt, I think he's comfortable among us. He's only staying one night. He'll fly in the morning on Tuesday and out in the evening on Wednesday. He'll book a room in Ajo for the night."

"Maybe he could stay with you," teases Crystal again.

"Am I going to have to raise your rent, young lady, to get you in line?"

Jack holds his beer bottle up as a signal to Julie he's dry. When she returns with another one, he says nothing. Thalia watches, wondering what their situation is now. She discussed it with Hector after returning from Phoenix on the baby delivery, but still has no answers. Hector's best guess was the Guardians and Julie know all about each other despite their rouge of privacy. Julie's peek into her past last week was most likely a sign of growing trust in Thalia. Julie told about herself and Jack, but not about the others. They would need to do that themselves when they felt comfortable. Julie probably suspected Thalia would share the information with Hector, since she never cautioned Thalia that the conversation was to stay between the two women.

Jack raises the bottle toward Smitty. "You are an enigma, Smitty. Why not just tell him no, that we don't have any information to give him? It seemed apparent last time, and God knows we've discussed it enough to be sure ourselves."

"Ah, Jack, I'm as transparent as the rest of you." He's joking, of course, because he knows he can piss Jack off quickly. He also knows that transparency is not the strong suit in Why. Unlike his friends, Smitty doesn't fear strangers despite his public protestations. "I've found the man interesting, both in person and as I've gained information from my sources. You know those sources, Jack, those spies who do my bidding in Washington and Boston. You asked me to keep digging, and I have. One of my old colleagues sent me a newspaper clipping from a few years back about nuclear accidents, something all of us are interested in being so close to Palo Verde." He lowers his brow and stares directly at Jack. "You especially, Jack."

At the bar Hector unconsciously squeezes Thalia's knee.

CJ slides his chair back. "Hold on, Smitty. I need to take a leak, and I don't want to miss where this is going."

Cocker lights up a smoke, and Julie refreshes the women's drinks. When CJ returns, he has Julie get him a beer, and he sits down next to Jade. "Okay, continue."

"I don't know what it means yet, if anything, but" and Smitty pauses for a moment as if drawing in his audience, "it seems Mr. Kramer, in addition to being the manager of a nuclear plant in northern Colorado, is a special consultant for nuclear accidents around the country." He pauses again and takes a drink of his scotch.

All the Guardians see the implication in Smitty's information, but none of the Auxiliary do. Thalia, since her conversation with Julie, sees it too. She looks at Hector and sees a man swirling in the wind of new information. Still, Hector's eyes don't indicate apprehension, but rather a gentle assent that another little piece of a larger jigsaw puzzle has been put into place.

Libby returns with the Auxiliary children at dinner time. She took them to Sells, the capital of the Tohono O'odham Reservation for a school fieldtrip, about an hour east from Rubicon. Cocker wanted to go, but Libby refused his offer, implying the kids feared him, and she wanted to make this fieldtrip all about the desert and her people. The children burst into The Call like the recent flash flood burst across the highway, bringing an end to the conversation. The younger children thrust their artwork on the Notajo table, proud of the cacti and mountains they have painted. To the children, Sells was not a rundown town, but a place where "Indians dress like us." Jade's three children are less enamored, but they enjoyed the day away from the classroom too. The visit to the Sells' elementary school was a highlight. "Mama, there were lots of chubby kids." Libby is herself overweight, but she believes there is a growing problem with the children's health on the reservation. "Government food!" she mutters, almost as curse words. "They think they're helping, but they don't understand our culture, so the food they send damages the bodies of our people. Other diseases will follow as our little ones' bodies lose the protections of our people's native foods. Because we're poor doesn't mean we don't see what their handouts are doing to us."

ભ

In the evening Jack and Alf sit at the table alone, still drinking, still talking about the return visit of the mysterious Walt Kramer. Julie listens to music from a Nogales radio station reading her Bible at the bar. *Out in the West Texas town of El Paso* compliments passages from *John*.

"So, what do we do, Jack?" asks Alf.

"The others don't see it, Alf; they just don't see it at all. Kramer's digging for something. He's like a roadrunner chasing a lizard. We can dodge all we want, but he's bound and determined to get what he wants. He cozied up to Smitty and convinced him he's just as lost as we are about life. It's not about some woman he or his buddy Dan met in the mountains on a camping trip; that's just the cover story. No, he's got something on one of us."

Alf turns in his chair toward the bar. "What do you think, Julie? Is this Kramer fellow dangerous?"

Julie puts a napkin in her Bible and closes it. Looking up, she runs her tongue under her lower lip. "I don't think so, Alf, but there's no convincing you and Jack about it. I agree Kramer wants something, but he doesn't seem angry about it."

"What do you mean *angry about it*?"

"When the Arizona cops were snooping around here, trying to get information about their missing colleague, they were angry. When the church guys wanted to reclaim Cocker's supposed fortune, they were angry. They all try not to show it, but if you look close enough, it's there. You know why we decided Thalia and Hector were okay, that we could trust them to listen in to our discussions? Because they weren't angry. It shows." Julie rises off her stool, places her Bible on the shelf beneath the mirror, pours herself a half glass of soda water, and walks around to the table. "Kramer and his scout, Dan, are smart. They intuit things. Men like them don't have to learn the information they came for to know it's there." Julie sips her drink, and they sit in silence for a while in the dim light of the bar. Finally, Julie asks, "If Kramer walked in right now and sat down, what would you ask him?"

"That's an interesting question, Julie, and I don't know," says Alf. He looks over to Jack, who shakes his head.

Julie rescues them. "You're going to get your chance next Tuesday, you know, so you might consider your words between now and then."

They sit in silence again, three people brought together from as diverse backgrounds as is possible in western America in the 1980s, people who are as close as kin, but whose backgrounds cause them to suspect even their closest friends. Fellow union members cross the picket line to work as scabs; idealistic eco-terrorists save themselves from jail by ratting out those who worked with them for years; lovers lose passion because of the strains of daily life in a harsh environment. A person falls into a place such as Why—"The wind blew me here"— and adjusts his or her behavior without ever understanding how it happened. A turn in the road. All of a sudden, a person has been in town for three, five, or ten years, and it's home. Sort of. And the wind wasn't strong enough to blow them out of town. Jack lays his head on

The Why Intersection

the table and falls asleep, something he does frequently, especially after hours of drinking. Julie finishes the last swallow of her drink and looks at Alf. He pushes his warm beer to the center of the table and nods. He and Julie stand and disappear through the narrow door behind the bar, leaving Jack alone, a one-legged idealist, drunk and splayed out on a table in a southern Arizona bar at a time when his beliefs are no longer in the ascendency in America.

∾

Thalia likes candlelight. She sits with her legs across Hector's on her couch, where she can see the candle flame reflected in his dark eyes. It leaves her face in the dark.

"What are you thinking in that mysterious head of yours tonight, Hector?"

Hector smiles gently. "It's never just one thought, but I was thinking about the finances of everyone at the bar tonight, especially Cocker and Alf. How do they support themselves?" He pushes a lock of Thalia's hair from her cheek to behind her ear.

"This is a pretty interconnected neighborhood, but I'll see if I can make some sense of it for you. None of this is talked about with certainty, but little bits of information leak out, and you know how perceptive I am." She smiles and Hector nods. "Cocker was here first, and somehow, probably through his church connections, he owned that warehouse across the highway, even if he didn't have the deed. When his ministry folded and his tiny congregation left, he was left with the property. Smitty bought it somehow and then bought it again from Cocker. Not for much, I'm sure, but enough to give him a nest egg of sorts. From what I can gather, Smitty set up an account for him at a Tucson bank to monitor how much he can use. I think Cocker even owns his house or at least doesn't pay any rent, and he has a small military pension. Smitty wants everyone to believe he got all his money from the government way back when, but I think he inherited much of his wealth. He's mentioned that his father was a self-made Italian posing as a Brit. Nonsensical but a clue. CJ works for the mining company in some capacity still, monitors the operations up in Ajo in some way. Jack and Julie run the bar."

Hector interrupts. "Which doesn't seem to make any money."

"No, but they don't spend much money either." She pauses. "They're not doing well. Alf is the question mark. I know he was getting a union payment for a while, but it wasn't much, and I think that's run out. He's an auto mechanic and services the Park's trucks periodically."

"And you, Thalia, how do you make ends meet?"

She smiles and tilts her head but waits to answer. "If I told you, some of the mystique might go away." She waits only a moment. "I get paid, I guess by Smitty, to tend the bar even though it comes through Jack and Julie, and I get paid a little as the teacher. I came here for a story; I'm a journalist, and while that story went away, I still send some articles to journals and newspapers about this part of America. Brings in a few dollars."

Hector can't see her expression clearly in the candlelight. This is an amazing woman, he thinks to himself, maybe with more secrets than the others who populate this isolated neighborhood. She came to Rubicon on some fuzzy journalistic assignment, but that seems to be over, and she remains.

"Am I getting too heavy?"

"Not yet."

"What about you, Hector, what do you do?"

"I work for Smitty." With that answer, Hector seems to travel from the room for a moment. The candle flame flickers.

"I know, but is it enough to get by on?"

"Smitty pays me enough. Actually, he pays promptly and pretty good." Hector lets out a soft laugh. "He usually asks how long I'll be staying and if I need a little extra for anything."

Thalia leans in and kisses Hector lightly. "Have you always worked with your hands?"

"Off and on. A separate part of me used to sit in a darkened room and watch a screen with dots that beeped. It wasn't a job with a connection to the real world." Hector pauses and returns to the room. "I like this work a lot better. More satisfaction." He pauses again. "The people here are real."

"That makes no sense, Hector. It doesn't sound like you."

"Maybe not, but like novels, it leads us to bigger truths."

"Hopefully," says Thalia.

"Can I read your book sometime?" asks Hector.

"Yeah, if you want. It's not anywhere close to being done, and it doesn't seem to have direction, but it is kind of fun to do. I have some other writings that might be of more interest." She touches his lips with her finger and then taps his forehead. "And your past, Mr. Jego?"

"If I remembered it daily, I could not survive. It's one of the reasons I work so much," answers Hector, again with a self-questioning look on his face.

"Are you as tired as I am each night from pretending all day? I fall into bed exhausted, but then I don't fall asleep, or at least not deeply. I toss and turn, I stir. I can't shut off my mind. Things are said at The Call. So much of why I stay here doesn't make sense. I just believe I'm supposed to be here."

"I'm glad you stayed, for whatever reason."

Thalia smiles a smile Hector can't see. She leans her head against his shoulder and lets out a soft sigh. "Maybe I'm your bridge."

"Over the Rubicon." The standard joke.

∽

"We tell lies." Smitty is sitting on his deck just after the sun has set. The sky is mostly orange as it often is in this desert.

"You just embellish," answers Geneva silently. "They're honest lies."

"Regardless, we lie."

"To keep our privacy. We just want to be left alone. There's certainly no crime in that."

"But over so many years?"

"I know you, dear. You know the difference between the truth and bullcrap. It's why you can distinguish right from wrong. You believe your eyes and ears and not the bullshit that some blowhard on the radio spews." Geneva reassures her husband often in the evenings under the stats.

"And this new truth protects us?"

"It's not a new truth. Truth is truth. Makes what we do possible," smiles Geneva.

Smitty extends his arm around the empty chair next to him. "The truth shouldn't be debatable, especially in a small town like Why, but it is. We're trying to do the right thing, but maybe we're doing it the wrong way."

Geneva stays quiet, but Smitty hears her anyway.

∽

"All airports need to be this size," says Walt Kramer. "No hassles. Get off the plane; grab your bag and go. It's not exactly summer here, but 60 degrees is a whole lot warmer than Colorado's ten degrees."

"January is our coldest month, along with late December, but it'll start warming up soon." Smitty looks over his left shoulder to check for traffic. "Cocker talks about population all the time. He believes the end of civilization is near because of the growth of population, which fits in nicely with his religious beliefs about the Second Coming. He'll tell you too many people cause us all to behave differently."

"Now, Cocker is the unkempt one, isn't he?" Walt knows, but he's making conversation.

"Yeah. He was the first to arrive in Rubicon. It wasn't called Rubicon back then; it was just plain old Why. Cocker tried to establish a revival church here, but he's not cut out for the organization required to run a church, the business end of a church. I suspect he could give a good sermon back in his day, but he chose a bad location. He'll tell you the Lord sent him there, but if He did, it just shows what a great sense of humor He has. After Tabernacle, as Cock called it, failed, he tried his hand at being a copper miner, but musicians weren't meant to do that kind of labor, plus he has a propensity for alcohol, so it didn't work out."

"Don't most miners lean toward the bar at the end of the day?" Walt remembers his days after the Korean War when the bar was his home.

"I guess they do."

"This weather is such a nice change. I can see why people, especially old people, move down here. I've got a yard full of snow in Colorado, and the drive to Denver last night was long and treacherous. A fella could get used to this winter weather." Walt watches South Tucson pass by as Waddell Smithfield steers toward the Tohono O'odham

The Why Intersection

Reservation. "How long's the drive?"

"Couple of hours at the speed limit," answers Smitty.

After twenty minutes of driving from the airport, Smitty comes to the Border Patrol checkpoint west of Tucson. He eases in behind four pickups as they all inch forward in succession. He notices Walt's acuity in collecting details: the number of agents, their dogs, the fact that all the vehicles in front are pickup trucks, the pedestrians on the opposite side of the road, two Border Patrol agents parked in a truck sitting perpendicular to the highway, ready to pull out in either direction in pursuit of anyone racing off without permission. "Seems pretty laid back, but there's quite a bit going on, wouldn't you say?"

Walt nods. "I would imagine most of the agents consider this pretty monotonous duty, but the variety of people passing through just this one checkpoint is fascinating. A microcosm of the Southwest, I would imagine." Walt finishes his sentence with the same words he started it with. *I would imagine.* Between his research and previous visits, Walt thinks he has a pretty good handle on Waddell Smithfield, at least his background, but background is a window into character. Waddell is a math genius who worked on some critical components of America's early defense system, but he resigned and headed west, and now goes by the name Smitty to his friends. He owns a neighborhood of houses in a rundown Arizona town in the middle of the Sonoran Desert, renting them out for next to nothing to a collection of people so different as to make one's head spin. He owns real estate in other parts of the country where he once lived. Walt's first impression was that Smitty pitied his friends, but he's not so sure of his initial assessment any longer. Smitty seems to appreciate their struggles and battles and certainly enjoys their company. Waddell Smithfield also has no passport.

There are no cars behind Smitty, so he makes small talk with the agent, mostly about the upcoming Super Bowl. Being an ex-East Coaster, Smitty favors the Giants. The agent takes the Denver Broncos, warning Smitty that John Elway will shred New York's defenses. The bet is a six-pack of beer. They shake hands and Smitty drives off.

"Those are good kids who get jaded pretty quickly," says Smitty. "The drug running is the worst; it taints the immigration problem.

The Indians and Mexicans from this area have been moving across arbitrary borders forever, visiting family or working or going to religious celebrations, but now they're suspect. All because of the drugs. Tucson accepts all of this, for the most part, but I'm afraid America won't. We believe in those hard borders, ya know." Smitty smirks.

"It's still pretty easy to move across the border right now, isn't it?" asks Walt.

"The Mountain" comes into view quickly and dominates the landscape to the south of the highway. Baboquivari. Smitty pulls off the road to allow Walt an unobstructed view of the peak from outside the car. Smitty talks as his guest takes it all in. "It's a pretty impressive rock, Walt. A granite monolith. Almost 8,000 feet high, although we start about 2,300 feet here. It's sacred to the Indians. They say their God lives in a cave near the top, that he brought his people to this spot. Big Brother, or something like it. The Tohono O'odham fight with the government over who owns it, who has the rights to it. Goes back to the Mexican War and the Treaty of Guadalupe-Hidalgo. Anyone with half a brain can see it belongs to the Indians, but then again, we're dealing with people in Washington who don't always have half a brain." Walt laughs or grunts; Smitty is unsure which. "Ready?"

Walt nods, but instead of getting back into the front seat, he climbs into the backseat on the driver's side of the car. "I want to watch this mountain as we drive, to see how it changes as we move on. You don't mind, do you?"

As they drive on, Walt verbalizes some of his observations. "Seems like all the scenery and action takes place on the south side of the highway, on the Mexican side." "Does anyone drive anything but a pickup truck around here?" "If I were God, I might choose a mountain like Baboquivari to live in too." He pauses. "Or to die on."

Smitty turns off the highway at Sells to make the loop of the town. "Libby grew up here and still lives here most of the time. Do you remember who Libby is?" Walt affirms he does. Waddell points to various buildings as he slowly drives through the worn-out town. "The nicest ones belong to the government, the Bureau of Indian Affairs mostly." He allows for Walt to process the capital city of an Indian reservation, a nation which doesn't control its destiny despite a history

The Why Intersection

of independence stretching over several centuries. The silence warms both men to each other, a growing respect born of age and ability. They know about one another; they each assume they will learn even more in the hours to come.

At the western edge of Sells, Smitty stops at a food cart and buys two tamales and two beers. The two men sit at a picnic table in the sun for lunch. "Not too long and I'll be looking for shade, but January can be pretty cool. The snowbirds come for this, this sun in winter. It was one of the things that hooked me when I first arrived." He takes a bite out of his corn-husked tamale. "You like the snow, Walt?"

"No, can't say as I do. I've just always lived in it in winter. Colorado native; got a job there after the war; went to college there; got my next job there." He remembers something and smiles to himself. "Married a Colorado girl. Guess you could say Colorado has been awfully good to me." They concentrate on their food for a moment before Walt asks, "You've been around a bit. Why'd you leave MIT? You were working on some pretty important stuff."

Smitty finishes his tamale, wads up his husk, and tosses it into the oil drum trash can. He leans into the card table to study Walt, but he already knows some things. "You've got government connections, don't you?"

Walt nods. "Good ones."

"You're not looking for any of us in Rubicon, are you?"

Walt hesitates. "Not directly, and this isn't a government job. It's personal." Walt tosses his husk and beer bottle into the trash and stands. The two men return to the car, Walt back in the front seat, and head for Why.

Smitty finally answers Walt's question. "I resigned because I couldn't agree with their plan. As I look back, I was most likely too hasty, but, damn, it frustrated me they would proceed with such an imperfect system. Any air defense system was going to be flawed, but it seemed they accepted too many flaws. We'd sit around and discuss those imperfections, and it always came back to having humans make the final call based on imperfect information. I wanted a better computer, one that would lessen the chances of error for sure, but also reduce the chance of putting the future of the world in the hands of men in Washington who'd never seen the cities they were about to incinerate. To them it was a board game, a math problem. The older I get, the less sure I am about my decision, not saying I would go back, but I don't see the alternatives any longer. It was what it was, but it hurt me that I was a part of it all. So, with MIT's blessing, I eased my way out."

"It meant you wouldn't have access to your computers any longer. Did it bother you?"

"No regrets there. I'd been a nerd, Walt, locked into all that from the time I was a teenager. Do you know what the first thing I did was when I walked away? I went to the YMCA and shot baskets. I hadn't picked up a basketball since junior high, so I shot baskets."

"You know, don't you, they still know where you are today?"

"Yeah. If you think the guys in Rubicon are paranoid, it's nothing to those fools in Washington." Smitty goes silent for a moment. "I don't know whether my life is a simple book with many chapters or a multi-volumed work, but I do know that I'm not proud of several of those chapters." Both men silently reflect on Smitty's words.

As Smitty speeds past a roadside cemetery, Walt turns his head to the rear. "Can you pull over and go back? I want to take a look at that."

A meager barbed wire fence restricts access to the cemetery from the highway, but all the 200 or so graves are visible. Most are framed with six-inch concrete or cinderblock enclosures, although many on the far side have no adornments except wooden crosses. *Even in death there is segregation*, thinks Walt. Several dozen sites have elaborate headstones with pictures of the Virgin Mary or etchings of Biblical quotes, but all the sites are adorned with colorful synthetic flowers. Walt is struck by the contrast of this cemetery from the one in Buena Vista where a simple river stone designates the spot where the dirt represents the passing of his son. These graves are taken care of on a weekly basis by the families, the deceased still part of the family. At one of the more ornate graves, a woman wearing a cowboy hat sits in a plastic lawn chair reading aloud.

"These are Tohono O'odham graves," says Waddell. "Indian religion mixed with Catholicism."

Walt nods like a bobblehead doll for a moment but says nothing.

The Why Intersection

Finally, "This is interesting. We can go now."

"You're a curious fella, Kramer. What else?"

"Why real estate in a poor desert town?" asks Walt.

"Seemed like Why might become an attraction, or at least I could make it one. You know, the last town in Arizona before the Mexican beaches on the Sea of Cortez. Besides, I like the weather, the desert, and the night sky."

"Do you own any other real estate?" Walt knows the answer. A half-dozen neighborhoods populated by people similar to Whyans. All a part of Waddell Smithfield's odyssey.

"A few places in other simple towns. Not just in Arizona. Places for people like," Smitty pauses, "like my people." He smiles like a grandfather at his grandchild's high school graduation.

∽

Hector catches Thalia before class begins. "I need to be gone for the rest of the day. Would you meet me for dinner in Ajo later?" He kisses her on the cheek and steps back.

Thalia says nothing, but nods and smiles. *A real date*, she thinks.

∽

Jade watches CJ watch Alf. He does it frequently, as if he's monitoring Alf. She asked him about it several weeks earlier when they were lying in bed, but he blew her off. "It's nothing," he said, but he was concealing something. It's what they all do in Rubicon, hide, and it drives Jade crazy. She stirs and paces. When she does, her Notajo girls know to keep a distance, like when she punched the lady in the union hall in '83. She walked away from her at first, up the aisle to get space, but the lady wouldn't shut up, so she came back and punched her. It happens in union halls, and nobody calls the police.

This evening, Jade's kids are in Ajo with friends, at least friends from before the strike. Jade barely speaks with their mother, but her animosity shouldn't keep her kids from playing with their friends. Besides, the pickings in Rubicon are slim, especially for Jade's two oldest, the oldest of the children in the neighborhood. Why has almost no children, mostly a hundred adults similar to the Guardians. Jade drove her kids to Ajo after school for play and dinner in the old neighborhood, in the company town. They'll be driven home after eight, three hours after dark has settled in winter, but Jade knows they're safe, so she ate a TV dinner and came to The Call to have a beer. CJ told her he needed to be at the bar, anyway, but she was welcome to come by. So, she sits at the bar watching CJ watch Alf, while Alf whispers to Jack and Jack whispers back. Julie reads her Bible behind the bar, and Cocker sings softly under his breath, a hum really. They're all waiting for Smitty to drive up with the enigma, Walt Kramer.

Jade will start her new job at the beginning of next week as a reporter and copy editor for the *Ajo Copper News*. She joked to Ruby and Crystal that she would need to drop out of the Notajo Auxiliary, because she would be driving to Ajo every day. Ruby told her that until she starts sleeping in Ajo, she wasn't a resident there. In the privacy of her Rubicon home, Jade is being pressured by her two oldest to let them attend school again at the junior high in Ajo where their old friends are. She sips her beer and wonders which direction her life will take next. She talked with Thalia and Hector about taking her kids out of school in The Call, explaining how easy it would be to drop them off each morning and how it would free up Thalia to teach only kids who were in elementary school. Thalia said she would miss them, but Hector thought it would be good for them. He said kids don't learn much about academics in junior high, but it is important for them to learn about puberty and social standing.

Cocker breaks out of his contemplative state and puts his hand on Alf's forearm. The others hear Smitty's Oldsmobile pull up in front of The Call and they straighten up, like they're about to be called into a formal interview. Julie prepared a tortilla soup in case Smitty hasn't fed Walt; eating at prescribed times isn't something Rubicon does. CJ looks back from his seat at the table to Jade, a look Jade feels is formal, almost a command to her to stay at the bar. She resents it but says nothing. Julie nudges Jade's arm with another beer, and Jade realizes Julie is also on the periphery. Jade is reminded of the early days of the copper strike, back in '83, when the women were kept off the picket lines and out of the union discussions, regardless of their status. That changed quickly as the women injected themselves into the middle of the confrontation with Phelps Dodge and began to walk the lines while their husbands, fathers, and brothers began leaving to find work in other mines of the West, or to cross the lines as scabs. Jade recalls seeing CJ at the PD gate back in '84, and she wonders if he knows how angry she is becoming at this moment at his dismissal and avoidance.

Smitty leads Walt into the bar, and after a brief hello, they sit at the table with Jack, Alf, CJ, and Cocker. While their attention is diverted by the grand entrance, Jade slides off her stool, pulls a chair from an adjoining table, and sits down just off CJ's left shoulder. "Hi. I don't know if you remember, but I'm Jade," she says to Walt as she raises her beer. She leans in and kisses CJ on the cheek. "Sometimes the men around here forget their manners." She sits back in her chair, crosses her legs, and holds her empty beer bottle up to her lips.

Jack speaks first. "Smitty told us you were going to pay us another visit. Three now and in the dead of winter. Must be pretty damn important."

Julie sets beers in front of Smitty and Walt and then returns to her station behind the bar. She wipes the counter with a damp cloth, leaves it at the end of the bar, sits on her high stool, and waits.

Smitty tilts his head from side to side, stretching. "Long drive for an old man. We stopped in Sells for a quick bite. Libby's tamales are better than her competition's. Looks like they've started excavating for the new elementary school."

"Can I buy a round?" offers Walt. "Feels like we need a little extra to loosen up." Without waiting for a response, he turns to Julie and waves his hand in a circle around the table. "Jack, it is important, but not for you guys. Just for me." Walt keeps his eyes moving around the table, not wanting to seem combative with Jack. This is his bar, his territory. Still, Walt knows there is a challenge, and he wants to know how Rubicon will rise to meet it, beyond denial and obscurity.

Julie sets the drink of choice in front of each man and returns to the bar. Jade clears her throat. "Excuse me, Julie. Am I going to be treated as a ghost by you too?" Her meaning is not directed at Julie, who understands and pulls a beer from the cooler. Jade stands and lets Julie hand it to her across the bar. Instead of sitting down, she leans against the bar. "You asked about me on your first visit, so I'm told, and decided I wasn't the one. I'm curious, Mr. Kramer, what I wasn't."

The Guardians listen, but don't turn to hear Jade's words. CJ watches Alf, who casts a side glance at Jack. Before Walt answers Jade, Cocker asks, "Do you like cats, Kramer? Nobody around here likes cats, except me. Everyone's a dog person. I tried to bring my cats in here, but Jack wouldn't allow it."

"I don't own either. Been too busy all my life to take care of one. My father-in-law keeps a dog at the house, a black lab, and I like him, but he senses I'm not his owner. How many cats do you keep, Cocker?" asks Walt.

"Three at the moment. I've had more. They don't need much care. As long as I feed and water them, they're pretty comfortable. I think they're the reason these guys don't visit me at my place."

"That and you don't bath often enough, Cock," jokes Smitty.

Walt turns to address Jade. "You aren't the woman my friend Dan asked about. I was hoping you were, or maybe Thalia was, but you aren't. I would have recognized you from a funeral I attended for an old friend. I'm looking for the connection to the man whose funeral it was."

"Is that all it is?" asks Alf.

It's a challenge, and Walt knows it. "What do you think it is, Alf?"

Alf sits up in his chair and leans across the table. "If neither of these women are the one, why do you keep coming back. Someone paying you?"

"Who might that be, Alf. Who wants to know about you? Or Jack? Or anyone else here?" Walt rolls his beer bottle between his hands. He's aware there's at least one man in the bar packing a pistol, one man besides Alf. Walt asks again. "So, who would pay me to be here, to find out what you're up to three years after you lost your job with Phelps Dodge?"

"I ought to kick your ass, Kramer."

Both Jack and CJ put a hand on Alf's shoulder. Smitty stirs. "Hey, that's no way to treat a guest."

"Whose side you on, Smitty?" asks Alf.

Julie brings soup to the table, two bowls. "Dinner time, and there are no fights during dinner." Jade brings two more bowls and sets

The Why Intersection

spoons in front of each man. Julie brings the final two bowls to the table, while Jade sets two more on the bar. "Now act civil, Alf, or I'll cut you off."

"Good soup, Julie."

"Delicious, Julie."

"Hits the spot. It always does."

The men eat without speaking, but not in silence. Cocker is especially loud in his slurping. The soup is disarmingly good, but Walt is working, so he barely tastes it. He needs to be wary of Alf because from the days of the strike, Alf has a history of being a loose cannon. "The Gatekeeper." Lots of fights and arguments; PD monitored him constantly and tried to get him arrested at each event. Law enforcement knew they could provoke him, giving them an excuse for an arrest. Walt wants to avoid a confrontation; he's interested in discovering what drives him to Rubicon, what it is he feels when he's here. He's intrigued by a feeling he's never experienced before. He's wary of Alf, but Alf is not the force. At different times, it seems to Walt that different Guardians are in charge. Smitty and Jack usually assume the role, but CJ has a presence to him, but he hides something too. Cocker on the other hand exists for the Second Coming, and because of that—or in spite of it—is comfortable. Cocker wants to be one of the Redeemed, but he believes it's in God's hands and will accept His judgment. Research and two previous visits allowed Walt to glean a good deal about these Rubiconers, but he's no closer in discovering his purpose here than he was before his first visit. Like the Guardians, Walt wonders why he keeps returning to Why.

Walt finishes his soup and pushes his bowl to the center of the table. "I can understand some of your apprehension about me. If some stranger kept showing up in my town, kept showing up at my house, I'd be suspicious too. I've never been comfortable revealing my past to anyone, including my wife. There's a whole lot there that doesn't need to be dug up; it's nobody's business but my own. The chapters in that book are closed. Having said that, you guys deserve to know a little more of what this is about. What I do know about you all is you can keep a secret. I'll expect this to remain one." He pauses and looks at Jade. "Can you be trusted, Jade?"

Walt motions to Julie to bring another round and points to himself for the tab. He takes a deep breath and nods, almost to himself. There will be gaps in his revelations, but it will also be more than he's revealed to anyone except Bellena and Mac, the people in the world whom he most trusts. "In the fall of '83, a Soviet nuclear energy plant in the northern Ural Mountains exploded under strange circumstances. All kinds of rumors circulated. Still do. It was denied by the Soviets at first, and to this day they continue to deny it was a nuclear reactor, but the facts are fairly well known, just not widely publicized. Yamantov, a secret city north and east of Pechora near the Arctic Circle." Walt pauses and looks at Jack. "Do you know anything about this, Jack?"

"Not much. Like you said, there are rumors. Nowhere near the yield of Chernobyl. Some of my associates want to believe it was an act of terrorism, but no one really believes that. Most likely, it was a faulty design. As you said, it's pretty well covered up."

"When I say the facts are well-established, I mean to the government and the nuclear insiders. Both the United States and the Soviet Union think it's best to keep the lid on this. I'm privy to some of the information because of my work, but I don't know everything." Walt pauses again. "I'm a semi-insider, and I can't reveal everything." He takes a swig of his beer and watches for reactions. "Now comes the part that utterly confuses me, the part I refuse to accept, except that it happened. A couple of years later, last year, a Soviet grandmother and her grandson show up in Colorado, in Buena Vista where I live halftime, looking for someone who might shed some light on the accident. The woman's daughter, the boy's mother, went missing in this accident, and somehow the boy connects them to me. I'm not a believer in fate; never have been. I don't believe in conspiracy theories or put any trust in people who do. I'm as no-nonsense as a person can be. Ask my wife. Anyway, this six-year-old boy gets me in touch with another man, a man, who as I understand it today, was a shaman, a carrier of souls, and he's evidently carrying the little boy's mother's soul and needs to deliver it to the grandmother. I only get to talk with the man for a short time, but in that brief time, it seems as if he does transfer the soul he's carrying to the Soviet woman. At least they believe that. Since he has accomplished his goal . . ." Walt pauses,

The Why Intersection

goes inside himself to remind himself of his practiced words here, and then returns. "Since he accomplished his purpose, he leaves before I can learn more and before I can tell him what I know. I can guess what you're thinking right now. Nice story, Kramer. Bullshit, but nice story." Walt's eyes study each person at the table. "The shaman was my son, the son I never knew from a teenage relationship, and he's gone. He didn't know I was his father, at least I don't think he did. Later in the summer, an old friend of mine died, a friend who knew my son briefly, but my son confided in the old man. There was a connection there somehow. My old friend died before he could explain it to me, but in his dementia before his death, he said some things to me and a few others that raised the hackles on my neck. About my son. It seems he said some of these things to the lady Dan asked about, the woman he came asking about last fall. As I said, I'm no believer in fate or shamans or even strange coincidences, so I should have let all of this pass, but I can't, so I'm searching for another explanation." Walt looks at Jade again. "The old man indirectly indicated my answers might be here, that the woman might be here. But it isn't you."

Jade smiles as if she's been flattered by a handsome stranger. "I wish I was. This is an incredible story. Weird, but incredible."

Alf reaches into his boot and withdraws a pistol. He looks at it before sliding it across the table toward Walt. "I wasn't going to shoot you, but I was going to try and scare the hell out of you. I don't want you here, but after hearing this, you're as crazy as Cocker, and he belongs here." The table laughs. Walt picks up the gun, withdraws the magazine, and empties the chamber, setting everything back on the table.

Cocker leans forward. "Shamans do God's work. There are some souls who aren't ready for Heaven yet and need to be carried around until their time." He looks Walt in the eye and nods.

"Here in Rubicon," says Smitty, "we try to divorce ourselves from some of those stupid actions, even though we discuss them daily."

"Hourly. Ad nauseam," adds Julie.

Smitty turns and shakes his head at Julie. "In a sense we are no longer just old fart Americans. We're . . ."

"Guardians," says Julie with a smirk.

Jack shakes his head. "Kramer, you're going to spend a lot of beer money tonight on this story."

∽

Jade leaves around 7:30 to be home when her children return from Ajo. CJ walks her to the bar's door, kisses her, and promises to drop by later. Jade's departure allows for a break, to use the toilet, to have a smoke, to simply walk around. Walt uses the pay phone outside the bar to call his wife.

"Hi, Bellena. How's our little princess? Yeah, everything went smoothly. Smithfield picked me up at the airport as planned, and we had a nice conversation on the drive over here. I may delay coming home by a day; we'll see. When I tell the story out loud to strangers, it does seem unbelievable, just like you said, but they're interested. Yeah, I love you too. Give our girl a hug for me."

Julie and the men settle in, again with their drinks replenished. She sits behind the bar, close enough to hear. She continues to drink tea, but she can get buzzed with her infrequent shot of tequila. Not tonight though, Walt's story fascinates her, a mid-50s father with children 30-plus years apart. She thinks about fate and predestination, about Cocker's beliefs and Libby's beliefs, and about her conversion to Christianity after an explosion in a garage almost killed Jack. Julie hopes Walt can shed light on his hunches, that this all doesn't turn out to be a desert mirage.

"Walt," says Jack, "you seem to know I'm against nuclear power. I know your generator in Colorado isn't performing as expected and there's talk about shutting it down and converting to conventional power. If I were healthy, I might be taking steps to close it myself. But I can't, obviously. What I'm curious about is what happened to the radiation released by the accident in the Soviet Union. How was it contained, or was it?"

"It wasn't contained, but fortunately, the winds were blowing to the east northeast, over the Arctic Ocean, which took the radiation away from any populated area. Were some people affected? Probably, but not many and to what extent, I don't know. The casualties were at the accident site, and they were numerous, although the Soviet Union

The Why Intersection

never gave a detailed account." Walt knows his use of the word "accident" is misleading, but it's part of the cover-up.

Cocker lifts his head from the table. "Bet you thought I was sleeping, didn't you, Mr. Kramer. I think God led you to our little spot in the desert. I'm curious, though, what sign did He send."

Smitty laughs. "He's not kidding, Walt. Cocker really wants to know what sign or indication you had that sent you in our direction. We kid him all the time, but he's serious about his faith, something the rest of us aren't. He takes God seriously."

"Was it sent religiously, Kramer?" asks Cocker.

"I'm not sure what you mean."

"Is this all a stupid, hopeful hunch because you feel guilty for something, or are there real signs directing you here?" asks Cocker.

From behind the bar, Julie stirs. "What he means, Walt, is this search going to change you or just allow you to feel better about yourself because you tried to find an explanation for the unexplainable? We all believe here . . . in something. Heaven? A world without the hope of Heaven is like a saguaro cactus. Though it might live two hundred years, in the end it withers, dies, rots, and disintegrates into the sand."

༄

10:30. Tuesday night, January 27, 1987. Walt sits at a small table writing notes into a dog-eared pocket tablet of this evening's discussion, a habit for over twenty years. The table is in the guest room at Waddell Smithfield's home, "the house on the small rise at the end of the road in Rubicon," referred to as 423 West Mesquite Place in the Ajo-Why phone book. "You can't miss it," says the owner of the convenience store on Highway 85. "Go south to the last street in Why, just past Ball Road, and turn right. The Call bar will be on your right and then one block of houses. At the end of the block is Smithfield's. Biggest house in Why. Seems too big for one old man. Rumors are the old man harbors ghosts." The owner of the travel store warned Walt about the crazy guy who lives across the street from the bar. He was referring to Alf. Alf's not crazy, but he is angry, and he does monitor who comes in and out of Rubicon. Walt understands. Alf promised his fellow workers the union would win and save their jobs, but he wasn't strong enough to defeat the corporate giant Phelps Dodge. Walt thinks about the men who sat at the table in The Call and listened to his story. Tonight, they all seem to be about his age, mid-50s, but they're not.

Smitty went directly to bed when they returned to his house. He showed Walt to the guest bedroom, pointed to the bathroom, thanked him for his story, and left Walt alone. "You can leave the hall light on in case you need to get up in the middle of the night." Walt isn't tired; he seldom is at any time, a habit which has served him well over the years. He and Bellena are compatible in that sense since neither of them needs much sleep. He thinks about calling her to describe the evening with the Guardians, but he decides to process it first. For a bunch of skeptics, they want to believe his story. Each one grasped one or two aspects of the story as his own, maybe applying it to his own experience. When Alf produced his pistol, both CJ and Julie reacted as if they could do something about it. Jack and Smitty barely stirred, like they'd seen this one-act play before. Walt remembers Cocker saying softly, "Oh Lord."

Cocker. An alcoholic, unemployed musician and Born-Again Christian. And the only Black man in the town. Light brown, really, most likely one grandparent with some African American ancestry. His attempt to establish a church of the Holy Ghost in Why failed. Still, Cocker stays, believing when the Rapture comes, he will be included. Yeah, Cocker needs to be in Rubicon, thinks Walt. What was it he said near the end of the night? "If any of your story is to be real, Kramer, it has to be confirmed through one's senses." Where in the world would he come up with a phrase that sounds so much like Barkley Abbott's *esse est percepi*? After several hours drinking with the Guardians—and Julie—this is what Walt hangs on. A thread really.

Walt hears a gust of wind. What he's noticed in his three trips to Rubicon is the air is never still. There is always movement, wind, and this Southwest Arizona desert, the Sonoran, reflects this movement in its plants and animals and people. He pushes the window curtain aside, cracks the window slightly, stands motionless, and waits for his eyes to adjust. A nearly full moon allows for various shadows to take shape. This window opens to the west, away from Rubicon and

The Why Intersection

Why, into the uninhabited desert. In a few moments, the noises begin. Walt assumes he hears the wind in the mesquite bushes; the street is appropriately named, but he hears a quiet gurgle too. Water. A patio fountain with its dripping and gentle flow. Walt remembers Smitty's backyard pool. Small, but relaxing. A toad croaks, at least Walt thinks it's a toad, probably drawn to the artificial creek. Bellena lovingly refers to him as a toad sometimes. An owl hoots and Walt hears its wings flap when it flies off in pursuit of a desert mouse. A symphony. The desert isn't uninhabited, but densely populated. Bellena would love this. There are more sounds that Walt can't recognize, and there is movement too. The movement he sees out of the corners of his eyes, never directly. Walt sees movement in the mesquite, near the fountain, and behind the patio wall. Whatever it is—coyotes, lizards, rabbits, deer, or simply ghosts—he is being watched in return. Walt understands he is indeed an intruder in this part of the world, and the Guardians' suspicions are grounded.

Walt closes the window but leaves the curtain back. He would like to leave the window open too, but there is no screen, and he's not sure what creature might choose to visit him. He returns to the desk to add a few more observations. Jack and Alf share anger beyond the nation's headlines, but there is something odd about their bond. CJ sees it. Jade feels it. These people protect each other, and yet they seem to suspect one another too. They hide their past lives, but they keep one foot there. They are creatures of the present, not the future because the future seems to hold little promise for them. Do they stay merely to protect each other?

Walt wonders where Thalia is tonight.

∞

He doesn't worry much about critters tonight as he stands motionless in the desert behind Waddell Smithfield's house, especially crawly critters. It's January, it's too cold, but still, he wears knee-high, rubber, irrigation boots as a precaution. He knows in which room Walt will be staying, so he arrives before Smitty and Walt and situates himself 30 feet to the west among the creosote bushes for concealment. When Walt opens the window, he peers straight into the observer's eyes, but there is no recognition, no realization as to what Walt sees is human; it's just an unidentified creature of the night or a saguaro cactus. The Tohono O'odham believe saguaros are people in another form. Tonight, this might be the case. This creature studies Walt, the intruder into Rubicon in search of his own ghost. Both Walt and the desert man look for someone who may or may not exist, but who holds answers to their next phase of life.

Libby turns right off AZ 86 onto a small dirt road on the west side of a cemetery. She does this each time she returns from Why to her home in Sells; she stops to visit with her daughter Ramona Delores. Tonight, it is cold and windy, but Libby is used to this. She sits in a white plastic chair that many mothers share, says a prayer, and then talks with Ramona, who tells her mother how her day went too. The visit can last anywhere from ten minutes to an hour. Each time as she prepares to leave, Libby looks to Baboquivari and says, "My heart hangs on that cloud," crosses herself, and tells her daughter that she loves her. "Goodnight, my Princess."

15

FEELINGS

"I drank way too much last night to remember anything," laments Thalia. "I have a vague recollection of dinner and dancing with a handsome man in Ajo at the American Legion or some such fancy restaurant." She rolls onto her side and kisses the man lying next to her. "You dance funny."

"We ate at the Copper Plaza Café, but we did dance at the Legion, and, yes, you did drink too much." Hector lays an arm around Thalia's shoulder. "Whether you remember or not, we had a good time. You move around a lot when you sleep. And mumble."

"Now, I'm embarrassed." She pulls the covers over her head for a moment before reappearing. "You never drink much."

"No, I don't. Anything past two leads to ten or more. My clan doesn't handle alcohol well."

The morning light shines through the east window of Thalia's house, the house she rents from Smitty, the first house west of The Call. Hector watches Thalia, her sheer size, six feet tall and athletic, fascinates him. Hector did not come to Why for Thalia, but for another. This feeling confuses him. He starts to ask a question.

"Shhh," she breathes as she moves into him.

He senses her desire for intimacy this morning, as well as passion, a desire that seems to transform in an instant. He's noticed this before, that intimacy is more important to her than pure sex, and he wonders what in her past necessitates this. Maybe all women need this at the foundational level, but Hector hasn't noticed this before in his very few encounters with younger women on the rez. He smiles internally at his lack of experience with women. Their kisses continue; she will hold his cheeks close to hers, dictating the rhythm and duration of each kiss. Most of the time, her eyes remain open for these gentler kisses, holding his eyes like a tractor beam as she searches for answers. As they move to climax, Thalia narrows her eyes and eventually squeezes them shut, as if her eyes are directly connected to her vagina.

They lay together in the morning light without speaking, just waiting for their breathing to return to normal.

When they are satisfied, Hector rolls to the side. "Don't you teach the kids this morning?"

"I've still got time. I just won't shower. I'll let them wonder what this odor is."

"Julie will know if she stands close enough."

"I'll just tell her it's dancing sweat, if she asks. Or I'll wear lots of perfume." Thalia gets out of bed and walks down the hall to the bathroom. "What do you have today?" she yells.

Hector sits on the side of the bed naked and repeats her question silently. "What do I have today? Well, Thalia, I have to make myself scarce again, to avoid the prying eyes of the intruder into Why."

She returns from the bathroom and stands before him. "Will you walk me next door?"

"No. I'm going to shower before I go out." He reaches out and touches her belly with his finger. "Are you on birth control?" he asks.

Thalia laughs. "I wasn't until after the first time, and then I drove to Ajo and started. My guess is we aren't quite ready for a baby just yet."

"Well, if we did conceive, Julie could sell it on the black market to a Christian couple in Phoenix."

Thalia shakes her head. "Not funny, Hector. If I thought you really meant that, I'd be pissed."

☙

Lizardo parks at the intersection of AZ 85 and AZ 86, eats his homemade salami sandwich, and watches. Something a state patrolman said about traffic through Why piqued Lizardo's attention. He is on his way to Lukeville at the border to pick up an embezzler who skipped his sentencing hearing. A little fish, but something seems to be transpiring in Why. And there's always that arrogant ringleader. "Fucking Smithfield!"

☙

Sometime in the early morning, Smitty made fresh coffee, but it appears to Walt as if Smitty then returned to bed. Nice gesture and

The Why Intersection

it's good, strong coffee. Walt sits on Smitty's back patio dressed in a light jacket, the same patio he looked out upon the night before. The sounds are still active, mostly birds, but different birds. He watches two grey-brown doves feed along the ground and listens to their sad woo-woo-woot. Walt understands where they got their name. Mournful. For all the discussion about the creatures of the desert, the most numerous seem to be rabbits. Hardly a dangerous critter. He's learning about the desert, how most of it is non-threatening if one treats it with respect, but with enough prickly cacti and venomous creatures to be dangerous if one gets careless. Today, when Smitty rises, he said he wanted to drive Walt out among the Organ Pipe cacti and see if Walt can understand his "hunches."

"You haven't seemed to be able to understand what all this is about just sitting in this dingy old bar with us, Walt. Maybe your old friend's words meant you would discover some answers in the desert. When I left Boston, I just sort of meandered across the country looking for a place to settle. It took me a couple of decades to get here, but not long to get comfortable here. My wife and I knew pretty quickly this was the place. Strange though, this desert has nothing I once thought was a necessity, and we were thinking about returning to Boston, but little things drew us in. The night sky in a place without city lights for a guy who loves astronomy is a pure gift. For my wife, she would sit on the back patio and turn on a symphony and drink wine and be entranced. The Arizona desert is unlike any other; it's alive and green. Well, green some of the time, but you get what I mean. And then I met Cocker and Libby and discovered a type of person I'd never been around. Libby's tribal philosophy is so refreshing, so genuine, so unneeding of a church building to gain a connection to God. Cocker discovered this pretty quickly too, being around her. If you remember, he came here by a circuitous route like I had, and he thought it was to establish a church to draw others here, but it didn't. Cocker's a goofy guy with so much baggage you would need a company of soldiers to carry it all, but he's got a true heart." Smitty had laughed when he said this last night. "His heart is what keeps Libby from running back to the reservation full time, because God knows his daily habits aren't an attraction. Libby has dealt with untrue hearts all her life, I think most of the local Indians have, but she can look into a person's eyes better than most and size him up. Anyway, Walt, I'll drive you a few miles into the desert on a dirt road and let you sit there and discover your true purpose in life." And Smitty smiled.

"Hunches," Walt says softly to a small rabbit. "Do you get those when you're hopping along in the desert, maybe warnings of impending danger?" He thinks about the residents of this neighborhood and wonders why they separate themselves from Why, which is basically a town of a hundred or so people much like themselves. And the name, *Rubicon*. One of the stranger things to Walt, though, are the women who now live here. Julie and Libby, he understands, but Thalia and Jade, Crystal and Ruby? Their arrival he gets, but their staying, he questions. *There you go again,* he thinks to himself, *analyzing the motives of others to avoid analyzing yourself. The question is, Kramer, why are you here? What brings you back for a third time?*

The smell of bacon breaks Walt's musings. His coffee cup is empty, so he rises and returns to the house where he finds Smitty in an apron hovering over the stove. A remodeled kitchen, a modern home on the inside, at the west end of Rubicon, yet it is a house apart, a house too large for one old man. Apart by enough distance to set it apart physically, two empty lots, but not so distant as not to be considered part of the neighborhood. After all, Waddell "Smitty" Smithfield owns every structure on the block. Walt remembers that Smitty owns property in other places besides the last neighborhood in Why.

"I was wondering when you'd pull yourself out of bed," says Walt.

"Every time I try to match drink for drink with those young guys at The Call, I pay for it in the morning. If it wasn't for you being here, I'd be even in worse shape. You know, I seldom got drunk before I moved here, before Jack and Julie and I started closing the bar down in the late 70s. My wife would have kept me from drinking so much had she lived, but maybe I was drinking so much because I missed her. She seldom drank, even though she liked to sit at the bars with me back when. She liked people; she would have liked you, Walt. How do you like your eggs?"

Walt refills his own cup. "Over easy works for me."

"Little bit of a change of plans this morning. I got you a ride-along with a couple of Border Patrol agents. Young guys. Good guys. They'll take you down to the border."

"My plane leaves at nine tonight. When will these guys bring me back?"

"You'll only be with them for three hours or so, enough to drive you to the border and on a dirt road into the desert for a bit. Maybe a little longer, but we'll meet up here in the early afternoon and get something to eat before heading back to Tucson," answers Smitty.

"Can we make it a family affair?" laughs Walt. "I know the rest of Rubicon wants to see me one last time."

"All right. This is what I've got." Smitty unfolds a yellow sheet of paper from a legal pad and smooths it out on the table. He sets his coffee cup on one corner of the paper to hold it down. "Walt Kramer is, at the least, who he says he is. He served in the Army during the Korean War and was decorated for his actions like many other soldiers: Bronze Star, Purple Heart. Got his college degree in Colorado in physics and began working in the energy field in the sixties. Eventually, he was assigned the position of control over the nuclear power plant in Platteville, just south of the larger city of Greeley, Colorado."

Cocker visibly shivers. He narrows his eyes trying to recapture an image.

"You've got something else, Smitty. What is it?" It's a question asked by each person at the table.

Smitty sips his coffee and nods. "Gray areas. Incomplete information. Stuff for us to get paranoid over. He travels a lot, all over the U.S. and Europe. Not for vacations, but in connection with the nuclear industry. My guess is he's been a consultant or what we used to call a troubleshooter. Someone has a problem that defies a solution, and you call this guy. Kramer makes those problems go away, which might explain Dan's story. None of my sources could name a specific problem, but they all said Kramer has this reputation. An energy plant manager shouldn't be traveling this much, but in the last four years, he's made the jaunt between Denver and Washington, D.C., several times, and these don't seem to be simply to meet with the Nuclear

Regulatory Commission. Kramer's a player."

"Why would a muckety-muck like that be interested in us? Makes no sense."

Smitty leans into the table. "One of my sources told me Kramer has absolutely no ego. He's a worker with a sense of duty to get the right thing done, whatever the right thing is."

"So, he's a bulldog, huh?"

"I wonder if he's on a leash or been cut loose," says Jack. Can't the damn government just leave us alone out here!"

The bar is silent for a time as each man contemplates Smitty's new information. In the background the sounds of the school children can be heard or Thalia's voice giving instructions. Finally, one of the men breaks the silence.

"What if he's not here for himself, but to help one of us?" asks Cocker.

Again, the table goes silent. Smitty folds his paper and puts it back in his shirt pocket but says nothing. The idea that Walt is in Rubicon to help one of the residents seems to be a thought none of the men had contemplated before. To this moment, it has always been that he was here to spy or collect information for the FBI or some secret agency, to help send one of the men to jail for a past offense. CJ rises from his chair to get the coffee pot from behind the bar, returns, and refills his own, Smitty's, Jack's, and Cocker's cups.

"Ever calculate how many cups of coffee we've drunk over the years?" asks CJ. He returns the pot to its base without an answer. Back at the table, he stirs in a bit of sugar and sips his cup. "He does strike me as that kind of man, though."

"How's that?" asks Cocker.

CJ doesn't answer directly because he doesn't know how to put it in words. "I don't know. We all assume, as we always do, that any stranger is here for evil purposes or on the run. I suppose it gives us a bit of notoriety in ourselves, that we've lived lives worthy of suspicion as opposed to lives of littleness. Rubicon becomes our Hole in the Wall where we fend off the posse." He stops himself. The newest Guardian, the only Guardian still working a semi-regular job, the Guardian who doesn't fit the Rubicon profile; CJ's use of the word "littleness" makes him recoil, and he sits back into his chair.

"It's been my experience, CJ, that most men want to feel good about their lives at a certain point, and we tend to embellish our deeds." Smitty speaks slowly. "Me and Cocker and Jack have a few years on you. We tend to look back a bit more. Your time will come. My heyday came early in life. Jack's got cut short because of some mishandled explosives, and Cocker had a good run with his music and preaching. None of us will make an encyclopedia entry, but most people don't." Smitty shifts his focus. "That being said, I might agree with your point. Kramer is here to help one of us, except we don't need any help, as far as I know. So, this just leaves us with the original choice; either he's here for exactly the reason he says or to secretly find evidence on one of us to turn over to the authorities." Smitty's eyes cloud over momentarily.

Cocker laughs gently. "I couldn't have said it better myself, Smitty." He turns to CJ. "Did you ever notice what a different fellow I am in the mornings with no drugs or alcohol in my system than I am in the evenings when the devil has gotten a hold of me?" It's a rhetorical question. "What's your devil, CJ?"

"Yeah, those drugs are evil," says Jack, and everyone nods.

The ride to the border, a distance of 27 miles, allows Walt to get comfortable with the two agents, Louie and Corey. Walt shows them pictures of his new daughter, and they tease him about his age as a new father. "You know, don't you, that you'll be 75 or so when she graduates from college?" The agents point to dirt roads they've used to chase down smugglers or illegal immigrants. "Seems to be ramping up, more and more illegals from Central America these days. The Mexicans get help from relatives or friends of relatives and avoid us around here, but these people from El Salvador and Guatemala get used by the dirty coyotes. They've been told the U.S. will grant them asylum, but we don't. We collect them and send them back mostly."

Walt knows about the politics. "The fight against communism takes strange turns, doesn't it. I'll bet you've said more than one cuss word about those politicians in Washington."

"No, sir, never," says Corey. "We know they're all wise and honorable and have a good understanding about what goes on here." He shakes his head.

On the American side of the border lies Lukeville, a town smaller in population than Why: a gas station, bar and restaurant, general store, motel, and post office with the name "Gringo Pass." Louie explains. "About twenty years ago, a man named Al Gay bought Lukeville, thinking it was a gold mine waiting to happen, what with the traffic from Phoenix and Tucson heading for the beaches at Rocky Point and further south on the Sea of Cortez. Al's a character. We're never sure if he's working with us or against us."

"Depends on the day," adds Corey. "At the moment he likes Louie and me, but he can turn on a dime. He thinks we're all corrupt, all taking bribes from the drug smugglers to allow certain Mexicans in without being inspected."

Walt slides up so his head is between the two agents who sit in the front seat of the Border Patrol SUV. "You mean the Border Patrol?"

"Yeah," says Corey, "but he hates the park rangers too. It goes both ways. He's shrewd and charming when he wants something, but an asshole when he thinks we're interfering in his operations."

"What operations are those?" asks Walt.

"He thinks all the Mexicans crossing the border should be left alone, but sometimes we're in pursuit of some of them through his town or the park," answers Corey.

"And we have this lingering suspicion he didn't make his fortune simply selling hotdogs and soft drinks out of his convenience store. Rumors are he's involved in the drug smuggling that goes on, but it's just that, a rumor," says Louie. "You hope it's not true, because he's mostly a good guy, at times the asshole part resurfaces, and one of those people who gets wrapped up in the border activities. He still sees America from the eyes of the 1950s when people crossed over the border with ease."

Walt nods. "Those days are long gone; that America is long gone." He goes silent and slides back, recalling his days after the Korean War. The fifties. Did they ever exist?

Louie parks the SUV next to the border gate and the three men get

The Why Intersection

out. Corey and Louie talk with some other agents while Walt meanders near the crossing. He shivers, a sensation that draws his head towards the Mexican side of the border, but past Sonoyta. He stares for a moment and then turns to look north up AZ 85, the road they just traveled. He raises his head and looks to the sky, a bright blue this late January day. Walt has had premonitions only twice in his life: in Korea in a ditch where his squad was murdered by North Korean soldiers in 1950, and last year in the moments before his son raised a pistol to his head and pulled the trigger. In both instances, Walt felt something else was going on beyond the immediate event. He stands at an obscure border crossing in a desert extending from the United States into Mexico, a border fated to become increasingly contentious in the decades ahead, but his intuition tells him one person crossed here a short time ago who had nothing to do with the coming illegal immigration crisis.

"Mr. Kramer, we have to go," yells Louie with immediacy. Already, two other Border Patrol agents are sprinting up AZ 85, Lukeville's main street. "We've got some runners in the Organ Pipe," he says when Walt closes the door. "They jumped out of a pickup when it reached the border and eluded the agents checking IDs. Three of them. If they make it to the park, we probably won't catch them."

"Did you think this would just be a leisurely ride through the desert this morning?" grins Corey.

"It started out that way," answers Walt. He slides to the middle of the back seat for a better view through the front windshield.

"They're wearing backpacks, so it's a good chance they're carrying drugs. We call these guys mules. They try to escape into the park or the reservation, somewhere into the desert and drop their load for someone else to pick up at a designated spot. The mules then return to Mexico to do it all over again next week." Corey flips open a notebook of photographs of captured drug runners.

As the SUV overtakes the two Border Patrol agents who are on foot and turns up a side street leading to foot trails into the park, a Cadillac pulls out from a driveway and blocks Louie's path, forcing him to brake suddenly. "What the fuck!" he yells, but he knows. It's Al Gay.

Al gets out and raises his arms to shoulder height. "Geez, guys, I didn't see you. You could've ruined this beautiful specimen," he says pointing to his Cadillac.

Both Corey and Louie know it was purposeful. They exit the SUV to argue with Al, knowing the pursuit of the mules will have to be done on foot, if at all. Before any capture, the drugs will be deposited and retrieved by men who will then deliver them to bosses in Phoenix and sold to Americans eager to get high. Walt can hear the raised voices but senses it's a ritual played out by Al Gay and the Border Patrol, real anger by the authorities, but an act by Gay. These mules don't run for Gay, but he's a player in this illegal drug running. Gay interfered with today's pursuit, probably to gain favor with gangs on the other side of the border. Live and let live, and if you don't agree with that, "You can kiss my fat ass!". Walt sits back and allows the one-act play to continue; he returns to the image he held while he stood at the border minutes earlier. He sees a man driving into Sonoyta, stopping before he gets to the gates into the United States, getting out to survey his landscape, to look backward and forward, and to choose forward. The man gets back into his car and passes unnoticed into America, driving north toward Why.

∾

Louie and Corey drop Walt off in front of The Call just before two. For the three men, it has been an enjoyable morning. Walt shakes both men's hands. "I don't suspect I'll be seeing either of you again, but I appreciate your willingness to let me tag along."

"It was our pleasure," says Louie.

"You guys have a tough job, but I hope you can keep your professionalism about you as it gets tougher in the years ahead," says Walt.

Corey laughs. "No, sir, I expect we'll both become frustrated and hardened and yell at our wives in the evening."

Walt nods. As the Border Patrol pulls away, he sees Thalia staring at him from the door of The Call. She shoves herself away from the jamb and steps forward. "I hear you had some excitement last night with the Guardians, especially with Alf. Sorry I missed it, but I had a date."

Walt extends his hand to greet her. "Yeah, he's a bit nervous about me. He thinks I'm here to expose their pasts and turn them in to the authorities."

Thalia smiles. "It's quiet inside. I think they all expected you to be back a little later. Care to buy me a coffee and tell me what you're really here for." Inside, Thalia pours two cups of coffee, and she and Walt sit at the table closest to the bar, the table about to be crowded in another half-hour. "First, tell me how you thought I might be the one you were looking for. It's flattering, you know, to think I might be someone special."

Walt opens his wallet and removes a folded photograph. "This." He slides the black-and-white picture across the table. "The man is Barkley Abbott, and the girl is his granddaughter. Barkley was a friend to my son, a late-in-life friend for both of them, and as far as I can understand, the friend my son needed. I tried to talk with Barkley about him, because I hadn't gotten to know my son very well, and I hoped Barkley could tell me some things about him. Unfortunately, he couldn't. He slipped into dementia rapidly and was mostly incoherent. Mostly. Those last days for Barkley when I was with him." Walt slows and sips his coffee. "It's like he was drugged and remembering snippets of his life and expressing them through poetry and parables. Anyway, never having experienced anything like that, I was intrigued by the words. Confused, but intrigued. On the last day I spent with him, he seemed to be talking about my son and how I could find out more information, that I could contact someone in the desert who could answer some questions." He sips his coffee again. "Why did I think it might be you? It was more hope than rational investigation. Barkley said to find the girl in the picture, at least I think that's what he was telling me, and I met her briefly at his funeral, but she was from back east and didn't know anything about what I was talking about. She didn't even remember the photograph. I was pretty sure she and her grandfather weren't close, and she was attending the funeral simply out of family responsibility. I thought that was the end of it, but, and here's where my father-in-law started thinking I was crazy, I saw a gravestone near my son's marking that connected me to Barkley's ramblings, to some place called Rubicon. That's where Dan came in. He had met some hiker in southern Colorado who said she was working in Rubicon. Did you meet Dan when he was here?"

"No, I didn't. Just learned about his visit from Julie." Thalia pauses. "So here you are, huh?"

"Yeah. Crazy, huh? I told my wife if I couldn't come up with something more than a feeling this time, I'd put it to rest. I think that's where I am. I want to find something, but it's just a regretful father's pipedream."

Thalia holds the photo up at eye level. "So, the woman you spoke with at the funeral couldn't remember this picture with her grandfather?" She lets her question hang in the air without a response from Walt. "These fifties pictures can be pretty grainy." Thalia moves the photo closer to her eyes. "What is it you regret?"

Walt's mouth contorts slightly. "I was in the Army when my son was born, and when I returned, I only spent a year or so with him before I left. He was raised by his mother into a fine boy and a fine man."

And he..."

"He died last summer."

Except for a soft "Hmm," Thalia doesn't visibly respond, but Walt sees a sudden tightening in the grasp of her coffee mug and a tic in her arm. She and Walt sit quietly for a few minutes sipping their coffee. In time Thalia asks, "How did your son die, if you will excuse me for being so personal? You don't have to answer if you don't want to."

Walt tilts his head to one side as he searches for a soft word. Thalia sees a man in distress for reasons beyond his story. "He fell," says Walt. Before Thalia can respond, before Walt can say "suicide," Jack emerges from the back room being pushed by Julie. Thalia's eyes remain fixed with Walt's for a moment, sharing her concern, before acknowledging Jack and Julie.

"Find out anything, Kramer?" asks Jack.

"It was an interesting ride. Got to chase some evil, drug running, foreigners through the desert."

"Did you catch 'em?"

"Nah, the guy who owns the town interfered. A scene right out of Hollywood."

Julie laughs. "That would be Al Gay, another weirdo who makes the desert his home."

The Why Intersection

"A rich weirdo," adds Jack. "Smitty's twin brother or alter ego."

Julie warms Walt's coffee, but Thalia puts her hand over the top of her cup. "Gay tried to get Smitty to let him use the golf course as a landing strip for his small plane," says Julie. "We all assume he smuggles drugs, but we don't know for sure. Makes a great story since every story out of southern Arizona has to have evil drugs as a part of the theme. Ask Smitty about it." She turns back to the bar and places the coffee pot on its hot plate. "Libby is catering this afternoon. Hope you're not tired of Mexican food, Walt."

"No. What time? I've got a plane to catch to get out of you people's lives."

When Hector and Thalia are together in the evening, Hector seldom drinks. His family and people have a terrible history with alcohol. During the day, especially when he works and is sweaty, he might have an afternoon beer. Tonight, after spending time at The Call with Thalia and the Guardians after Smitty drove Walt Kramer to Tucson, Hector borrows Diego's car and drives Thalia out to the desert on a dirt road west of Rubicon, west of Smitty's two-hole golf course. Sitting mostly in silence and darkness, Thalia traces the contours of Hector's face with her fingers. "Seeing in the dark," she calls it. Earlier, everyone's thoughts centered on Walt Kramer. "What is he looking for? Who is he trying to uncover?" Thalia thinks she knows now; Hector feels he always knew.

Hector takes Thalia's hand from his face and holds it with both of his. He turns it in his hands, an intimate act of exploration, of discovery. Without words he tells her to reveal her thoughts. Hector can see in the dark and watches her eyes search for him only inches away. She begins generically.

"One's life paths are interesting. Everyone's, I suppose, but some more interesting than others." She goes quiet momentarily. "We live in chapters, and this seems to be one of mine and one of yours. I'm pretty sure it's not a whole book." He keeps his eyes focused on hers while hers search. "A moment. Our moment. At some point we will need to transform back to our prior selves, which will be our future self."

She takes her left hand and covers his hands. Lightly. "Some morning, after a night where we fit together, after I have kissed you one last time before leaving to work, you can mount the wind's tail out of this eddy we call Rubicon. That time is not yet, but it's approaching." Intuitively, she leans her forehead into his.

"I've ridden that wind before," says Hector. He would like to be sitting on a carpeted floor where they could intertwine more easily, instead of in a cramped compact sedan.

"You often seem like another person in the dark. Are you ever just you, Hector?"

"Maybe when I fish." It is a real response. "I was born in the desert. It's never just one thing, and the people who live here aren't either." He feels Thalia's pulse through his hands. He pulls them to his lips and kisses one hand. "Before I came here, I rode with a Catholic priest and an empty can that once held a damaged man. It could have been anyone." They go quiet. A minute passes. Two. Three. "It could have been me."

Still with their foreheads together, Thalia asks, "Do you know Diego's real name?"

"Today it's Diego. Today is all that matters."

Thalia laughs so gently. "I should have known you would answer that way, so let me rephrase. Do you know what Diego used to be called?"

"It's never mattered to me who he was, only who he is now, but it certainly matters to him. He's locked in a small space, and he can't get out. His time has been violated."

"God, you've got an old side to you!" Thalia pulls her head back, lifts one hand to Hector's lips, and pushes in. She shakes her head in the dark and then reconnects her forehead to his. "I think . . . you are here for him. I think . . . I am to, but not in the same sense you are."

"Of all the hidden souls passing through Why, Diego is the most hidden. Rubicon sees him in the shadows. He never joins at The Call. He is more wary than a desert rabbit that knows predators are lurking. He knows that he has no completely safe space, and Mr. Kramer has sharpened his senses to an even higher level."

Thalia takes a big breath. "Kramer told me a story. He's looking for a woman who may give him information about his son, a son he didn't raise and who died. Diego may also have insights for Mr. Kramer. He showed me a photo and I think it was of me with my grandfather nearly 30 years ago. It's all so weird."

"Mr. Kramer is a good man, but he needs to go home and raise his daughter, live that new life. He looked at you and didn't see the woman who has his answers, and that's the way it should end here. Diego's life needs to be his own, and we need to ensure that."

Thalia nods slightly against Hector's forehead. "Hector, do you believe in fate? Do you believe in things you can't see or verify through your earthly senses?" She moves her arms around his shoulders, sliding her head onto his shoulder. She is curious about his thoughts, but strangely calm with her emotions. She has never asked this question of anyone in her life, but from the time she was little, she has believed."

16

BURNING OF THE SOCKS

Wearing a Hawaiian shirt with a plastic lei, Waddell Smithfield enters Rubicon Elementary prepared to explain the meaning of the Burning of the Socks festival to four students, four older men, three women, and two Border Guards. He has celebrated this day, the first day of spring, since the fifth year of his arrival in Rubicon. "On this day, the sun crosses the celestial equator heading northward, and this marks the end of winter." He marks an up-arrow on his simple diagram on the blackboard. "Here in the Sonoran Desert, winter ended earlier as temperatures rose into the 70s and 80s weeks ago. But back east, the boating community marks the end of winter by taking off their winter socks and burning them in a community bonfire. Back there, they still may experience snow and freezing temperatures, but here in our desert paradise, this day marks the explosion of blossoms on the cactus plants. Yellows, reds, oranges, purples, whites, blues, every color imaginable. It is the best time in the desert, as it comes to life and shares itself for those of us who live here. On this day, I make my New Year's resolutions, because today is truly the first day of the New Year, full of promise. March 21, 1987. Our festival will commence at five o'clock at the end of the block in front of my house with the bonfire to burn whatever article of winter clothing you wish. Cocker will lead us in a singing of *Auld Lang Syne*, and then the barbeque will start. Several non-Rubiconers will be joining us."

"Who's the band this year, Smitty?" asks Alf.

"A young group out of Tucson. I heard them at a county fair and offered them the gig."

"What kind of music?"

"Mariachi. For the children. Make it happy and lively. It was the only instruction I gave them. Paying them 50 dollars plus expenses and all the food they can eat." Smitty smiles at the students. "Miss Libby will cater the meal, so you are assured of lots." He looks up to Thalia signaling he's done, and she can have her class back.

The Why Intersection

"What resolution did you make, Smitty? To quit aging?" asks Cocker.

"No, to expand my golf course to four holes."

"It's Friday, class, so let's dismiss early." Thalia smiles. "We've survived the short winter days. Spring has arrived."

Flames from the bonfire can be seen a mile away at the RV campground, the neighborhood of comfortable retired folks, happy with their America but apprehensive too. Cocker feeds the fire with dried mesquite wood from the desert trees, while the children dance around it, and nobody tells them to be careful. Off to the side, CJ talks with Louie and Corey, who are not in their border patrol uniforms. All are drinking beers and laughing.

"We get word of things. People tell us things because of our jobs," says Louie. Corey knows where his partner is heading. "Evidently, Lizardo has been doing some snooping about someone in Why, but I have to warn you, CJ, Lizardo's dirty. He's not bound by the same rules as the sheriff's department or the Border Patrol." The three men stand quiet and drink their beers. Louie speaks again. "He's onto something. Just thought you might want to know."

CJ nods but says nothing.

"Well, CJ, Louie and I need to give our regards to Mr. Smithfield before we leave. Early start tomorrow morning. We've got duty in the Altar Valley. Must have pissed our boss off to be assigned there." He shakes CJ's hand as does Louie and they walk off, making small talk to a few others on their way over to Waddell Smithfield.

CJ allows little to show on his face. *The Stoic*, as Cocker calls him. As CJ watches the two Border Patrol officers walk past the flames, he sees another man, a man standing in the shadows away from the flame. Corey and Louie were warning CJ about a coming event, one without reality yet. CJ doesn't need the information about Lizardo; he already knows, the table knows. He is startled by the arms that surround him from behind, but he quickly recognizes the touch.

"I wondered when you would get here. Newspaper work or the kiddos?"

Jade stays behind him, laying her head on his shoulder while maintaining her hug. "A story about Phelps Dodge and the continuing shadow it casts over Ajo. Remember the fight we had over your working there still? Well, I'm sorry."

CJ turns into her body and smiles. "Forgotten long ago. I was just happy you didn't slug me. You have a reputation." He grins and kisses her.

"I almost did. All of us have this anger over PD. It never goes away. My story is about PD; they've begun marketing company houses to Snowbirds. They sold Crystal's this week. She'll be devastated." Jade's body tenses, a feeling CJ knows is anger. "Her family lived in that house for three generations, and now, an old couple from Minnesota will live there for five or six months each winter." Jade pauses. "Don't tell her; let me. I'll do it tomorrow morning in her kitchen over coffee. I'm glad she isn't living in Ajo anymore; glad none of us are."

CJ knows Jade considered moving back, but her work with the newspaper and time in Ajo has opened her eyes to the hostility remaining among the people who still draw lines between union and scab. "Why did you apologize tonight?" asks CJ.

"Because I discovered what you do today. What you did. The EPA."

CJ relaxes. "Can we keep it as our secret? The others don't need to know."

Jade's eyes say "yes," and she kisses him. "But it's a cool thing and I'm proud of you. How do you get PD to pay you?"

"It allows them to say they have Ajo's interests at heart, that they've begun cleanup at the mine, but really, they're being forced to do this by the EPA. It was a compromise of sorts. A stranger, someone from Washington, wasn't going to be sent in to dictate the conditions."

"From what I've been able to gather, you piss them off frequently."

"Yeah," says CJ, "but I can keep it behind closed doors and threaten them with that *Guy From The Government*. The known bad guy is always less threatening than the secret bad guy. What's that line from *Moby Dick* about better to sleep with a sober cannibal?"

Jade laughs out loud. "That's not always true. I have this reputation in Ajo, and there are plenty of people there who would gladly exchange me for someone else."

The Why Intersection

∾

Hector studies Lizardo as the bounty hunter works the small crowd at the bonfire. Lizardo wasn't invited but somehow found out, much like bounty hunters are supposed to do. Hector knows it was Lizardo who went through his house back in January, but he didn't find anything because there was nothing to find. Lizardo is sniffing for information, just as he did earlier in the evening with him. He didn't discover anything, but he ended up asking him open-ended questions, hoping something would slip out. No, thinks Hector, Lizardo wants information from him, but not so much about him anymore. Nothing on the radar about a handyman Navajo drifter with no APBs out on him. Lizardo moves confidently in the dim evening light, as if he has sensors in his skin.

Alf, Cocker, and Smitty sit on plastic lawn chairs smoking cigars, enjoying the festivities. Smitty fueled the fire with new socks, probably purchased at the thrift store in Ajo. Alf contributed a head cover he wore under his helmet in the mine. Cocker tossed in three old sweaters, ragged sweaters from an earlier decade. Hector watches the flames cast shadows across the three men's faces, noticing how age creates different images. Since Julie left, these three Guardians, especially Cocker, have taken care of Jack. Cocker has the time. Jack isn't at the bonfire; he chose to stay at The Call and watch a basketball game on the tube. An excuse. He won't talk about why Julie left, and the others wonder if he knows why. They don't, but it is the hot topic when Jack isn't part of the conversation. Taboo when he is. Thalia sensed something in Julie's demeanor in the days prior to her flight; she even talked about it with Hector. Hector understands flight and about the apprehension preceding the lam. Because of Thalia's earlier conversations with Julie, she was aware of Julie's unhappiness, but Thalia, like the others in Rubicon, was stunned when she vanished. Not Hector, though, he saw it coming.

Corey and Louie, *La Migra*, pay their respects before thanking Mr. Smithfield for the invite.

"Those two fellas are good guys," says Alf.

"Most of them are. Like any large group, you get some bad apples, but there aren't many in the Border Patrol," adds Smitty. "It's become a dangerous job and getting more so."

Cocker nods. "The drug money tempts all of them. It's a wonder any of them resist, but as you said, most remain professional."

"Getting back to your question on Reagan, Smitty, if there's anything I like about our president." Alf says *our president* with a hint of sarcasm. "I'll pass on any caveats and just say this. He loves America; no doubt about it, and he's a big improvement over Carter."

Smitty shakes his head, possibly in disagreement, but he lets Alf's comment pass. "He's sure taking a firestorm of criticism over his arms-for-hostages admission. It seems like he's losing it; not as sharp as he once was."

"He was once sharp?" says Alf. "Never noticed."

Lizardo takes a seat with the Guardians without being asked to sit, a tactic he uses to raise suspicions among them. His presence alone is enough to do that.

"I don't recall anyone offering you a chair, Lizardo," says Smitty.

Lizardo swivels his head to take in the entire celebration scene before responding and then lights a cigarette. "I know your kind, Smithfield. You look down on people like me, just like you did at the restaurant in Ajo a few years back, back when I first came to town. Yeah, I know you."

Smitty has a slightly puzzled look on his face. "What the hell are you talking about, asshole?"

"Don't play ignorant; you remember. I was talking with your wife, and you took offense and had me thrown out."

Smitty tries to remember and shakes his head. "I vaguely remember when some loud, drunk-ass jerk was hitting on the wife of one of my friends at the country club just after the strike, and management removed him. Don't recall it was you though, but it wouldn't surprise me."

Alf makes a sarcastic grunt. "Nooo. Lizardo getting thrown out of a nice restaurant? What a surprise."

Lizardo ignores Alf. "This is a strange festival you celebrate," says Lizardo. "I looked it up. Guess you experienced it when you lived in Massachusetts, huh?" Lizardo inhales his smoke and goes quiet only for a moment. "You guys still staying mum about the shooting of the

The Why Intersection

little girl in Ajo?' The Guardians know the bounty hunter wants to claim the reward money offered by PD for information about the shooter. Lizardo has asked the question a few times in the past.

"You're putting a pail on the celebration, Lizardo. You know that, don't you?" says Alf. He doesn't look at the uninvited guest, but instead, looks at the ashes of his cigar before flicking them to the ground.

Smitty also looks past Lizardo. "I think you mean pall, Alf, but you're right, Lizardo is a downer." Now, Smitty does look at the uninvited guest. "You see, Lizardo, you don't have any scruples; you don't care who you hurt as long as you get paid. You have a good time doing something, get you rocks off, and move on."

"Oh, Smithfield, you don't need to flatter me; it's my civic duty." Lizardo blows a smoke ring and grins. There is quiet for several moments before he speaks again. "Your repair guy, he's a question for me. Can't seem to find any information on him. It's like he has no past. No work record, no military service, no hometown, no family, no nothing. Just a common drifter Injun. I even borrowed a glass from Libby's that your man had drank out of, but there was no record of his prints. That's pretty strange, if you ask me."

Cocker slides up in his chair to defend his lone parishioner. "What's strange about it? Hector is a good man. A fellow never does anything wrong, there doesn't have to be a record of his life. God knows about him, I'm sure. You don't need to." Cocker looks to the heavens and crosses himself.

"What if I told you all it was him who spooked Julie, made her run away?"

Alf turns to challenge Lizardo. "I'd say you're a damn liar. What if I told you I was about to kick your ass?"

"I ain't worried about it. I know you'll find some excuse not to, like you don't want to disturb your leash-holder's celebration or alarm the children." Lizardo grins again and leans to the ground to snuff out his cigarette.

Before he can rise up, Alf leaps out of his plastic chair and tackles Lizardo, pushing him to the ground. Alf hits the bounty hunter twice in the head before Lizardo can break free. Alf charges again and grabs Lizardo around the waist. Lizardo clasps his hands together and brings them down hard on the back of Alf's neck, but it doesn't seem to deter Alf's momentum. Alf drives Lizardo back to the ground and thrusts his forearm into Lizardo's throat. All the people at the bonfire gather around the fight, Smitty and Cocker stand and cheer on Alf, and CJ and Jade run to see what's going on. But it's another man who breaks up the fight, who pulls Alf off the bounty hunter and physically turns him away, who forces Lizardo to his truck and warns him to drive away tonight.

∾

Jade, who said before Christmas she would never be a waitress again, brings bottles of beer to the Guardians, Hector, and Thalia as they crowd around one table in The Call. She then pours tequila into everyone's shot glass and raises hers for a toast. "Damn, a little excitement in our neighborhood. I'd like to propose a toast to Alf for kicking that son-of-a-bitch's ass."

When the glasses have been emptied, Alf turns to Hector. "You sure have a way of making your presence felt. All these months with barely a word and just when I'm about to strangle the jerk, you step in and haul his ass away." Alf eyes Hector and pauses. Then, "Why'd you do it?"

Before Hector can speak, Cocker says, "Cause if he hadn't of, you'd have killed him, Alf, and then where would you be? That temper of yours..." Cocker's voice trails off and he shakes his head.

"I wasn't going to kill him," says Alf.

"Yeah," says Smitty quietly, "you could have. Cocker's right. You have a temper that doesn't know any boundaries; it has a life of its own. The scar on your neck is just one piece of evidence, but we know, and we just stood around and cheered you on. If Lizardo is killed, it would just bring dozens of law officers to Rubicon, not because they particularly like him, they don't, but when people associated with the law are murdered, the law itself frowns on it. The sheriff of Pima County and his deputies would ask questions you would rather not answer, and your ability to live in Rubicon without scrutiny would be destroyed. Probably ours too."

The Why Intersection

Hector's clears his throat. His voice is so quiet that each person in the bar has to sit still and lean forward to hear. "From what little Thalia has told me, each of you has a past you don't want overturned by unwanted investigations. Any new face here is a big enough distraction as it is. I know Lizardo researched my past, and I know he didn't find anything, because there isn't anything to find." Hector takes a deep breath and whispers something in Thalia's ear. She smiles and kisses him on the cheek. He wonders where his remarks are coming from, but he continues.

Hector purses his lips and sniffles. "I didn't force Julie away, but I did offer her a bit of advice. She's safe." Hector turns his head, his eyes, to Jack. "I need to tell the table about your talk with Lizardo. Hear me out, okay?" Without taking his eyes off Jack, Hector continues. "He has no intention of hunting Kramer, too big of a fish. He's afraid of Kramer, but he did make some calls about Julie's past in California. I think you know all about her youth, but those records have been expunged. She was a minor and was never arrested after that. She left partly out of fear of Lizardo, which could have been a real concern if there had been more substance behind it. She left more so because she was lost here just now. It's spiritual mostly, but she doesn't have you, and you've been her life. She blames herself. She also decided her work with the baby groceries needed to end. She didn't explain how she arrived at this decision, just that it had to end." Hector goes quiet, watching for a reaction from Jack.

Alf stands abruptly, his chair falling backward onto the floor. "You son-of-a-bitch, Jack!" He stares at the old man in a wheelchair, his jaw clenched, and his eyes narrowed. CJ stands quickly to place himself between the two men. "Go outside, Alf, and walk around."

"Who's the real son-of-a-bitch, Alf?" challenges Jack. "Get the fuck out of my bar."

Alf wants to hit Jack but remains motionless. Finally, he shakes his head to Jack and walks behind Hector and out the front door into the street. Hector looks to Thalia and nods. She follows Alf into the street, and CJ sits down.

After a few moments of contemplation in the bar, Cocker speaks. "He'll get over it. He has too much invested." Cocker turns to Hector.

"You got a way about you, you know." He allows his statement to float above the table for a moment, and a couple of others nod their heads. "I thought I was the only one who was this way, but you come to give me company and a little comfort. I thought it was Thalia, but it isn't, it's you."

Hector's expression shows he doesn't know what Cocker is talking about. He turns to Smitty. "Your neighborhood is both a refuge and a jail for all of you. I've never been around so much anxiety, and I don't understand it most of the time. It seems self-imposed." His statement is a question. "What do you people have to fear?" The room is silent like the moments after a demanding math teacher has challenged a class on an unfamiliar proof. The quiet breaks when Thalia and Alf reenter the bar. She takes her chair next to Hector, while Alf pauses behind Jack. Alf reaches down and rests his hand on Jack's shoulder for a minute before returning to his chair.

"The Burning of the Socks is supposed to be a celebration, you know," says Smitty. "How about if I buy another round?"

Jade starts to get out of her chair but is held down by CJ. "I got this, babe."

∞

Two men hundreds of miles away from Why study an old mine map and a report from a company that no longer exists. Their comments reflect a new understanding based on new evidence, but each man refuses to draw an unfounded conclusion.

"So, it's possible?"

"Not really. The mine is a hundred years old and up to 700 feet deep."

"How far did you explore?"

"I crawled in for a ways, but it's not safe. As you see here," he points to an adit on the map, "there was once one more entrance, but unless we want to risk our own safety, I would recommend against it. Finding his revolver with prints and blood should be enough, but . . ." His comment rests on the map for a moment while the other man considers the implication.

"But it's that one loose end, and they want certainty."

"You're good at keeping secrets, Walt. I've known that since college. Sorry I couldn't help more."

"Could you have missed anything?"

Dan shakes his head. "Sorry."

Walt grunts and pushes a pencil to the middle of the map. "Yeah, I know what I saw."

∽

Lizardo's eyes blink rapidly as he stares at his bruises in the mirror. *Gonna fix those bastards*, he promises.

17

ARREST, MAY 1987

The *Newsweek* cover shows a distraught Mexican teenager with her arms outstretched reaching for her baby. The background displays mounds of garbage in the Guadalajara slums. "The Illegal Baby Trade." It is the feature article for the weekly news magazine and covers four pages, citing several sources, including the *Arizona Republic* out of Phoenix. Lizardo stops by The Call and leaves a copy for the Guardians.

"Only the names have been changed to protect the innocent. In case you forgot, that was *Dragnet* and Sergeant Friday. Seems like a lot of little people get involved in this scheme to make a few extra dollars. Despicable, don't you think?" Lizardo's last words are said with no empathy, but as a veiled threat."

"Haven't got a clue what you're talking about, scumbag," says Jack.

"The article says AZ 85 is a prime route for moving these babies north, along with the drugs and Mexicans. If I remember correctly, 85 is the highway just a block to the west of where we're sitting. The article doesn't mention Rubicon, but it does mention Why. Probably a good thing you guys never go there, or someone might get suspicious." Lizardo laughs. He's poking the bear again. "How long's Julie been gone now? Couple of months?" He laughs again. "Do you ever miss her, Jack?"

As he turns to leave, a beer glass whistles past his head and shatters against the wall near the door, causing Lizardo to flinch. "Damn, I missed," says Rose. She leans into the bar with both hands below the bar. "Get the hell out of here." When the door closes behind Lizardo, Rose grabs a broom and dustpan from behind the bar and begins to sweep up the glass.

"I can see why Phelps Dodge feared you, Rose. I can also see why the Dodgers never signed you. You missed his head by three feet." Jack smiles. Rose works for Jack since Julie left. "Thanks for your support. I won't dock your pay for breaking the glass. We'll call it an accident." He pauses. "Did you make sure the shotgun was loaded?"

The Why Intersection

Glass shards are strewn across most of the bar's floor. "I should have thrown a mug; it might not have broken." As she sweeps, CJ and Alf walk in, and their expressions ask the question.

"Rose here is still learning how to treat the customers. Lizardo dropped off a magazine, and he always has a comment to make. Rose took a bit of offense and sent a beer glass past his head," says Jack. "I think if you'd have been here Alf, we would have had to call Hector to pull you off him again."

Alf picks up a *Newsweek* and peruses the cover article. In time, "This article is pretty specific. A lot of this comes from an anonymous Arizona source." The implication is clear.

Jack nods. "Julie? Only she would have some of this information."

"Hector still won't say?" asks CJ. He knows the answer and respects Hector's ability to keep a secret. An important trait for a man in Rubicon. It was CJ who sat with Jack and Alf a few months back and got them to settle their differences, to share beers together again without the animosity. It was about the larger picture. "I see where Cocker's fixing up the warehouse again."

"Cocker mentioned something about holding services again, but his time has passed, I think," says Alf, "but then, he's always fixing up the Tabernacle."

From behind the bar, Rose adds, "Libby thinks he's preparing for the Coming, thinks it will be soon."

"Those who believe that are always preparing," says CJ. "They see the Rapture in every Middle East event, see the imminent demise of Israel, and believe Jesus is on the way. He's not the only one who believes around here."

༄

Thalia doesn't openly pry. She's a keen observer, but not a snoop. She leaves the second bedroom door closed whenever she visits Hector, allowing his roommate to remain private. No name, not Diego, just "roommate." Tonight, Hector is reading her romance novel, *Other Lives*, the first draft, while she works on a short story. For two years, Thalia has observed the people of Why, taken notes, and written articles. Her first one, *The Baby Trade,* recounted the adoption of a single baby from Mexico purchased from a poor mother and adopted by Thalia's sister. It was the story that Thalia was hired to investigate as an independent journalist. *Newsweek* picked it up, expanded it, and published it. An expose, under an alias, one of a handful of contributors covering the trade nationwide. Thalia's second story brought to light Phelps Dodge's decision to sell off company homes in Ajo, to drive out the remaining miners and especially the women who stayed to continue picketing. The national news had wearied of unions and strikes by early '87, but Thalia's story ran in the Tucson newspaper where copper mining remains a part of the economic picture. Now, Thalia's curiosity is on the religious beliefs of the recluses who populate southern Arizona, men and women like Cocker, who wait impatiently for the Second Coming, believing the signs point to His imminent arrival. These stories are Thalia's secret, and only Smitty knows who writes them.

She puts her pen behind her ear, slouches in her chair, and watches Hector. Despite the age difference, he has become her lover, and yet they both have secrets they have kept from each other. Thalia's latest research, though, pushes her to want to disclose these expository essays to Hector, to lift the curtain on her other life.

"Hector." Occasionally, during intimate moments she will wonder if he can channel others, but he is Hector for the most part, and certainly in public. That's a secret they do share. Hector looks up. She rises and goes to the couch where he cradles her manuscript. "I want to talk with your roommate."

Hector folds a corner of a page in the three-ring notebook and closes it. He nods his head. He places the notebook on the end table and turns back to Thalia where he finds her eyes alive with anticipation. "You've been patient." He curls his lips inward as he always does and bounces his head, almost in embarrassment. "I hope you won't be disappointed."

"I haven't seen him sitting on the roof for a while, not at all since you and I have been together. I wondered if he had left, and you haven't spoken about him," says Thalia.

They sit in silence for a moment until Hector takes Thalia's hand. "Mr. Smithfield has him working on a house in Ajo. He leaves early.

The Why Intersection

He's been sleeping up there when he works late. He has a sleeping bag. He doesn't always stay here." Hector pauses. "Come with me." He leads her to the closed door, still holding her hand, where he pauses, resting his free hand on the doorknob, not looking at her. "This is going to be really strange." Without turning around, he opens the door and leads her in. The room is sparse, a single bed, a wooden chair, a nightstand with a small lamp, and an old photograph of Pancho Villa hanging on the wall.

She waits. Then, "I don't understand."

Hector leads her to the bed and sits down with her. He puts his hand over his chest. "He's here. Try to remember the first time I came into the store when we first met."

Thalia stares at Hector, but his eyes are distant. She remembers. Translucent. She understands to a point. A minute passes. She continues to hold his hand, a hand which has gone soft, unlike the hand of the hired worker who was reading her novel just a short time ago, more like the skin of a long-term hospital patient. She wants to squeeze his hand, to reassure him, but she fears she may damage it, so she slides her other hand over to cover Hector's hand. And she waits.

Finally, he speaks in the gentlest of voice. "I don't know what to do about Diego. I'm overmatched. He was here before me, I think, waiting. There are moments when he's so depressed, that's when I sit on the roof with him. The starlight he sees comes from the past, and it seems to allay his grief. But it comes again. He experienced something terrible." Thalia stays quiet. "I've spoken with Cocker in the abstract, while I paint his church. He's trying to repair the windows and add a second door. I think he's trying to help me understand all this, but..."

Thalia leans over and kisses Hector's shoulder and makes a soft murmur.

"He comes and goes. Never far. He is who you see on the roof, gazing into the heavens. He left around Christmas, not sure where to, but away from visitors."

An image forms in Thalia's mind. "Kramer's missing person?"

"That's not for me to know, but it's out there too." His sentence hangs in Thalia's head. Hector continues. "He transforms me. I was walking down a road, a dirt road in northern Arizona up on the reservation, when a gust of wind blew me over. A microburst. I laid there for a time, I don't know how long, but when I started walking again, I was changed. I know the exact moment. Ironically, I was given a ride by a priest to town. We didn't talk much. He was driving back to Mexico. Short drive into town. When he dropped me off, he spoke with a couple of the elders briefly and then left."

"The wind again," mumbles Thalia. She remembers a walk they shared earlier in the year when his gait seemed unsteady. "When?"

"Early last summer." Hector pauses while he attempts to understand this journey himself. "I've told you things I didn't do, about events I shouldn't know, but I think maybe they were Diego's words. They just fall out of my mouth." Now Hector's eyes lock in on Thalia's. "Like when I saw you with the baby. I left The Call and wondered where that came from. Hard to believe, I know."

Thalia's eyes reassure Hector. "No, not at all. Not anymore. We're here for a reason, I guess. You. Me. Cocker. The Guardians. We seem to have eddied here in Rubicon. I came here to get information for a story on a single event, about a safe house for my sister's adoption of a Mexican baby." Hector's eyes blink with a question, but he waits. "Yeah, I have a connection to the family in this drama, but my gut tells me it's something larger, something directed by fate. I've been directed to this place all my life." She shakes her head. "Rubicon. How quaint." She sees the question in his eyes and responds. "You once asked how I make my living in this place. Besides the massive amounts of money Jack pays me for my meager work at the bar, I write stories for journals and newspapers. I'm a free-lance journalist, something I've done for years. I'm good at investigating without being suspected of it. Rubicon has given me a couple of stories so far, and I'm working on another. Still, I arrived here with a larger purpose, one still unfolding."

"The hidden past no one in Rubicon wants to talk about," says Hector. "I'm an orphan who was living in Gallup, New Mexico, one of those unclaimed Indian kids raised in an orphanage just outside the reservation. Somehow, I managed to graduate from junior college, but like lots of Indians, I didn't have much drive. I liked to drink. Instead of getting out of there, making a success of potential, I stayed. A few of the tribe's elders believed in me. I became an odd jobs man.

The Why Intersection

Construction. Road work. Pipe layer. Nothing fancy. I lived by myself most of the time somewhere near where the job was." Hector speaks not out of self-pity, but in earnest to provide Thalia with background. He shifts his weight on the bed and stretches his neck. "Those things don't matter, except I try to see why I was selected to carry another's burden, if that's what it is. Does any of this sound reasonable?"

"Is he with you all the time?"

"He's real. He has his own body. I don't always feel him. I don't know for sure. It's not like he's in me or me in him, more like I can channel his... his pain. I wish I knew what he wanted, what he needs from me. He's changed me... for the better."

Thalia smiles gently. "Did you always believe in this kind of stuff?"

Her smile eases Hector and he laughs. "My tribe's elders always told me I had powers. I'm Indian; it's a part of my makeup. Did you?"

"No, but I've been talking with Cocker about his beliefs while I work on another story. He thinks I'm just searching for answers for myself, mid-life concerns over God and faith. He would have no problems with all of this."

"Cocker." Hector smiles. "Talk about a damaged soul." He shakes his head to negate what he just said. "Maybe a damaged person, but not a damaged soul. He's one of the few around here who accepts his own soul without guilt or doubt." Hector looks away from Thalia, aware her eyes are searching him. He comes back. "Diego is damaged, maybe beyond repair. I went through a period where I believed I was special to have been selected to be this unique friend, to carry him, if that's what I'm doing. But I don't believe it anymore. I think it was more like I was available. I need to stay here for a reason, for him, and I don't know how long it will be."

Thalia rises from the bed and stands before Hector. She wraps her arms around him and pulls his head into her chest, at the same time dropping her head so her cheek rests against his head. He doesn't feel exactly like the man she has made love to several times over the past months; that man is partially there, but at this moment, it's not him. Hector's arms hug Thalia's waist and he breathes deeply. She recalls information from Walt Kramer, about a son who died for an unspeakable act, and she wonders what that act was. What is Kramer searching for, besides a woman at a funeral, the funeral of her grandfather she failed to attend? Unconsciously, she moves her hands up and down Hector's back while her cheek remains unmoved. Can Cocker be correct about shamans? Could this simply be a chance case of availability or is there more to it. Indian, huh? Navajo, not Tohono O'odham. Some college. What was his major? She realizes he is holding her tighter than she is hugging him, almost as if he is holding her up. "What are you thinking just now, Hector?"

"Just now? About how good you feel to me. I can hear your heartbeat. I wasn't thinking about the rider, which might seem strange since it's what we were discussing, which is what I think about most of the time. You've been good for me, the best thing I've ever had, but we both know it's temporary. You will go."

"You won't?"

"Not sure. I don't know what my destiny is. It's certainly linked to Diego for now."

A loud knock at the front door startles them both, and Hector stands quickly. "Stay here." He closes the bedroom door behind him, pushes a curtain aside to see who it is, swears under his breath, and opens the door.

Lizardo and a Pima County deputy sheriff smile arrogantly at him. "This officer has a warrant for your arrest, Hector, for assaulting an officer of the court a while back. It's time we find out who you really are."

18

DETENTION AND REUNION

Most of Rubicon had been there at some point in their lives. Jail. Cocker experienced incarceration several times in Texas, usually because of alcohol or drugs. Drunk and disorderly was a phrase encrypted in his DNA. Often, he could not remember why he was sitting in a cell, the resulting confusion lasting beyond his release. Alf ended up in the local jail in eastern Arizona for his actions during The Strike, and his anger was stoked whenever he was forced into a small cell. His mood swings attested to the acrimony between the union and Phelps Dodge, between the workers and the company. The residents of Why are wary of the Gatekeeper's mood swings still. Julie learned of the indifference of jailers during her three experiences with juvie in California. Before she met Jack, who gave meaning to her rebellious behavior, Julie spent brief terms in juvenile detention. Jack's one experience with confinement was in Sacramento after a decade of eco-terrorism. When a couple of his co-terrorists ratted him out, he became depressed and disconnected, and it sent him to Alaska to battle a larger enemy on his own. Ruby, Crystal, and Jade, "The Women of the Line," all spent a night or two in jail for their strike behavior, for threatening the police or scabs in front of fences keeping the ladies from working in the mine. Waddell Smithfield spent five weeks in a Birmingham, Alabama, jail for riding a bus with other Freedom Riders. Smitty's days were a crash course on the dehumanization that can occur when people are incarcerated. Jail for Smitty inspired him, brought out an awareness that lay dormant in his soul prior to his participation in the Civil Rights Movement. Even Libby admitted to a short stray in jail in Nogales, but she never said why, implying she felt guilty for her behavior and bringing shame to her family.

ॐ

"They'll book him in Tucson, haul him before a judge tomorrow, and set bail. We'll be able to pick him up later in the day." Smitty paces in front of the bar while the others sit. "If necessary, I'll get him my lawyer. In fact, . . ." He walks behind the bar, picks up the phone, and dials.

"You have a lawyer?" asks Alf.

"All rich people do," says Jack.

Smitty ignores them and turns to Thalia, covering the receiver with his off hand. "Is there anything more we should be worried about, other than the fight? What else do you know about him?"

"There's nothing else. He is what he is. He's a carpenter, a handyman from Gallup. As far as I know, he's never been arrested. Didn't Lizardo tell us once Hector didn't even have any prints on record." She slides off the bar stool and walks behind the bar to get a soda from the cooler. "It's all bullshit! He didn't start the fight; he just broke it up. Why would Lizardo arrest him instead of you, Alf? It makes no sense." She halts her rant and sips her soda. She remembers her episodes with the police when they would come to her house late at night after neighbors had called about another domestic fight with her ex, but they were always on her side. Hector didn't say goodbye; he stepped outside where he was handcuffed and put in the officer's car and driven away. Thalia bets he never said a word in his defense at that moment or on the ride to Tucson.

"It's not Hector, Thalia. Lizardo's sending a message, laying down the gauntlet," says Alf.

"Doesn't he get one phone call?" asks Cocker.

"Legally he does, but it wouldn't surprise me if he didn't use it. Hector's never been one to intrude on us," says Alf. "When Phelps Dodge would have me arrested, legalese never seemed to enter into the equation. Fortunately, the union always came to get me." He smiles and grunts. "Have I ever told you the value of unions in America?" It's rhetorical and he lets it go. His friends have heard it many times before both from him and the Notajo women.

"We have to go get him," says Thalia.

Smitty holds a 3 x 5 notecard up to the light and slips a pair of reading glasses over his nose. "My lawyer knows some people in Tucson who will make some calls. Said he'll get right back to us. He seemed to think it would be better if just me and maybe Thalia went to pick him up. Certainly not you, Alf." There are more notes on the card, but Smitty just nods to himself and tucks the card into his breast pocket. "I assume you'll want to go with me," he says to Thalia.

Jack speaks. "Why would Lizardo have Hector arrested instead of you, Alf, if he truly was sending us a message? He hates you and barely knows Hector?" There's the usual tone of conspiracy in his question.

Cocker stirs. "I have a feeling about this, about Hector. Not a good feeling either."

"We all have that feeling today, Cock," says CJ. "It's not often we all agree with you, is it? Lizardo's plotting something; we just need to figure it out before he springs it on us. He's such a lowlife. He throws out a net just to see what he can drag in hoping he can stumble onto something of value."

"No," says Jack. "He's got a bead on one of us."

"What are you thinking?" asks Alf looking at CJ.

"First thing we do is get Hector out of jail. Smitty and Thalia need to be in Tucson early and be at the Sheriff's office to follow everything going on. My guess is the Tucson sheriff doesn't know Lizardo well, since that scum has always worked out of Phoenix, but I'm not sure. Regardless, they'll take his word over Hector's, as will the judge. If your lawyer has any pull at all, have him use it." CJ turns to Thalia. "You might want to warn your news people you could have another story for them from this little village, something about a corrupt bounty hunter preying on us losers."

Thalia's face shows surprise. "Wait. You know about what I do?"

"Hell, girl, we all do. We like your stories, even Julie did. Gave us all a little temporary fame. You seem to be sympathetic to our side in those articles," says Jack.

༄

The desk clerk at the sheriff's office does not have an explanation. Yes, Hector was brought in on a warrant yesterday and booked. Within the hour, however, he was freed in a rather unusual circumstance. Obviously, no bail had been set and there was no court appearance, but he was released into the custody of another man. Quite irregular. Prints and photo, of course, but those were whisked up and not filed. Strange."

"Who authorized it?" asks Waddell Smithfield.

"I don't know," answers the clerk. "The sheriff just ordered me to release him."

"Where was he taken?"

"He wasn't taken anywhere as far as I know. A man came in, spoke with Sheriff Harr in confidence, and then I let him out of the holding cell. Like I said before, strange." The clerk pauses. "That other man was pissed beyond belief."

"What other man?" asks Smitty.

"The bounty hunter who had the papers."

"He was here when it happened?"

"No. He came back after dinner and found out. Started yelling at me. Asshole."

"Yeah, that would be Lizardo, and he is."

Smitty takes Thalia's arm, and they step back from the clerk's desk to consider what has happened. They talk quietly, discussing their options, before Thalia turns back to the clerk.

"Under what name was Hector charged when he arrived?"

"Hector Smithfield."

༄

The comfortable bitch sessions that are the norm at The Call have been replaced by a more personal tone. Rubicon has been violated. A person falls into a place such as Why and adjusts his or her behavior, "gets on with living," while the problems that swirled these people into an isolated village remain just outside its boundaries. Hector's arrest, however, has demonstrated just how porous its city limits are. Sort of like the U.S.-Mexico border. The standard line, "The wind blew me here," might have worked for the Guardians once, but doesn't seem to be the answer now. A week has passed.

"I'm still confused as to why Hector would give Smithfield as his last name," says Cocker, "although I don't recall he ever gave out his last name."

"Jego," says Thalia. "It's pronounced differently than it's spelled." She chooses not to explain.

"Real or an alias?" asks Jade. "You all have aliases." She smiles and kisses CJ on the cheek. "Except maybe you, dear."

Each night, the Guardians have contemplated Hector's disappearance. Smitty's sources have no answers either. The tables at The Call have been rearranged to provide a measure of privacy to the discussions. Patrons from the area's ranches, RVers, and infrequent tourists are relegated to the tables near the juke box and door, but the Rubicon regulars settle in the corner nearest the bar and the dartboard and talk in hushed tones.

"It would make sense," says Alf.

"What?" says Jack.

"That he would say Smithfield. Who better to help him out of a jam? Smitty employs him and has money and influence. And, as Jade alluded to, it's at least a real name, unlike some of ours. Hector could claim to be Smitty's son, and it might carry some weight, at least in the early stages of the process." Alf pulls his mouth to one side as if to acknowledge his response is just one possible answer, a stab in the dark at best. "They'll find out pretty quickly, but it appears that it bought him some time."

"How hot did it get today?" asks Jade.

"One-oh-seven. Supposed to be hotter tomorrow," answers Jack.

"Why do any of us stay here in the summer?" asks Alf. "Ought to hold up over in Morenci where it's lots cooler. I'm sure PD would love to see me over there."

"It's a dry heat," kids Thalia.

"Where are the kids tonight, Rose?" asks Smitty.

"Spending the night with Crystal's darlings. I get them tomorrow night. Sort of gives each of us a break." Rose roams the bar getting orders rather than stationing herself behind the counter, and she enjoys the camaraderie of The Call.

Jack turns around to face Rose. "Who's going to work tomorrow then? Crystal?"

"How about if I do?" From behind the counter, from the entrance to the living quarters, Julie emerges. "About time I earned my keep." She is immediately hugged by Rose. A chorus of welcomes comes from the entire bar, and she walks into a sea of hugs: CJ, Jade, Smitty, two local ranchers, and Cocker, who whispers he knew she would return. She says hi to Alf and exchanges a shoulder-to-shoulder hug briefly. She faces Thalia and the two women clasp hands and smile at one another. She walks behind Jack, leans over and hugs him warmly from behind. He reaches up and takes hold of her head and they share a moment in this awkward position.

"I'm sorry, Jack," she whispers into his ear, words no one else in the bar can hear.

"No, it's me who needs to apologize. I've missed you a lot." There is a moment of silence until Rose asks if anyone needs another beer. Jack turns his head into Julie's cheek and asks, "Are you okay?"

"Yeah, I'm good. I needed to go, but I should have told you."

CJ pushes a chair into Julie's thighs, a signal to sit next to Jack and join the discussion. Rose touches Julie on the shoulder and then hands her a shot of tequila. "On the house."

"So, what have I missed," she asks.

Julie's return seems to alter the tone of the table; unexplained events turn out okay. No one asks where she was; she'll tell them if and when she chooses, but she has returned and now sits next to Jack with her hand on his forearm. Alf's expression indicates almost relief that Julie is back in the fold and shows no sign of regret or animosity towards Jack. CJ takes note immediately, as does Smitty, who wonders if The Call will react to Hector's return in the same manner. Probably no hugging if he comes back.

"We were trying to figure out a way to get in touch with Hector," says Thalia. "Lizardo had him arrested and now we can't find him. He's not in the legal system, . . ."

"That we know of," interrupts CJ.

". . . and he hasn't contacted us. We don't know where to turn," finishes Thalia.

"Hector was arrested?" asks Julie. Her hand squeezes Jack's forearm slightly, and she bites the inside of her lower lip. "F-ing Lizardo got him, huh? He was trolling for us."

"Cuss jar," says Jack.

The table goes quiet and watches Julie. They wait. Cocker begins to hum-sing an old Pete Seeger tune.

The Why Intersection

Jack hasn't asked, but Julie tells him anyway. She cradles her hairbrush in her lap and looks over to Jack as he maneuvers to lift himself from his wheelchair into the bathtub. "I stayed in Libby's home with her family first." She laughs slightly. "Extended family. A dozen or more people seem to live there. I didn't know her husband died in Mexico, in an auto accident south of Nogales. First her husband and then her daughter. She's a strong woman. His picture is on her mantle. Nice looking man. Of some importance on the reservation once, I guess." She puts her brush on the counter and pauses. "It made me wonder about how our lives would have been with children."

"I'm sorry about that. I always had the bigger picture." Jack sits in the tub with his head on his chest. Julie steps over and kneels beside the tub. She takes a washcloth from the bar, dips it into the water, and begins to wash Jack's body lightly.

"I couldn't stay with Libby for long. Two men, older than Smitty, came and drove me to their home up on the Navajo reservation, in Chinle. Hector's people in a way. So stark." She raises Jack's arm and washes his side and armpit. In time, she runs the cloth over his entire body, taking care around his damaged penis and testicles, ending where his leg without the knee and foot stops. "We need to get your prosthesis refitted." She talks as she washes the nub. "The men were elders, and along with their wives, they cared for me. Each week, I went to a different church. Baptist, Mennonite, Seventh-day Adventist, Mormon, Jehovah's Witness, and a few others. They took me to their sacred places and cemeteries. Libby must have told them my spiritual self was in need. They never lectured me or counseled me, just exposed me to all that was happening in Chinle and Canyon de Chelly, where they left me one day. Gave me a jug of water and a plastic chair, and I sat by a creek and thought. Two days ago, I told them I was ready to go home, so we drove all day today and they dropped me off at the gas station."

"I'm sorry I'm always angry. I just can't seem to let go of it." Jack's jaw tightens.

"It's how you are. I know that. I'm glad I'm back." She wrings out the washcloth, unwraps it, and washes his face gently. Then, she leans back onto her haunches and smiles.

Hector doesn't know where he is being detained, but it's not a jail. More like a military base. What's the name of the base in Tucson? It's been a major base for the deployment of Titan II missiles if he remembers correctly, only these either are in the process of being decommissioned or soon will be because of the agreements with the Soviet Union over strategic arms. He remembers. Davis-Monthan Air Force Base. An unarmed guard sits by the door in this spartan room, and Hector assumes an armed guard is on the other side. When the meals are served, Hector is instructed to go to the far side of the room and sit behind the table. The food has been delicious and plentiful. Hector thinks his captors are confused about him, which doesn't surprise him because he knows it is not Hector Smithfield they want. They want to know what he knows, what's inside him. If they can get to it, they will release Hector Smithfield/Jego/Dehiya. Dehiya: the Navajo brave who went upward. Hector laughs, and the inside guard looks up at him. Hector laughs at this too. Except for leaving Thalia with no explanation, Hector finds his captivity intriguing, nothing to be put out by, just another life experience.

Hector sits across a metal table from the man whom he assumes will question him eventually, the same table where he ate his breakfast an hour earlier. They have been sitting for fifteen minutes and the man has yet to look at him, so Hector studies him. He is short, maybe five-six and possibly 55 or 60 years old. Military, thinks Hector, but having never been in the service himself, Hector doesn't know for sure. It would make sense and would put him in the Korean War—if he ever served in war. The guard stands alert by the door, not quite at attention, but close. He has been Hector's only in-room guard during the day, but they have not spoken. His pressed uniform has no insignias, no rank, no name tag, and no medals. Hector sits with his hands in his lap, back straight, with both feet firmly on the floor. He wears the same clothes he came in with, and they're beginning to smell. The stack of clothes the guard placed on the counter remain folded in the small pile. Khaki. Maybe later today after a shower.

The Why Intersection

"My name is Cooley." He pauses and finally looks up, into Hector's eyes. Cooley has deep blue eyes, almost as if he is wearing colored contact lenses. "Thomas Cooley." Cooley looks again at his folder of papers before closing the folder and sliding it off to his left. "Your written answers to the questions when you arrived are a little confusing, so I'm going to try and clear some things up." Cooley pauses again but does not avert his eyes. Hector moves his eyes to Cooley's mouth and watches as Cooley forms his words. "Which is it? Jego or Smithfield or Dehiya?"

Cooley has mispronounced both Jego and Dehiya. "Dehiya. It's Navajo." Hector has promised himself he will not volunteer any information but will give accurate information when asked. He has broken his pledge with the first question.

"Or is it Elkington?"

By the manner Cooley has asked the question, Hector thinks the interrogator already knows he is not Elkington. Lots of ways he could have gained this information; most likely by a simple description, although Hector doesn't think it matters to his interrogator. Unless. Hector suddenly is bothered that he never thought of his roommate's physical characteristics. He just was. "No sir," he answers. "Dehiya."

"Do you know why you're here?"

"No, not exactly, but I guess it has something to do with Mr. Kramer." Again, Hector has given more information than was asked.

Cooley nods his head. He stands and walks over to the guard, says something, at which time the guard nods his head and exits the room. Cooley returns to the table. "Did you meet Kramer?"

"No."

"How did you know about him?"

"He visited Why three times."

"Do you know why?"

"From what my friends said, he was looking for a woman who might have a connection with his son."

Cooley opens the folder, turns three pages, reads them, and then closes the file again. "Did you ever see Kramer?"

"Yes. All three times. I made sure he didn't see me, but I watched him."

"Who told you Kramer was there?"

"My friends were nervous about his arrival and talked about it like they talk about every stranger in town, but I always sensed it."

"Sensed it? Nobody told you? What about Thalia?" Cooley leans into the table just an inch or two, but Hector sees it. He probably knows what she does, where she's from, and her family history.

∾

Thomas Cooley cups his hands over his mouth and nose. He sits alone in a makeshift office pondering his subject. Never in his two decades as a Navy investigator has he encountered an enigma such as Hector Dehiya. A Navajo brave who speaks of things he shouldn't know. Cooley recalls the Navajo Code Talkers from World War II. Very few people understood what they were saying either. Maybe Cooley can break Hector's code. Cooley shakes his head at his previous beliefs, none so glaringly wrong as that Hector might have been Sam Elkington. Why did he believe anyone could survive a gunshot to the head and the fall into the mine? Maybe the paranoia of the Cold War, of dealing with men who are out to destroy America. Still, there is something about Hector connecting him to the secret. Cooley's eyes remain fixed, staring out the window at the runway where jets practice touch and go landings.

∾

"Reagan's losing it!" says Jack.

"Never had it," replies Alf, "but what makes you deduce that this morning?"

"Watching him trying to tell us about the arms-for-hostages fiasco. He doesn't know what's going on around him; seems confused. The certainty he had during his first term seems to have dissipated."

"It's a job I don't want, that's for sure," adds Smitty. "An impossible job." He leans forward and looks into his coffee cup where a fly is swimming. He makes a face and then spoons him out, only to squish him in a paper napkin. "What do you do in that situation, Jack? You're an avowed anti-communist, but the Congress won't fund your programs in Central America, so you maneuver covertly."

"Shit, Smitty. Those governments we back in South America are thugs. Brutal fascists who kill the poor in the name of God knows what. Maybe fascists is too strong; but ultra-right wing thugs regardless," says Jack.

"Strange bedfellows for sure," injects CJ. "From Central America to South Africa and apartheid; what a clusterfuck. The Cold War colors every action the government has taken during our lifetimes, at least since WWII."

Julie puts her hand on CJ's shoulder while she refills his cup. "I'm not sure, but I think my retirement fund is growing with the cuss words this morning. I ought to double the fine for the f-word." She warms each man's coffee, returns to the bar where she pours a cup for herself, picks up her Bible, and returns to the table to sit next to Jack. "Did you hear our Border Patrol is going to be expanded to keep this Red Menace from crossing the borders in larger numbers?"

"Mexicans aren't communists," says Alf.

"No, but to beef up border security, the government says they're doing it to prevent Central Americans from coming here. Our groceries. Sort of dovetails on what this conversation started with," says Julie.

"The tragic part of all this really is what happens to those poor farmers from Guatemala, Nicaragua, and El Salvador. The Contras are evil." The table nods at CJ's statement, and then he adds, "And to the integrity of the Indian reservation."

"How much longer before I can get a beer?" asks Cocker.

Julie looks at her watch. "Close enough. I'll get you one. Anyone else?" There are no takers, so Julie grabs a single bottle from the cooler. "I haven't tapped the keg yet."

"Is Thalia any better?" asks CJ.

"No." Julie pauses. "Worse than a breakup."

Jack turns to Smitty. "Anything?"

Smitty shakes his head. "This is confusing. I can't get any information on Hector or Lizardo, like they just dropped off the face of the earth. Feels like I'm failing Thalia."

Cocker picks at the label on his beer. "You can read it in her face." He pauses. "You know this is all connected, don't you?"

He has the table's attention.

∾

At the Ajo library, Jade and Thalia pour over articles from the Phoenix and Tucson newspapers dating from the early years of the current copper strike. Jade found it before Hector was arrested, but even then, it piqued her curiosity. A letter to the editor in the Phoenix *Arizona Republic*, just one paragraph long, suggesting the authorities were being misled in their search for the man who shot the little girl in Ajo, signed with an obvious pseudonym.

"Why wouldn't he have written to the Tucson newspapers too?" asks Jade. "After all, they wrote as much about the strike as Phoenix did."

"My guess is they had a preconceived notion and weren't going to allow for deviation. An unknown union man shot into the house of a scab, accidently hitting his daughter. That by itself is a great media story. Turns the sympathies of the state away from the strikers and allows for Phelps Dodge to gain support, as if they needed it in this environment."

"That didn't answer my question, Thalia. Why wouldn't a similar letter show up in a Tucson paper? Or here in Ajo?"

Thalia holds her index finger on a specific story as she looks up. "Maybe whoever wrote the letter also sent one to other newspapers, but they declined to print them."

"Who would know? How can we find out who wrote this? Even now in podunk Ajo, we verify the letter writer even while protecting his identity. Wouldn't they do the same thing in Phoenix?"

"Initially, Jade, they would. But too much time might have passed to find out who wrote this one. Have you met anyone here at the newspaper who might be willing to speak in private about such a letter?"

∾

"Do you have any idea what I do, Hector?" asks Cooley.

"You mean beyond this interrogation?"

"Yeah, the bigger picture."

"No." Hector shakes his head slightly. He's wondered about that bigger question but hasn't come up with an answer. This is his third day of confinement, and, except for these moments with Cooley, he hasn't spoken to anyone. He worries for Thalia. She was there when he was arrested and probably heard the short discussion. He didn't say goodbye, didn't want to draw attention to her presence in the bedroom. She sensed the extra soul; maybe she can sense this. Whatever this is.

"That was a long pause for a simple no answer," says Cooley. "I work for The Government. Capital G government. More specifically, I'm a naval officer, always on special assignment. From the time Walt Kramer parked an RV in the park in Why, Rubicon has been my special assignment. I have a dossier on everyone in the neighborhood, including you and Libby, who don't exactly live in Rubicon, but interact with them. I've been keeping an eye on Kramer because he was working on suppressing a leak, a leak that if allowed to get out would cause an international event. To be honest, I think he plugged the leak, but he wasn't 100 percent sure. Kramer's as good as they come in dealing with these kinds of problems, and if he wasn't completely convinced, then I can't be either." Cooley pauses. "Are you following me, Hector?" Hector is and nods. Cooley draws his words out as if he's speaking to a child, but there is nothing condescending in his attitude. By telling Hector this, Cooley is still probing. "I was in no hurry, you see, but that bounty hunter Lizardo forced me to take you out of the system. He was pretty excited about having you arrested, getting some satisfaction for the fight."

"You know I didn't start the fight, don't you? I broke it up?" says Hector.

"Oh, I know. I watched." Cooley watches for Hector's reaction. "You know how to handle yourself."

"I fought a lot as a stupid kid. I didn't see you there, and no one mentioned it."

"I stay in the shadows; it's what I do. I watch. I collect information. I form hypotheses."

Hector drops his head to the side and scratches his forehead. When he looks up, Cooley is still staring into his eyes. "What do you need, sir?" asks Hector.

For the first time, Cooley's posture loosens, and he leans forward a tiny bit. "I need to be convinced about the security of that secret, and I'll do whatever it takes to lock that secret up. I mean anything." A minute passes between them. "Do you know anything about a secret Soviet city known as Yamantov?"

❦

Thalia listens to Libby.

"Before the strike I sold my burritos and tamales in Ajo. Very profitable, but the town became a war zone, and I was uncomfortable. Neighbors turned on each other overnight, and everyone became suspicious. I witnessed everything, it seems, but shared nothing, so I decided to stop selling there and set up in Why only." Libby returns her spatula to the beans in her metal pot and rolls six burritos into their final shape. She slides one across the table to Thalia. "Yes, I saw things I never talked about. No one ever asked me."

"You wrote the letter?"

❦

Thalia and Libby sit with the Notajo Auxiliary in Crystal's kitchen. Rose crochets, but the others sit and drink. Margaritas tonight. The tone is serious, a follow-up on Thalia's question to Libby.

Thalia's butt rests on the front of her chair, her body in a seemingly relaxed position. She holds her margarita with both hands and speaks. "One night, back when I was about twenty, I was driving home from school, college, to see my mother. The weather had turned really bad, blowing snow across a two-lane hilly country road in Michigan, one of those storms where the snow seems to be coming straight into your windshield and your headlights only make it worse. I'll bet I wasn't going ten miles an hour. I remember looking in the rearview mirror and seeing my father's face smiling at me, almost reassuring me I would be all right. Not a big deal except my father was dead." She looks at the four other women. "Somebody else's turn."

Rose looks over her reading glasses. "It all gets back to souls, doesn't it. Thalia, dear, the four of us have sat here lots and discussed this. We hold prayer sessions. It's a part of who we are, so you don't need to be uncomfortable bringing this up."

Jade reaches over and places her hand on Thalia's forearm. "We all hurt about Hector, but he's going to be okay." Both women smile.

The Why Intersection

Libby reaches down into her handbag and withdraws a joint. She lights it, inhales deeply, and passes it to Crystal. "All those crosses and memorials by the side of the road," she looks at Thalia, "most of them died too early, and I believe their souls weren't ready for Heaven yet. So where are they kept? Asleep in those shallow graves? Unconscious? We can argue their state all evening and never agree, but the four of us believe those souls are still hanging around, waiting for their time to rise up. My people believe they are aware, not simply sleeping in the ground, but it doesn't matter. Details. The bodies are in the ground, but the souls are being held by another."

"Are you a shaman, Libby?" asks Thalia.

"Lord no, dear, but I believe your Hector might be." Libby's eyes offer a mild challenge to Thalia. "Tell us."

"Hector told me of another, maybe the one Kramer was here to find. Whenever Kramer was here, Hector hid or would leave Why. It wasn't that he was afraid of Kramer, more like he didn't want to give up what was inside him."

"Who, not what," says Jade.

"Yeah, the one inside. Hector was confused about it, but clear about when it happened. He was walking down a road up north, and suddenly he was carrying another."

"Say it," says Libby. "A soul."

"Yeah, a soul." Libby offers the joint to Thalia, who shakes her head and raises her margarita glass slightly. Jade accepts the joint and takes a hit before passing it back to Libby.

"This is one reason why Cocker and me are so compatible." The table laughs. "Cocker." Libby's voice trails off and she smiles and looks back to Thalia. "Are you in need of another story for your journalism papers? Write about Cocker. What you see at The Call . . . that's not him. He's able to contact spirits. Souls. He's a channeler. Many people believe shamans hold the souls, but I don't. They aren't housed in another's body, but there are people who can contact these lost souls. It's as if the Guardians are holding the souls of the Central American refugees, protecting them on their perilous journey. Smitty and Cocker started it, but Rubicon is a sanctuary." Libby's eyes narrow, but they miss not a single beam of light.

"If these souls don't go directly to Heaven or aren't kept in others' bodies, where do they reside?" Thalia sits up. This is new territory for her. Her mother always told her friends what a curious girl her daughter was, and what a considerate, respectful girl also. Never has she considered herself critical, and now Thalia wonders if her friends deem her questions disrespectful. She remembers her discussion with Julie about stolen babies, the closest she's ever come to openly challenging another adult about contrary beliefs. Always before, her challenge came in print form. Thalia is uncomfortable. "I'm sorry, but we come from different backgrounds, and even though I mentioned my one experience with my dad in the backseat of my car and my questions about Hector, I've never been around people who," she pauses searching for the correct words, "who actively communicate with spirits."

Crystal sits off to Thalia's left and is out of view from Thalia once she moved forward in her chair. Crystal moves her head slowly toward Thalia's ear. "Boo!" she says in a slightly elevated voice, startling Thalia. The table laughs, and Thalia realizes the moment.

"That gullible, huh?" asks Thalia.

"No, dear," says Crystal. "You're just so darn fun to be around, and so open, that sometimes it sets you up. We love you."

"Welcome to my world," says Jade. "Until you, I was this White woman in a Chicano world and never understood the subtle differences. You being here takes the pressure off me."

Rose laughs. "Little bit of difference, don't you think, Jade? We tease you and you get mad. You strike back and storm out." Jade pulls her head back in mock surprise. "Yes, you, girl. Never let anyone take advantage of you. You're angrier than any Mexican woman I ever knew."

Libby pinches the joint out and returns what's left to her purse. "You think what we think about the dead is a little weird, but we think what your kind thinks about the dead is so simple. A person dies, you bury them, and their soul goes straight to Heaven or Hell. You visit their grave once a year on their birthday for a time in a cemetery crowded with dead bodies, to remember them when they were alive. Not us. Those spirits are not just a memory; they live among us. Doesn't matter where. We're connected."

"All those roadside memorials aren't simply a reminder not to drink and drive," adds Jade. "I didn't understand that either. Now, I do."

"Well," says Rose, "as much as a White woman can." Crystal high fives Rose.

Thalia laughs. "I wonder if a living person can surrender his soul for a time?"

Libby nods. "Honey, it's not Hector's soul you're feeling. Maybe it's the soul of this Kramer guy's dead son, or at least the soul of someone he's lost. Kramer's not a believer either, but unlike you, he would have a harder time accepting these beliefs." Libby shakes a loose fist at Thalia. "There's way too much coincidence for this to just be coincidence. The winds have swirled everyone here for a reason," she smiles and nods to Thalia in a caring way, "and this, too, is hard for you to wrap your head around."

Jade laughs out loud. "It's not Hector's *soul* Thalia's feeling anyway. Something much more intense."

ဢ

A sedan parks a hundred yards north of Cocker's warehouse. The driver turns off the engine and sits, watching for movement. Satisfied that he is alone, he exits the car and strides quickly to an obscure side door. He takes one last look before entering.

ဢ

Lizardo circles three more names on his list. He despises the haughty crew that calls themselves Rubicon, which separates itself from the rest of the God-forsaken outpost of the stopover at the junction of two desert highways going nowhere. *Petty criminals. Liars. Drunks. Union sympathizers. Losers. Julie returned; Hector isn't charged. They spit on me. This isn't over. Down the road, Smithfield, you won't have a following. I'll get them all, and then you can ride around in your stupid golf cart by yourself. The cripple, the Mexican, the drunk: they're all going down. They all have a past, and I'll find out what it was. Aliases, new names, police records for sure. And CJ, that arrogant sellout. Joe Jacoby and his new girlfriend. The band of bums who live their little lives protecting each other's secrets.* Lizardo speaks out loud to no one.

"You're temporary and your time is past."

∞

The Sierra Vista police chief seems to remember a man with a golden voice who used to pal around with Reverend Allen before "that phony" left for California and died. Wasn't named Cocker though. Michael. Mark. Something like that. Good guy for the most part, but the police chief is pretty sure he recalls something about Allen's assistant and a younger staff member that got swept under the rug. The chief will ask around.

∞

There is no record of an Alfonso Galvan working at the New Cornelia Mine in Ajo, no record of an Alfonso Galvan anywhere in the Phelps Dodge records. No one by that name in the various union logs either. Lizardo knows Galvan is an alias, but what was it before, and where did he work? He doesn't seem to be working now, so what does he do for an income? Lizardo wonders if Smithfield keeps records.

∞

Lizardo stands at the bar sipping a coffee staring at the map of Alaska. He's the only one in The Call this morning. He parked at the gas station in Why and walked over, hoping to avoid notice and hoping one of the Mexican women was working instead of Julie. When the two border patrol agents left, Lizardo entered. He studies the Alaska map, notices a red dot, and writes a name down. Livengood. An old mining town, maybe? A red line marks the path of the pipeline. Lizardo doesn't know his Alaska geography, but he does understand the great distances between places there. Livengood has to be a couple of hundred miles north of Fairbanks. Why would Jack and Julie display an Alaska map with an insignificant town marked in red?

Rose returns to the bar after sweeping the front porch. "You know you're not wanted around here."

"Bounty hunters aren't welcome anywhere, it seems, darlin'. I'm used to it. Just consider me an independent contractor looking for business, you know, looking for the bad guys." He takes a drink from

The Why Intersection

the paper cup and looks over the top at Rose. "You wouldn't happen to know of any around here, would you?"

Jack London wheels himself into the bar. He levels a .45 at Lizardo. "You get the hell out of my bar, asshole."

Martin Lee Wagner, Fallon Andrews, Alonso Peru. Statute of limitations on Cocker and Jack, and no charges were ever filed on Alf, but the suspicions are still out there. Lizardo wraps his long fingers around his short file. His eyes blink rapidly. A possible connection between Alf and CJ? Throw out the net and see what it drags in. Aliases! And Livengood?

19

EDDYING, SUMMER 1987

Thalia jots her thoughts on a yellow legal pad: one side labeled "Hector" and the other "Finances." She sits in an Ajo breakfast diner across the street from the Ajo *Copper News* where Jade now works, the diner Jade's family used to own before the strike. They sold it and moved to California. Jade pops in periodically to check on Thalia's progress and to have a "free" cola. Hector has been gone for a week, and his whereabouts is the focus of Rubicon's thoughts and discussions. *The Government's got him!* seems to be the general consensus, voiced most strongly by Jack. "He's either done something far worse than we ever suspected or he's got information on us and they're protecting him." The other Guardians and citizens of Rubicon don't go so far. The government's got Hector all right, but for what reason, they still don't know. Under "Hector" Thalia has noted: Navajo from northern Arizona, junior college degree in construction, Shaman?, protector, avoided Kramer. Under "Finances" her notes include Phelps Dodge profits for 80-86, decertification of the union, shooting of the child, EPA, CJ, and PD-Rubicon connections.

Regarding her last notation, Thalia has learned that each one of the Rubicon residents is a treasure chest of knowledge about the events surrounding the copper mine in Ajo. Prior to '83, they all lived or shopped or socialized or worked or golfed in Ajo on a regular basis. Thalia throws out an event and each one has a recollection. Small town, common experiences. Why did this group end up drinking beer together after the strike began? Libby is correct; too many coincidences to be a coincidence. Thalia curls the fingers from her left hand around her lower lip and apes the movement with her right hand on the table, her eyes unfocused, but her brain racing. Jade should be returning shortly with information from the newspaper from the night the child was shot four years ago. Thalia has read the article over and over, but something is missing besides the obvious. No one was ever charged, but Arizona believes it knows who did it; not by name,

The Why Intersection

but by association. An angry union miner. Case closed. Libby says it wasn't but can't say how she knows this. During a violent strike, a bullet is fired into the home of a scab with the intent of scaring him, hits his daughter, probably by accident, but nearly killing her, nevertheless. Obvious.

Jade arrives and the waitress automatically sets a cola on the table. "Why do men fly off the handle and fire off their guns?" asks Jade. "Why not just slug it out?"

Thalia smiles remembering a past she'd rather not. A quick nod. "Over women. Jealousy."

"Yeah, maybe. What if the shooting had nothing to do with the strike?"

"So, even if the gunman was a union guy, but he fired for a reason unrelated to the strike, everyone would assume it was related to the strike." She pauses. "Another wild theory."

Jade leans over the table. "So, preconceived notions over facts? But he was jealous?"

"Can we prove this?" asks Thalia.

Jade shakes her head. "Probably not. Nobody wants to come off the official story because it's so ingrained, because they don't want to be seen as a snitch or a coward for not coming forward earlier. But there are lots of cowards in small towns, Thalia, and they don't believe pursuing this line further is of any value. The little girl's father died a few months later in a car accident and the girl survived. Let it stay buried."

"There are cowards in big cities, too, Jade, bigger cowards with bigger secrets. Did you get this from the deputy?"

"Yeah. He won't give me a name, probably doesn't have one to give, and I used my most persuasive charm. Must be losing my touch," says Jade. She flutters her eyes. "Maybe he's just telling me the office conjecture or telling me what I want to hear."

Thalia smiles again. "Who would the town want to protect, and by town, I mean the establishment, the PD people. Not a local miner. Not an Indian from the reservation. Probably not even a border patrol officer, although law enforcement usually wants to protect its own. No, Jade, my guess it was someone important who hid under the cloak of *The Strike*."

"Why would Libby know then?"

Smitty sits with three ministers inside a south Tucson church, three men he has now known for a few years. He delivered another grocery late in the night, a unique delivery in that this grocery is not from Central America. Smitty moves this grocery around at various times, never allowing it to become a permanent member of any community yet. This is not the first time that this grocery has spent time at this church, this sanctuary, and always he keeps himself busy repairing broken or damaged church parts.

Cooley watches the lady. She sits in her car across from the sheriff's office. The sheriff called when she arrived demanding information about Hector Smithfield. The sheriff had none to give; nothing had changed. Hector was brought in, and the booking process began, but before charges were filed, he was removed from their custody and whisked away. Since then, they have received no information. "Sorry, but it's out of our hands now." She persisted, but the sheriff really didn't have anything to give her. Hector was truly gone.

Cooley knows who she is, knows she must be suffering, but thinks her journalistic skills will keep her going. He knows her real name. Not really an alias, just an alteration. Maybe she is more than just Hector's girlfriend. Maybe she could help crack the enigma. Cooley has read all her articles. She's liberal and her research is first-rate. Her first articles, the ones that appeared in Detroit's *Free Press*, stressed facts, demonstrated her research. Later, she allowed her research to lead to speculation and a certain slant. Water quality, housing, inner-city schools, Detroit's homeless. Cooley holds some opposite views, but he respects her in-depth research. Not enough American journalists have the guts anymore to dig for a story, to get down and dirty, to tramp through the slums of Detroit or confront an evangelical church organization about accepting dark money for its religious activities. Brave. And now she's sitting in her car about ready to cry.

The Why Intersection

I have Hector; she wants him back. She may know the answers I seek—or at least has a path to those secrets—but doesn't have Hector. Cooley wonders if it is Thalia he needs to deal with. Is her relationship with Hector professionally based, or is it a love affair that developed while she was researching her work on the baby trade? Her disposition indicates the latter. He puts down his binoculars, looks at a photograph of the two of them he took last winter, and jots down a note. The photograph shows them standing in Rubicon Wash, holding hands. They're happy.

∞

Cooley taps on Thalia's car window to get her attention. She is startled, but not scared. Cooley's appearance is not threatening, and she rolls down the window. He steps back to indicate he wants only to say something.

"Yes? Can I help you?" she asks.

"Quite possibly, Miss Fisher, and I may be able to help you."

∞

"Jade," asks Libby, "how well do you know CJ?" They are sharing a morning pancake at the diner across from the newspaper where Jade works. Peanut butter and pecans cut in half. Jade has whipped cream on her half. Libby sprinkled seeds from her purse on her side.

Jade throws Libby a look of surprise. "I met him in Rubicon at The Call after I moved there. Before then, not at all. I think I used to see him around here in Ajo before the strike began, but I'm not sure about that. We date. It's not serious." Jade smiles. "He's *way* too old for me," she says, emphasizing the *way*.

"Are you and Thalia still researching the shooting?"

"We've kind of reached a dead end. Why did you ask me about CJ?"

Libby adds a bit more syrup to her pancake. "I was telling Cocker about our earlier talk, and he said you might want to ask CJ about the shooting. It was one of those things he just throws out and doesn't explain."

The doors and windows at the Tabernacle are wide open for ventilation. Cocker shows Alf, CJ, Crystal, and Rose where Hector painted and what remains. "If you'll notice, he's very conscientious with his work. No paint on the ceiling, he tapes around the fixtures, he moves the furniture around where he's working. Leave that square alone."

"The one that sort of looks like a windowpane or a door?" asks Rose.

"Yep. I'll get it later. I appreciate your help. I think we can get it done if we work all day."

"Do we get a bonus if we do?" kids CJ.

"This is volunteer work," says Rose. "God's work."

"Beers at The Call when you're done," says Cocker.

"What will you be doing while we're working?" asks Alf. "Drinking?"

"I ain't going anywhere. I'll be cleaning up the altar area, sanding and staining."

"Praying for our souls," says CJ.

"Ain't enough prayers for you and Alf. Besides, I think God has heard enough from me over the years. You might ask Rose and Crystal to put in a few words for you."

∾

As a boy on the reservation, Hector had been raised by relatives, but the relationship soured before he reached his teen years. Then, that sort of orphanage. Eventually, he was taken in by another Navajo family living south of Farmington, New Mexico. He never found out for sure about his birth parents, just rumors. Both were alcoholics, it was said, and had never married. Hector didn't bother to search, was told not to bother, and again the stories were that they had died early. All he retained from them was his name: Dehiya, the *one who went upward*. Whatever that meant.

∾

"Hector," says Cooley, "I can't keep you here forever. I've spoken with a person who seems to think you are who you say you are, a

The Why Intersection

carpenter from Gallup, New Mexico, who has an undefined past which allows for others to imagine or create a more defined past for you." Cooley smiles awkwardly and shakes his head. "This person implied I might be one of those people too." Hector sits without responding, his hands clasped before his chin, his eyes focused. "This person said I should try to listen past your words."

※

"Did you find out anything?" asks Jade when Thalia joins her at The Call.

"No," replies Thalia. She will need to fudge on her answers for now to keep her agreement with the naval officer. Lie at times. "The sheriff doesn't know where Hector went. He's out of the loop too. He's going on the assumption that Hector returned to the reservation up north and that we won't see him again." Thalia knows that isn't the case. While the winds around Why have been stronger recently, they haven't been strong enough to blow Hector away. Unlike most of the residents of Why, Hector didn't escape from somewhere to this tiny southwest Arizona town seeking refuge. Thalia believes Hector will return.

"I'm sorry, but I did get Libby to talk again about the shooting. I threw out some additional questions, things that just frustrate the hell out of me about this cover-up. She won't answer anything directly, just answers questions with questions."

"Are all Indians like that?" asks Thalia.

"Finish your beer. The gang is over at the warehouse painting and needs extra hands. Libby thinks Cocker is about to try again, thinks he's planning for The Rapture. Besides, she thinks CJ may know more about the shooting than he's ever let on."

※

When Jade and Thalia arrive at the warehouse, they find the painters sitting outside eating sandwiches and drinking iced tea. Lunch. Julie brought it over. "I'm not painting, but this is my part. Jack and I are driving over to Tucson for a date." The three men and two women have been joined by Libby and are laughing or giggling at something

Cocker must have said, but that the others added to. A common event. "What's funny?" asks Thalia.

Crystal can barely contain herself, and her roundish body shakes like the Pillsbury Doughboy. "Cocker said he could tell when it's going to rain because his bone gets hard the night before." They laugh again. "Pretty sure that's not quite what he meant, but it's what he said."

"We think we need to check the long-range weather reports and tell Libby when to sleep over," says CJ. "Libby says it would save a lot of time."

A part of every day in Why is set aside for bitching, Thalia wrote during her first months in the small town, *but most of the day is commonplace.* Simple chores, family interactions, making ends meet, filling the hours of each day with laughter or routine tasks. Watching her new crew work together to help a fellow Whyan fix up his place reminds Thalia of her earlier words. *Commonplace.* Hector is missing, but life must go on. It's easy to disappear from Why since most of its residents were mostly invisible there anyway, at least to the outside world. Smitty constantly brings balance to the bitching sessions that occur over beers that Rubicon is simply trying to provide a small corner of the country with a bit of justice. Cocker reminds his friends that "God has a plan."

Cocker feigns hurt feelings and a bit of anger. "Lunch is over, you losers! Pick up your paint brushes and get back to work."

Thalia smiles to herself and wonders how hard Hector would be giggling at this scene. Then he would shake is head and tell Thalia again about how Why is weirder than his reservation. Yes, thinks Thalia, Rubicon defies description.

Rap Sheets. Martin Lee Wagner. Fifteen citations for some form of drunk and disorderly in both Texas and Arizona from as early as 1957. Fines and short jail stays. Possession charges in Arizona in the seventies. No convictions. The charges don't surprise Lizardo, but the failure to receive a conviction does. Resisting arrest: October 1982, Sierra Vista, Arizona, Christ Miracle Healing Center and Church. Lizardo remembers. The shootout between the Cochise County

The Why Intersection

sheriff's department and the Pentecostal group that occupied a tabernacle established by Reverend Allen in the 1960s. So, Cocker took part in that. He must have driven down from Why because he had set up his own church in Why several years earlier. Two church members died in the confrontation.

Fallon Andrews. Six aliases, most recently Jack London. Vandalism, breaking and entering, sabotage. A tree hugger. An ecoterrorist before there was a term for it. Jail time in Arizona and California. Clean record since he left California in 1974. Alaska. Lizardo doubts Jack became a law-abiding citizen. Livengood, Alaska. What was in Livengood, Alaska?

Alonso Peru. Alf Galvan. A dead man's name, a name Peru stole from a miner who died underground in the sixties. A union leader in Morenci, Arizona, who might have known Peru and his family. Nothing on Alfonso Galvan, but plenty of petty offenses on Peru's record. Assault, drunk and disorderly, illegal assembly, crossing police lines. Lots of union actions during the early years of the strike. Found guilty of them all and served short jail terms. Misdemeanors. No outstanding offenses. Lizardo looks at another set of notes on Peru. Married with children. Where is his family now? If they left, why is he still living in Why, near Ajo, where the mine is closed up? What keeps him there?

Lizardo draws a triangle on a piece of typing paper. At each corner he writes in a name: Jack, Cocker, Alf. Near each name he adds pieces of information. Next to Jack, Lizardo writes Julie, Alaska, eco-terrorist, cripple, The Call. Next to Cocker, minister and Miracle Valley. Beside Alf: union miner, wrong town, Chicano, angry. Lizardo studies his diagram but can't see connections. He lays the paper down, rises from his chair, and refills his coffee cup. He walks to his office window and looks out to I-10, the busy interstate running through the heart of Phoenix and connecting the capital to Tucson—and California. Connections. *Think, man! Connect the dots.* He returns to his desk and his diagram. He taps his pen on the desk while he rubs his lips with his left hand. He writes the name Smithfield inside his diagram and adds a question mark. No police record. At the bottom of the page, Lizardo adds the names of the three women miners who resettled in Why:

Rose, Crystal, Jade. He writes Thalia and Libby and finally Hector. Lizardo resumes his pen tapping. Shortly, Lizardo exes out the three female miners, circles Hector's name, and sends an arrow up to the triangle. What about Libby? Anybody I'm missing, he asks himself.

Tap, tap, tap, tap.

∾

"I didn't meet Diego for a few weeks after I arrived," says Hector. "I just kept getting these thoughts. I sensed Kramer's arrival before I actually saw him, or I should say, this thing sensed his arrival. I know you don't believe this crazy shit, sir, because it is . . . I don't know . . . tribal nutty." Hector pauses while Cooley writes a note on his pad. "Look, I'm an Indian, a Navajo, so maybe that helps explain this, but up until the wind knocked me over early in the summer, I didn't believe it either. Navajo mythology. I still don't know what happened, but visions and words come to me I'm unable to explain. I've always heard voices, but don't all Indians?" He smiles, as much to himself as to the interrogator. "They certainly aren't from my past. Whatever it is you're trying to discover, I can't tell you. There's no conversation occurring between this person and me; I can't ask him anything." Hector thinks about what he just said and corrects himself. "That's not quite true. I ask him all the time, but he never responds. The biggest question I ask him is 'Why me?' But so far, he's always ignored me. We aren't best friends, and I seem to have no input."

"Could this person you're carrying be Samuel Elkington?"

"I really don't know. I've never heard that name. He's just Diego now. I didn't choose, but I'm not carrying a person, just channeling him—or his spirit."

"Did Diego ever talk about his job in the Navy?"

"No sir."

"Any talk about submarines?"

Hector looks puzzled and doesn't answer.

"Did he ever mention living in Colorado?"

"No sir."

"And he never mentioned anything about the destruction of a Soviet city named Yamantov?"

"No sir. He never spoke about his past. His current job, the weather, a laugh about the people in Why. Only small talk."

Cooley leans back in his chair, folds his hands together on his stomach, and confirms to Hector his story is a bit crazy. He holds this posture for a few minutes while he thinks. Finally, he sits up straight and speaks. "Hector, I'm going to have Warrant Officer McHale drive you to a spot west of Tucson where you will be reunited with Miss Fisher. Understand I can pick you up again if any of what you've told me is a lie. Also, if these messages you're receiving from within tell you anything about Diego's past you might consider to be important to me, that is, relevant to our conversations over the past week, then I insist you call me. I can't stress this enough." Cooley's eyes tell Hector he is not to respond, but to accept the order. Cooley means what he says.

༄

"Kramer, we need to talk."

༄

Thalia stands next to her car, her hair blowing in the wind back toward Tucson, when Hector arrives in a white, unmarked van. The Navy officer returns Hector's wallet, an arrowhead necklace, and a pocketknife, but says nothing and drives off, back in the direction of Tucson. A small plume of dust is kicked up by the van's back tires. Hector gives a brief nod in the direction of the van before turning to Thalia with a sad, sheepish smile.

"Sorry I put you through this," he says.

Thalia steps forward into Hector's arms, the first human touch he has experienced in over a week since he and Thalia sat on the bed in Diego's bedroom. "You have nothing to apologize for, except maybe for leaving me so suddenly while I was just getting to understand you." She pulls back from the hug to see if her mini sarcasm registered with Hector. "I'm sorry for that, Hector. This past week can't have been fun for you. I learned from Cooley you were being held incommunicado all this time."

"It's okay, I expected it." Hector anticipated this months earlier when he balked at Thalia's overtures, when he warned her about having any kind of a relationship. His wave of guilt doesn't prevent him from moving to find her lips, and she responds in kind. They pull back, but their eyes remain locked.

"Come on, let me take you back. There is a neighborhood of people concerned about you."

∾

Cocker walks around Tabernacle's main hall. Except for a single square, the painting is complete; the repairs are done. Chairs and benches have been dusted, windows washed, light bulbs replaced, although the floor needs swept. He nods his head as if he is satisfied, but he wonders if God is. Early in life, at least in the life since becoming a minister, Cocker thought he knew what God was thinking; not anymore. Cocker has learned the lesson of over-confidence. That sin has been knocked out of him. Faith is just that: faith. Not surety. A belief, a hope, a plan, an expectation. As far as Tabernacle's preparation goes, it's ready. Cocker knows he has done all he can to this point, now he will have to wait. He walks out of Tabernacle, lights a cigarette, and heads across the highway to Rubicon, to The Call where he can get a beer.

∾

Jack rubs his hand over his entire face, a sign of fatigue and concern. His government paranoia has been rekindled by the arrest of Hector, but he knows his friends are tired of his complaints. The incursions into his territory of Walt Kramer and Dan intensified his suspicion. Instead, as they wait for Thalia to return with Hector, Jack returns to a familiar complaint. "This country . . . these pockets of poverty . . . belies America's promise. It robs our potential . . . always has."

"It always will, Jack," responds CJ. "Some people work harder than others or are born with a silver spoon. Besides, we're in a worldwide economic adjustment which is only accelerating. Automation and the movements to international trade will invariably leave some workers behind. It's not really a conspiracy, just a new place in economic history. That's not to excuse greed, because there are some nasty people

The Why Intersection

who will game the system to their advantage and think nothing of hurting the little guy. Phelps Dodge Corporation exemplifies both of my responses. It's caught in this new technology transfer, but it also cares very little about its workers. It has no heart, no conscience." CJ fiddles with his spoon and empty coffee cup.

Jade sits at the bar listening to the men, also drinking coffee. Since becoming "a newspaper reporter," she has quieted, become more observant in her behavior. Not less angry, just maybe more controlled, less openly agitated. Less likely to punch someone on the spur of the moment. "A professional woman, I suppose," she told Thalia—and then laughed. "Still, it's only been a few months." Jade admires Thalia and looks forward to the frequent times when they work together on this recent story: the shooting of the little girl in Ajo during the strike, searching for sources, checking their credibility, researching, interviewing random people for a clue. Thalia told Jade that being a journalist was more like being a detective.

Smitty arrives on one of his golf carts. More and more, the local communities in Arizona are providing traffic lanes specifically for golf carts, recognizing that old people find them an extension of their retired lifestyles. In Why, in the Rubicon neighborhood of rutted dirt roads and arroyos, Smitty is the only person who owns a golf cart, and nobody gives a shit what kind of car one drives around. Having a new car would be an embarrassment. Several of the local ranchers have all-terrain vehicles for work or hunting.

"Thalia called from Sells," he reports before sitting down with a drink. "Says Hector was hungry and is just sitting at a picnic table eating and staring at Baboquivari. I guess he was denied any outside time for over a week; never felt the sun." Smitty takes a heavy drink from his beer as he sits. "Imagine, not being allowed to go outside for that long."

"Hector's an outside guy, for sure," says Julie. "I could add that being Indian accounts for it, but that would stereotype him, and I wouldn't want to do that to anyone who sits at your table." The Guardians laugh. Julie turns away from the bar and remembers her time away from Rubicon. She stayed at Libby's early on but walked the town and drove the back roads in an attempt to clear her mind. *Babo*, she recalls, that looming mountain which dominates the whole Tohono O'odham reservation, gets into one's psyche and makes a person think about spirits and souls. Julie picks up her Bible and remembers where she got it: Alaska, when Jack nearly killed himself and she stayed with the religious group. She pictures Hector sitting at the table trying to understand this all. She considers her work with the baby trade and wishes she could have carried souls of the dead instead of babies from their mothers. She pulls her Bible up to her chest and walks out of the bar into her living quarters in the rear.

"Where's Alf?" asks Smitty.

"Said he had a job?" answers Cocker.

"A money-paying job or a task?" asks Smitty.

"He didn't say, only that he was going over to Ajo. He didn't know when he would get back, only that he wanted to hear what Hector has to say." Cocker puts his finger in his ear and shakes it. "He was worried about what information Hector might have given the government about us when he was being questioned."

Thalia and Hector continue to sit at the picnic table after he has finished his lunch, her hand at his elbow. He seems in no hurry to get to Rubicon. They are shielded from the sun by a beach umbrella at the outdoor burrito stand, probably the same one where Walt Kramer ate several months earlier on his way to Rubicon. Just as Kramer was, Hector is awed by Baboquivari, the stately granite monolith where, according to the Tohono O'odham, life began. He seems humbled.

"You're Navajo and you're sitting at a picnic table on an Indian reservation in southern Arizona possibly carrying the soul of someone who is the focus of attention of the government, which makes you the center of their attention, since governments don't recognize souls." Thalia pauses. "And I'm a journalist who is following the 25-year-old advice of my grandfather who told me I was to come here to help a wounded soldier." She leans in and kisses Hector's cheek. "It doesn't get any weirder than this, does it?"

At the same time, Hector shakes his head and says, "No, not really believable when you say it like that." He slides his arm back and takes

The Why Intersection

her hand from his elbow, turns to face her, and smiles. "What's this about your grandfather? You haven't mentioned this before."

"Oh, I have this memory from my childhood. Whenever he would visit, before he stopped coming back to our home in Michigan, he would tell me great stories about what I was to become. The one remaining in my head is about me saving a soldier, carrying his load. I've told you about my grandfather, a pretty wonderful man. My part in this current drama is connected to his late-in-life friendship with Kramer's son. I wonder if my grandfather had his own destiny to go somewhere to meet him. Have we all been directed to Rubicon?" She looks closely at Hector, trying to determine if any of this is true. They share a common question: What is this all about?

"You know, we could turn around, catch I-10, and head east until our cash ran out; get a reprieve for a while," says Hector.

"Do you want to escape?"

"Eventually, yeah, but I need to stay in Why to protect Diego."

"Why you?" asks Thalia.

"I guess I'm the only one who can."

"Heavy burden."

"Yeah, maybe." Hector pauses. "I think Diego has zoanthropy. He believes he's a creature of the desert." Hector lowers his head to hide his smile.

"Which kind?"

"A spider." Hector looks up, smiles at Thalia, and nods, affirming his tease.

Thalia shakes her head. "I've met Cooley and he's not going to let this go until he's convinced the answer, whatever it is, is uncovered. It would be nice though, wouldn't it, to just forget about this whole drama for a week or two."

"I was teasing about escaping east. I know we can't." He smiles at Thalia, but his eyes have a long-distance stare. "What's so important about him? First Kramer, then Cooley. Maybe you should use your journalistic skills to find out who they are," says Hector.

"Smitty already has. He has a theory. I couldn't find anything about Kramer beyond his profession."

Hector squeezes Thalia's hand. "I've never had a best friend to share my secrets with. Never been engaged. A few casual girlfriends. I assumed I'd be one of those Indians who never partnered with a woman and just led a lonely life with no purpose. My experience in life has been the reservation and the nearby towns. I tried Albuquerque and was like a fish out of water. Gallup was way better for me, more comfortable. I almost joined the Army but realized the discipline wouldn't be for me. His wind changed me." He looks into Thalia's eyes. "You've changed me. I don't want to be a drifter, a paycheck-to-paycheck guy, or lonely. You and me are temporary, I get that, but . . ."

Hector's pause lets Thalia interrupt. "Let's not get ahead of ourselves just now. Lizardo and Kramer are forcing the issue, so let's go find out. Besides, we can't sit here. The monsoon rains are moving in."

∾

Tap, tap, tap, tap. Lizardo studies his triangular chart. He crosses off Cocker's name, draws a circle around him, and moves him to the inside of the chart. He replaces Cocker with Smithfield. He was in Alaska, too, for a short time. Now, the chart has Jack, Alf, and Smithfield at the vertex and base points with Cocker and Hector in the center. Geometry. Tap, tap, tap, tap. Lizardo's long fingers pinch his lower lip. Suddenly, his eyes blink rapidly. Livengood, Alaska. The seventies. The Pipeline. The bounty hunter picks up his phone and dials. "Can you book me a cheap flight from Phoenix to Fairbanks? I'm looking to go back in time."

∾

"What did you find?" asks Cooley.

"It's still impossible to go down. Too old, too dangerous. Your people found the secondary adit and were able to get close to the shaft, but it was blocked. You probably have this information already, but it looks like a semi-recent cave-in, maybe caused by Sam's fall. I heard a sound just after he fell." Walt Kramer curls his lips inward before he speaks into the phone again. "Same conclusion. His body's down there, but the shaft is just too deep to make recovery possible. I think he knew what he was doing."

"So, what will you do with your hunches and the old professor's strange words?"

"I'll make one more last trip to Arizona, talk to those guys in the bar to try and convince them I'm an old fool too. I'd like to spend a little time with the one lady, Thalia Fisher. Maybe she'll reveal something new. Maybe it's just as you surmised, a journalist who's poking around for more stories. She's still there, isn't she?" asks Kramer.

"Yeah. I'd like you to spend a little time with Hector Dehiya. He's got an interesting take on all of this."

"The Navajo worker?" asks Walt.

"Actually, he's part Hopi too. Clean record, but what made him remarkable was Lizardo the bounty hunter had him arrested. I didn't want it to be a distraction as I watched the drama unfold in Why, but when I talked to him the first time, he proved to be a fascinating man. Battling a demon of sorts. Says he's communicating with another's soul. Right up your alley, Kramer. Maybe you can get him in touch with the Soviet boy again." Cooley laughs briefly on his end of the phone, but he does want Walt to talk with Hector. "My theory is your son met Hector somewhere, maybe at a bar in the Four Corners area or in Mexico when your son was on the lam, and they talked. Hector knows stuff but doesn't have a framework for it. Just random information swirling in his head that's just now coming back to him. Maybe the two of them got drunk or stoned together."

"Sam spent a year in Hermosillo, Mexico, working at a Ford plant. Could they have met there?" asks Walt.

"Maybe, but I don't think so. I found nothing about Hector ever being in Hermosillo. He told me some strange things, but I never felt like he was lying to me. Mistaken maybe, but not dishonest. When I observed him in Why, he worked all day long. Seemed like a good man, probably a lot like your son was. Besides the physical similarities, it's what made me consider he was your son. I gave up on that strain immediately though."

Walt Kramer considers Cooley's words. When Walt was observing the collection of people in the borough of Rubicon, he heard mention of Hector, but he didn't follow up. Is this what he missed? Barkley said, *Across the river*. "What river? It's a desert."

"Did you say something, Kramer? I didn't quite hear you," asks Cooley.

"Just talking to myself. My wife says I do it often. Thanks, Cooley. Anything else?"

"Lizardo. Don't let him get in the way. He got beat up by Peru one night and now seems to want revenge on the whole group. It's why he had Hector arrested; to get back at Peru. Now, he's gathering information on everyone in Rubicon. Lizardo's smart enough to follow a trail, but not smart enough to connect any larger dots, if indeed there are any dots in the desert." Cooley makes a note to himself. "Let's talk again, Kramer, after you get back. In the meantime, I'm going to see what more I can find on Lizardo. I have a tip that he's angling for the reward money PD is offering for info on the shooting of the little girl."

∽

Bellena sips her wine and lightly sings in unison with the songs on her dad's tape deck. She lays her head on Walt's shoulder occasionally and touches Babette, the Princess, who lies sleeping on Walt's chest. "Last time?" she asks.

Walt leans his head over onto his wife's head. "I said that once before, so I won't promise. It's an itch, Belle."

"Maybe you could relocate the whole group to Buena Vista so we could keep a tighter watch on them."

"Could you find them a neighborhood where they could live in close proximity? It would need a bar."

"Oh, Walt, this past year plus, you've become a gentler man. Princecella, for sure, but also your feelings for Sam. If this is the essence of fatherhood, I like it." Bellena closes her eyes and ever so slightly snuggles closer to her husband.

Family, thinks Walt, but only for a moment. His thoughts move deliberately back to Rubicon, Arizona, a neighborhood now sweltering in the summer heat of the Sonoran Desert where he hopes a missing piece might still be found.

20

A MONSOON THUNDERSTORM, LATE JULY 1987

The storm is hit or miss, as monsoon thunderstorms tend to be. Tucson and Sells receive a drenching, but, so far, Why remains dry. 1987 will be remembered for the latest start to the monsoon season on record in Arizona, and one of the driest. The last few days of July. "A line of thunderstorms," says the Phoenix weatherman, but already a month late, this one provides no moisture for the desert sands near Rubicon. Still, the dry lightning sends the desert creatures scurrying, hopping, and scampering for shelter. The sky is alive and magnificent as the strikes dance from the heavy clouds to the desert floor. Maybe the next cloud in line will drop rain on Why and bring out the creosote smell that defines the Sonoran Desert, sweet and earthy.

Smitty arrives at The Call wearing golfing shorts and an expensive golf shirt. "Ninety-eight," he proclaims to the Guardians, who understand breaking 100 at the Ajo course most likely included several mulligans and gimmes. Still, they know breaking the century mark is a rare occurrence for him under any circumstance. Smitty hugs both Julie and Crystal at the bar on his way to the table where CJ, Jack, Alf, and Cocker sit, all with a beer in front of them. Julie moves behind the bar to get a mug from the cooler and fills it with draught beer. She hands it to Crystal who walks it over to where Smitty has sat down and places it in front of him. Her other hand rests on his shoulder for a moment.

"Any birdies?" asks Alf.

Smitty shakes his head. "No, but a handful of pars and no quads. Consistency is my game." The table laughs. He makes a satisfying sound as he drinks from the mug, then lifts his glass in a mock toast; more of a "Good to be with you guys" salute. A good round of golf eases lots of concerns. "Any word?"

"No," answers Jack. He leans into the table, angling toward Smitty.

"Got a long-distance call from a friend of ours in Fairbanks this morning. Said a tall, skinny guy asked about me before renting a car to drive north." The sentence is phrased in such a way as to expect a knowledgeable response.

"Ah, must be our old friend Tabor. Did he give Lizardo anything on us?" asks Smitty.

"Nothing incriminating. It's nice to have friends in the right places," says Jack.

Smitty nods, takes another long drink, and removes a folded paper from his breast pocket. He holds it at arm's length both to read the small print and for effect. "It says here . . . 'anonymous Soviet sources reveal the city of Yamantov in the northern Urals near Pechora was being constructed as a secret military base, contrary to official Soviet sources.'"

The table goes silent: wondering, considering, waiting.

Finally, Jack asks, "Anything else?"

"No, but if it was military, then it raises questions as to its purpose. It wasn't a power plant for the region, contrary to what we were first led to believe, so it becomes . . . suspect." Smitty looks over the heads of his friends at the table to the dart board on the wall. One dart is in the triple one spot, a second in the five segment, and a third has just missed the triple twenty. Twenty-eight points. All close to the most prized triple twenty, an area comprising less than one percent of the board, but none inside. "Kramer's son was Navy, right?"

"He said he was," answers Jack.

"Record says he served on a destroyer in the Pacific fleet." Smitty gets up, walks to the dart board, removes the three darts, and steps back behind a line marking the spot where a person stands when playing. He's skeptical about the navy file. His first toss finds the triple twenty bed, as does his second. His third dart strikes the metal divider between the one and twenty slices and falls to the floor. Smitty walks over, picks it up, looks at it suspiciously, and then pushes it into the board outside the scoring zone. "One hundred and twenty points. Not bad." He returns to his chair and sips his beer, while the others wait. He looks to Jack and nods. "How many years have we been paranoid about the government?"

The Why Intersection

From behind the bar, Julie gives a sarcastic laugh. "Too long. Decades. Made us all afraid of our shadows."

Cocker sits up and nods. "Yep, even me, and I'm the most rational person here." Alf leans over and punches Cocker in the arm, but nods in agreement.

"Are you saying we're fools, Mr. Smithfield," says Jack.

"Oh, we're fools all right, but only because our horizon has been limited. We've all had problems with the local police in various places, but they haven't sat in their offices plotting our every move, and we've been forgotten. We're a bunch of people who had big dreams about this country and where it was headed, but we got caught up in our own importance, I guess. We're not real fools, just a collection of guys . . . and you, Julie, who let our fears take over our dreams. We got scared away. For you, Jack, it started in Alaska when you tried to blow yourself up. Those were real government people who investigated the explosion, but they couldn't prove anything and went away, except in our own minds. For over a decade, we've been seeing them behind every cactus here in the desert." Smitty looks to Jack and raises his eyebrows. "But, my friend, for important things, the government is out there spying on us, and this is one of those things. It ain't Lizardo, but it's been looking in on our little borough of Rubicon, and it's about to show its reach."

"Lizardo's in Alaska, you said, trying to find stuff on us, but now you say he ain't *The Government*?" says Alf.

"That's what I'm saying. He's smaller than us and of less consequence. He's a pain in the ass, but I don't think he's connected to anything above the courthouses in Phoenix and Tucson. He is what he is, a hunter. He's got no philosophy, just adrenaline."

"Jesus, Smitty, you break a hundred, and now you've got all the answers," laughs Jack.

"What if you're wrong about Lizardo?"

"It wouldn't be the first time, but I don't think so."

A sudden gust of wind rattles the screen door at The Call, and within seconds a hard rain begins. Rubicon's first monsoon thunderstorm. A thunderclap explodes over Mesquite Avenue.

Thalia and Hector sit in her car waiting for the water to subside. Flash flood, a common occurrence, common enough for road signs to warn drivers not to enter a wash when water is present. The storm didn't drop a single drop on them, but they could see it off to the west and knew a flood was possible. It's a minor delay.

"You looked at Baboquivari pretty hard back there," says Thalia.

"Must have been the Indian in me," says Hector.

"Any answers?"

"Just that that granite block makes me see how small and transient I am, how small everyone really is. Not to say unimportant, but it makes me reflect. Up north, it's those monoliths on my reservation rising straight up out of the desert floor like Shiprock."

"I've passed through your reservation, through your desert. I like this one a whole lot better. Not so desolate," says Thalia. "You have a way of deflecting the conversation away from yourself, you know. You hide yourself."

"Thalia, I'm not naturally outgoing to begin with, but now I've got people seeking me out for reasons I can't comprehend. I seem to be in touch somehow with the thoughts of a man the feds believe is dead. A man that only Rubicon sees who's placed his soul in safe keeping. Not really his soul though. Another man from Colorado, an important man, has visited Rubicon three times to get information about the person I'm channeling. And to top it all off, I don't believe I'm a shaman or someone who carries the souls of dead people. People don't carry around other people's souls; that's witch-doctor stuff." There is exasperation in Hector's tone. "A strong wind arises suddenly and knocks me down. The next thing I know, I'm sensing feelings and thoughts I've never contemplated before, and these are directing me to go to the desert in southern Arizona for God knows whatever reason. If I was the only one experiencing this, then I could say I'm crazy and get on with my life, but my gut, *the soul within*, tells me I'm not crazy, that this journey has a purpose. What I want to say is, 'Screw this,' and go home, go back to Gallup and build highways. I want everyone to leave me alone, everyone except you, and I fear when this is settled, I'll lose you and be who I once was." Hector's emotions cause him to bite

The Why Intersection

the inside of his cheek. "Why me?" He looks at Baboquivari, the big rock that defines the reservation.

Thalia takes his hand and waits. She remembers the day he first came into The Call, when he seemed both curious and vulnerable. At this moment, only the vulnerability is apparent. She decides to respond from a different angle. "You can't buy peanut butter and bread any more at The Call. You know that; you haven't been able to for a year. It's just a bar now, except in the mornings during the school year. Since you arrived a little over a year ago, Rubicon has closed in on itself, even more so than it already was. But it's still five paranoid men and a couple of their women." She humphs. "Then there's the supporting crew: me, Jade, Crystal, and Ruby, and the children. That's Rubicon, and it's a hoot. I came to write a single story about the baby trade, but I'm still here, and you know why?" She pauses. "You. I've written a second story, and both have been published, and I'm writing a third. I can find other stories in places a lot more beautiful and social than Why, Arizona. Trust me on that, but not more intriguing or mysterious or captivating, and at the heart of it is this guy who's carrying around the soul of some guy who is mostly invisible. If I lived back in Michigan, I would never concoct or believe such a tale, but here in the desert, it's not so implausible."

Hector smiles. "People will think the heat has melted your brain."

She squeezes his hand. "If you're going to live in Rubicon, you need to learn to ignore what others think about your motives. We're as far from government as a person can get in America, and yet it sits on the shoulder of everyone who holds a regular chair at the table in The Call and most of those loners and ranchers who come in for a once-a-week beer."

"So, what are you telling me?" asks Hector.

She nods to the road ahead which has dried. "That carrying around a stranger's soul isn't so strange in this desert."

☙

Planting drugs on the unsuspecting involves no deception or genius. For an envelope of cash or a once-strong friendship, a baggage handler wraps a key of weed and a packet of cocaine in a pair of socks and returns it to the suitcase. Authorities are notified to be aware of the unsuspecting carrier when he deplanes in Phoenix, to run a cursory check for possible recreational smuggling. The marijuana might be overlooked if one has the proper connections, but cocaine will land you in jail for a time. Even a bounty hunter with extensive knowledge of the system, with connections to lawyers, judges, and bail bondsmen will be placed in a sticky situation. The message is delivered to Lizardo at his cell in Phoenix.

Surprise. Two can play your game. Some have more to lose than others. You might want to consider returning to your day job. We live where we do for the purpose of being left alone.

Alf fiddles with his ring, a silver band with Native-American designs, the type of ring one might buy for a few dollars at a Saturday morning farmers' market in Tucson, except Alf's is pure silver and an original piece of art. His wife had it made especially for him by an artist from Chihuahua, Mexico, part of her extended family when they married. It is not as snug as it once was when he was a miner, and his wife fixed him three meals each day. Alf has lost weight in the past three years and has not been in the mine since 1983. The Guardians haven't talked about the strike recently; speculation about Hector is center stage. Early on, when Hector first appeared in Why, Alf thought he might be a scab or a rat for Phelps Dodge. Another example of the paranoia living in Rubicon. Still, suspicion remains as to who Hector really is and why the government wants him. Alf wonders about Hector's brief jail time and his transfer after his arrest. Doesn't ring true to Alf. Cahoots, but with who . . . and why? If he's coming back, then maybe Hector hasn't discovered everything. Alf snaps his ring between his thumb and index finger again.

When she returned from northern Arizona, Julie replaced the Alaska map behind the bar with one of Arizona. Today, while everyone waits for Thalia and Hector to return, she studies it. Completely surrounded by the great Navajo reservation in the northeast portion of Arizona is a smaller Hopi reservation. Their borders were drawn by White officials two thousand miles to the east in Washington. During

The Why Intersection

her recent stay, she heard talk about relocation of some Navajos living near the Hopi borders. Their borders have to be more open than the one between Mexico and the United States, and especially the southern border of the Tohono O'odham reservation. But maybe not. "Borders!" she spits out.

Jade's oldest boy enters The Call. "Have you seen my mom?" he asks Julie. She points to the table on the far side of the bar. He walks over quickly and whispers into his mother's ear. Jade rises, says "A little accident at home needs my attention. I'll be back as soon as I can" and leaves.

Cocker looks to CJ for a response. CJ smiles. "It's over, Cock. We're from different places, and she's got more questions for me than I have answers. Not like Libby, who accepts you for who you are. How do I get one like her?"

"I'm a fortunate man, CJ. I stumbled into it and keep stumbling, but she keeps forgiving me. God didn't seem to make many like her, and for that I am truly blessed."

"Yes, you are, Cock. Yes, you are."

A line of traffic follows Thalia and Hector; all had been waiting for the water to recede in the wash. Six trucks and one white van, none of which seem impatient with the speed of the caravan and getting longer. Thalia drives at the speed limit, a speed at which she is often passed on the long, lonely roads traversing the Sonoran Desert.

"It appears we have company," says Hector.

Thalia looks out her rearview mirror and studies the procession for a few moments. "How can you tell?"

Hector smites his chest and smiles. "A ghost warned me. Slow down a bit and see if anyone passes."

When she does, the first two pickups pull around her, but the white van maintains its distance, slowing its speed to match Thalia's. Two more trucks pass both the van and Thalia, leaving two pickups behind the van at a considerable distance. "It could be a coincidence," says Thalia.

"The van maybe, but not the pickups. Indians on the reservation have no patience and need to win the road race," says Hector. "It's in our genes."

"Now there's a stereotype if I ever heard of one. Are you implying the people in the van and those remaining trucks aren't Native-American?"

Hector reaches over and squeezes Thalia's neck, allowing his hand to remain there. "Let's see how this plays out as we approach the junction at Why."

"Or I could simply pull over and let them pass."

"I'll bet if you do, they'll be parked at the convenience store or The Kitchen just waiting for us." Hector looks back to the van. "If you see a spot where you can pull over, let's try that."

Within a mile Thalia pulls to the side of the road, allowing the van, two pickups, a Border Patrol green and white truck, and two sedans new to the caravan with California plates to pass. She waits until they are down the highway a mile before pulling back onto the road. "Okay, let's see what develops."

He smiles as he passes Thalia's car; he knows she and Hector noticed a tail, but he doubts it's him they suspect. For sure they will notice Cooley, but they will drop their guard when the remaining vehicles pass by. Cooley does have the resources available; a van filled with sophisticated, high tech listening devices, but it shouldn't have been following so closely. Probably a rookie driver, an Army pfc or a Navy seaman. Why Cooley is driving a second vehicle surprises the man though. He scratches his chin and pushes back his baseball cap. This will be an interesting afternoon and evening in Rubicon.

"They should be here by now," says Julie.

"Soon," responds Jack. "Soon. Finish your thought, Cocker."

"Just sayin', our problems aren't race or ethnic groups; it's all about poverty. Rich blacks or Mexicans fit in and can be mostly accepted anywhere. They have all the advantages as rich people anywhere, but if you're poor, it don't matter. Maybe if you're poor and black, it's multiplied, but it's poverty, plain and simple."

"You're naïve, Cock. Here in Arizona, it's poor and Chicano. No chance," injects Alf. He snaps his ring hard against his thumb. The sound of a car stopping in front of The Call halts the conversation.

"They're here," says Julie. She wipes her hands on the bar towel and then dries them on her jeans before stepping out from behind the bar. When Thalia and Hector enter, Julie gives each one a hug. "How's jail?"

Hector smiles. "Cleaner than my place, better food, better air conditioning, just a little lonesome."

"You saying you missed us, young fellow?" says Smitty. Along with the others, Smitty rises and shakes Hector's hand. "Welcome back."

Crystal brings two beers and sets them on the table in front of two empty chairs. "Anyone else?"

"Just bring a couple of pitchers, Crystal, if you would please," says Jack. As the crew settles in, Jack lifts his mug. "Jail time, Hector. You're one of us now."

Hector is clearly embarrassed. He broke no law, doesn't know what charges would be filed, spent less than an hour in a real jail, and was treated well, even during the interrogation by Cooley. A thought crosses his mind. Why are all his pursuers called by one name? Cooley, Lizardo, Kramer. The eyes of each person at the table are on him, and it makes him self-conscious. He shouldn't be the person of interest here. More than when he told Thalia in the car an hour earlier, he wants to be rid of this and return to the reservation. Is there such a thing as a reverse wind? Could he walk backward along that dirt road and give back the soul, or whatever came to him on that day?

"I doubt," he begins, "that I deserve to be in your inner circle."

Thalia notices his discomfort, feels his discomfort too. She wants to slide her hand onto his thigh beneath the table to reassure him but isn't sure it would have that effect on him. It might just make him more uncomfortable. She wants answers too; she's as eager as Jack or Alf or Smitty to hear his story.

The door opens and Jade returns. "Have I missed anything?" Her question typifies the mood of Rubicon.

༄

"Are you getting it?" asks the seaman to Cooley, who nods.

"Your reach extends farther than mine," says Walt Kramer. "No legal search warrant for this wiretap?"

"*I'm The Government*, Walt." Cooley turns back to the naval technician. "If you hear any of the key words, let me know. Make a note of who references them." Cooley and Kramer exit the cramped van into the blazing summer afternoon heat. A substantial portable air conditioner pumps cool air into the van. "How anyone can stand this heat is beyond me. Care to join me in my trailer for a beer?"

Walt politely refuses. "I need a nap and to call my wife. Maybe my daughter will say something over the phone. I appreciate the amenities you've provided in my RV, especially the extra-strength air conditioner. This heat is oppressive." The men enter neighboring trailers, recently rented by fake old men to avoid suspicion. Walt's is an Airstream Excella, luxurious by any standards. Cooley's is also an Airstream, but his is an office on wheels, fully equipped for rapid communications between Why, Arizona, and Washington, D.C. Neither man completely trusts the other, although both are seeking answers for the death of a Navy middle grade officer who held secrets no individual should know, a man who committed suicide, a man Walt Kramer believes could not accept his actions that led to the death of 10,000 Russians four years earlier, the "Keyman" whose guilt transcended his will to live. Cooley, on the other hand, is skeptical of the sun's appearance an hour before dawn. Until it happens, there is doubt. With no body in tow, Samuel Elkington may still be alive, and if he's alive, the nation's most closely guarded secret is vulnerable, a U.S. first strike on a Soviet military base.

Inside his trailer Walt takes a beer from the miniature refrigerator and sits at the cramped table and picks up the telephone. Before he dials, a thought comes to him. Has Cooley bugged his phone? He sets the phone back into its cradle, takes a sip of his beer, and nods. Most likely, but he'll need his call to Bellena on record, and somehow, he needs to warn her to monitor her words. She's in on the plan. Walt drinks his beer. When he finishes, he steps outside to retrieve a pouch from under the front seat of his truck. Inside his trailer he unwraps the secure mobile phone and remembers when he instructed a young boy to fetch it for him outside of a mine near Buena Vista, Colorado, while a distraught man sat in the darkness of an abandoned mine. Walt dials his wife's number.

"Hey, it's me. I miss you and our Princess."

"We miss you too. She's napping at the moment. Everything going okay?" asks Bellena.

"Too good. I'm calling on the bag phone, because I think the phone in the trailer may be bugged. After we finish this call, I'll call you on it but watch your words."

"The reach of the government even reaches into its own, huh?" says Bellena.

Lightning flashes near Rubicon and within seconds, rain pours down. The noise on the roofs, some of them tin, makes hearing difficult. The lights in The Call flicker, but don't go out. The rain turns Why's dirt roads to muddy paths, nearly impossible to navigate while it rains, but they dry quickly. This monsoon rain will create flash floods in the washes and arroyos for miles; floods in areas that receive no direct rain, much like the flood that blocked the highway near Sells for Thalia and Hector. Because of the noise, the people in The Call stay quiet and drink. They wait for the rain to cease so they can ask Hector questions they've been pondering since his arrest. Monsoon rains arrive quickly, but they leave rapidly, and the desert comes alive.

"So, Hector, how was it?" asks Alf.

"Since I've never been in jail before, I can't compare it to anything, but it was comfortable." Hector smiles, almost in an apologizing way. He knows several of the men at the table have spent time behind bars. He wonders if Julie has. "In truth, it wasn't jail, it was detention for my unknown transgression. It was a guarded military barracks room; quite comfortable."

"No intensive questioning?" asks CJ in a semi-joking manner. "No torture?"

"It was serious questioning, but they didn't use pliers to pull out my fingernails." The table laughs. Hector volunteers the information he has, from his arrest at his house a couple of blocks over from The Call to being retrieved by Thalia earlier in the day. "The interrogator was an interesting man. Polite, yes, but focused. He wants something, or should I say, someone, but it isn't me. He doesn't for a moment believe in the supernatural; he's like a soldier seeking the return of all his men after a battle and wants an accounting of each one. If he had wanted, he could have broken me down, but that wasn't his way, at least with me. I got the feeling he knew every response I was giving him before he asked the question but was probing for a response he didn't expect. I've never been questioned like that before. It was unnerving." The men nod their heads and listen. "I have a question for you guys. How did Lizardo react when his prisoner disappeared? I can't imagine he was too happy."

Jack looks at Smitty and smiles, a look of accomplishment, and Smitty smiles back. Alf pinches his nose and nods. CJ places a hand on his brother's forearm. Julie steps into Thalia's back and puts both hands on her shoulders. In a moment, Jack answers. "It seems he got arrested himself. Up in Phoenix when he got off a plane. Seems he was carrying some drugs in his suitcase that he couldn't explain."

"You'd think he would be smarter than that," says Smitty. "You know, a law officer smuggling drugs. Even a bunch of losers like us here in Rubicon who have a history with drugs know you can't do that."

"I hear he got bail, but the judge was none too happy with him," adds Cocker. "Damn shame, Lizardo's such a nice guy."

A slight smile crosses Hector's lips. He nods. "So, I think I owe a round then." He looks to Crystal.

As she begins to pull beers from the cooler, Jack says, "On the house."

The two doors into the bar are open to allow for the breeze to penetrate the heat. Walt Kramer enters the open front door, and without giving a greeting, he sits on a stool at the bar across from Crystal. He nods for a beer. When she hands him a Corona, he swivels to the table. "Don't mind me; I'm just here to drink."

"Well, look what the wind blew in," says Jack. It's not a challenge, but a subtle welcome. "How long's it been, stranger?"

"Let's see. Five, six, seven months or so. It gets lonely back in Colorado. Those people I work with are too focused on their work to take time off for small talk and beers, so I thought I'd drive over and say hi." Walt knows exactly how long it's been, to the day.

Hector, whose back is to Kramer, slides his chair out and gets up. He turns to the man at the bar, studies him for a moment, and then looks over at Thalia. "I didn't feel Kramer today," he whispers. Hector takes the three steps over to the bar to face Kramer and raises his hand to shake Walt's.

Kramer takes Hector's hand firmly. "Seems like we've been missing each other on my visits, son."

The two men study one another, while the rest of the bar watches carefully. Thalia notices a relaxation in Hector's cheeks as the two men continue to grip each other's hand. She can see the side of each man's face, and their expressions seem to mirror the other's, like they're seeing something that's always been there, but hasn't been recognized before. A discovery. A warmth. Thalia thinks Hector has something to say, but can't figure out how to begin, so he waits. From behind, Jade puts her hands on Thalia's hips and her chin on Thalia's shoulder.

"Why don't you join us at the table, Kramer?" says Jack.

Walt nods. Before he moves, he takes a pen from his front pants pocket and scribbles a few words on a napkin. He stands, hands the paper to Jack, sits in the chair between Jack and Smitty and raises his beer bottle to the Guardians and their extended family.

Jack reads the napkin silently and shows it to the table, *"Watch your words; we're bugged."*

21

DINNER IN AJO

"You are full of surprises, Kramer," says Smitty.

Rubicon sits in the banquet room at the All-American restaurant in Ajo. Semi-private. It's a public restaurant in a town on life support tied to a shuttered mine and a discredited, defeated, angry union. It's a room that used to hold celebrations of all kinds common to small towns, from Little League to bowling leagues, weddings to quinceaneras, job promotions to graduations, baptisms to retirements. Not so much any longer, not since the mine closed, and like every other business that hasn't closed down, the All-American restaurant barely hangs on. Old Ajo, a mining town, will pass on. In its place a different Ajo, a retirement community, will arise, but it will take time.

"My father-in-law jokingly calls it pathetic. I know what I saw, saw it with my own eyes up close and very personal, but because others demand greater proof, I keep allowing myself to get sucked in." Walt looks across the table to where Thalia sits between Hector and Jade. Thalia is not the woman he met briefly at Barkley's funeral, nor is Jade. That much he had previously established, and Hector is, well, Hector. Still, he thinks. Walt counts the people at the table.

"Kramer," interrupts Smitty, "do you always go off by yourself in the middle of a conversation?"

Walt laughs. "As a matter of fact, I do. My wife constantly tells me about this, but she tolerates it nowadays."

"What were you counting just now?" asks Smitty.

"People here at the table."

"It's a quorum. The total population of Rubicon is seventeen, ten adults and seven kids. Eighteen if you count Hector, but he doesn't actually live in the neighborhood. He's over by the oil tanks, a few blocks over. I don't count Libby even though she's here a good part of the time, but she technically resides on the reservation."

Walt nods. "Does anybody ever move out of Rubicon?"

"People come and go. Julie tried earlier this year but was drawn back. Libby's oldest daughter tried to move in, but she was killed in a car wreck about five miles into the reservation. Happened one evening when she was heading back to Sells after moving some furniture into one of the rentals, the one Ruby lives in now. Her marker is on the eastbound side of 86. Libby keeps it up regularly. Just a nineteen-year-old kid." Smitty pauses before adding, "That was a half-dozen years ago, not long after Libby lost her husband too. I'm not sure Libby has ever gotten over it." The earlier buzz at the table ceases as they tune into Smitty's words.

Cocker drops his head, takes a hold of Libby's hand, and mumbles a prayer. When he finishes, he crosses himself and says amen. "You want me to say a prayer for your boy, Kramer?" he asks.

Before Walt can answer, Libby speaks. "Losing a child hurts like no other pain. It never goes away, not even if we are sure our child has been taken up to the mountain, or in your case, to Heaven. My Princess died too early; she had been drinking. Her soul is not on the mountain yet; it wasn't ready. I hadn't prepared her properly."

"Hush on that, Libby," says Cocker. "You were a good mother to her."

Walt slides forward in his chair. "Your daughter's name was Princess?"

"Not was, is." Libby's eyes catch Walt's, and she adds, "Your daughter's middle name is Princess."

Walt's breath catches. "Babette Princecella. Prince-cella," he says breaking up his daughter's name to account for her unique spelling. "She's named after a nearby mountain in Colorado."

Slowly at first, but more quickly, each head at the table turns to Smitty. Jack's. Julie's. CJ's. Alf's. Crystal's. Jade's. Cocker's. Libby's. Thalia and Hector keep their eyes on Walt who has noticed the turning of the heads but stays with Thalia and Hector. There is a secret at the table, in Rubicon, that Kramer doesn't know, but he now knows exists. Smitty waits until he gets the attention of the last three.

"This isn't the place, too many ears. With the arrival of that government van, it appears as though Rubicon has grown another pair. We kid Jack about his paranoia, but maybe he's been right all these years." There is a soft laugh around the table. "This evening, we will enjoy the meal, the companionship, and later tonight, after midnight, one of us will come get you and let you observe our ritual." Smitty's smile promises more. "Whose turn is it to say the blessing?"

∞

Cooley hears Walt's truck drive up to his Airstream. The Navy officer watches as Walt turns off his engine but remains in the driver's seat. If there is one thing Cooley has learned about Kramer, it's he leaves no stone unturned as his mind plays every scenario over and over. The dossiers on him were accurate. Cooley grabs two glasses and a bottle of scotch from the cupboard over his workstation and heads out. He taps on the truck window, mildly startling Walt. Cooley lifts the scotch to eye level, and the pondering man lowers the window separating him from the government man.

"Nightcap?" asks Cooley.

Inside, a single nip moves toward a few.

"They know they're being monitored, don't they," says Cooley, not as a question but as an observation. Walt nods and Cooley continues. "This is an interesting dynamic, Kramer. You and I work to move this country forward and to keep it safe, you especially with your work at that nuclear power plant and your, shall I say, consulting work with the entire nuclear field." Walt understands and allows Cooley to continue. "I pegged you for a completely objective man; that's the report I got, but you're much more complicated. My guess is it's the family part of all this. Then, there's this group of vagabonds here in Why. What a collection. I'm not sure you could imagine a stranger group."

"They're united in their suspicions. Jack and Alf are angry, Thalia and Smitty and maybe Jade are as curious about the world as all get out, Cocker and Libby are spiritual. Crystal and Rose can't get past the strike, although Crystal may be moving ahead slowly. And then there's CJ. He and Jade were together for a few months, maybe a bit longer, but not anymore. He's the loner in the group and the one who has no easy handle. He has no outside ties of note. I don't know if you found this out, but he and Cocker are half-brothers. By their dad."

"You left out Hector," says Cooley.

"That's because he's not himself, and saying this, I'm not sure I

The Why Intersection

know what I mean. I'm good at what I do because I size up people fast and accurately." Walt reaches across the small table, takes the scotch bottle, and pours himself another half inch of alcohol. "My guess is Hector looks in the mirror each morning trying to decide if the image is reflecting his life back at himself or reversing the image like a camera does."

Cooley follows suit with the scotch but doesn't immediately drink from his glass. "When I questioned him back in Tucson, he would say the most unusual things, as if he was telling someone else's story." Now Cooley drinks from his glass.

It seems to Walt as if Cooley is conversing with his scotch rather than to him. Walt waits until Cooley looks up before he answers. "Hector doesn't comprehend it all, the depths of this. He holds no judgements about the goings on in Why. Remarkable fellow. I spoke briefly to him tonight after dinner, and he indicated he wanted to sit down with me and tell me all he can, to answer any question I might have. He's very confused about this."

Cooley nods. "He's trying and I know he bounces things off Thalia, but even his Navajo experiences haven't helped. Naïve and totally honest as far as I could discern. He told me he came here because the wind blew him over, and he took it as a sign from Nature. In the year-plus he's been here, his appearance has been altered. His weight has fluctuated; his skin tones even seem to change from reddish to brown to pale. He's like a mood ring. You probably already know this, Kramer, but Rubicon relocates people. It's like a safe house along the freedom trail. It's what binds this neighborhood together so closely. Alf and Jack started out as fugitives; Smitty and Cocker took them in. As I just said, now, it's the whole neighborhood."

Walt tilts his head in agreement. "Central American refugees mostly, some babies a while back but no more, a few protest fugitives." He knows. "What about souls?"

Cooley laughs out loud. "So, you heard the story too? Hector was sure he was channeling a soul and offered it might be someone else trying to avoid capture." Cooley catches himself. For over three years, he has referred to his fugitive by his last name. Elkington. But with Samuel Elkington's father sitting across the table from him, Cooley now sees Elkington in a different light. "Sam's. Sorry."

"No apology necessary. We both know my son died in the mine. I saw it. You and your men examined the evidence and concluded the same. Pistol with his blood on the barrel. Except for there's one missing component. No body."

"Yeah, no body." Cooley shakes his head in a way that indicates there is still one loose end, and that missing piece keeps his task incomplete. "Your son was a good sailor, Kramer." Cooley amends his statement. "No, he was an excellent tar. He couldn't have been a keyman if he wasn't. He released that missile to protect his country, thinking we were at war. When his boat returned to port, he found out we weren't. It was a preemptive strike. Lots of non-military people died. A heavy pack to carry. The psychiatrist in Seattle listened to a man tortured by his role in the destruction of Yamantov." The Navy officer gently pauses. "Take my advice, Kramer, and let it go with that. Your son did his duty. He was a casualty of the Cold War too."

Walt pours himself another inch, certainly not enough scotch to drown in. "So, you're following this one last lead. My movement to this remote outpost set off a warning bell—and you got the call." Walt shakes his head before he continues. "It will haunt you, you know. You'll get an unconfirmed sighting from Seattle and fly there. Or from Chicago. Or Hermosillo. You'll make a career out of this futile search. Take your own advice, Cooley, and let it go."

"And you, Kramer. I know you're about to retire, just tying up loose ends. Why do you keep coming back?"

"Homage."

"To whom?"

"To Sam. To Barkley. To Yamantov. I don't know. To a guilty father mostly."

"Go home to your wife and little girl." Cooley smiles wryly and lifts his glass in a toast to this unspoken bond between two old soldiers. He stands and nods knowingly. "I'll have my partner turn off his listening devices so you can go witness that 'ritual' later tonight."

☙

Cocker moves around the Tabernacle using only the light from a

The Why Intersection

single table lamp. He stares at the unpainted square looking for understanding. He bends to the paint can, pries it open, dips his brush, and paints a door frame, extending to the floor.

From behind a free-standing closet, a man steps silently toward Cocker.

∽

"I guess this soul is a big deal," says Hector. Since returning to Rubicon after the dinner, he hasn't sat down, and now he is referring to his passenger as a soul. Hector paces, pauses, and verbalizes segments of his thoughts to Thalia, who listens without comment. She understands the difficulty of his position and his uncertainty of his future. When Hector first arrived a little over a year ago, not in Rubicon, but in Why, there was the usual suspicion. It was Libby who cautioned the Guardians to tread lightly, that something was occurring in his life creating instability. Not distrust, but an air of uncertainty. "A passage," was how she referred to it. Thalia felt it when Hector first bought supplies. Libby's warning kept Waddell Smithfield from renting out the last house in Rubicon to Hector even after he showed his value as a worker, allowing him to stay just outside the neighborhood all these months. Libby's words carry clout. To the residents of Rubicon, she is the Voice of the Desert, its spirit incarnate, and when she cautioned Smitty and Jack, they heeded her words. To Cocker, Libby provided a different message, but Cocker's heart is not Jack's heart—or Smitty's. "He is your congregation. Help him find his path."

"What if what I have isn't a soul?" asks Hector. He stops, turns to Thalia, and for the first time since she sat on the couch in her house, he wants her to respond.

"What else could it be?" She laughs. "I have never believed in this kind of... stuff, and now I say that, like I am a follower of Shamanism." She stands and takes Hector's hands in hers, forcing him to look her in the eye. "Was there lightning when the wind blew you over?"

"No, just wind. Like a very strong dust devil." Hector smiles. "Jego, remember."

"These things you tell me, these things that aren't you, where else could they come from?"

"Jack might say the government implanted a chip in my brain and is programming me to say these things."

"Jack says a lot of ridiculous, paranoid things." Thalia pulls Hector into a hug, not a lover hug, but a big sister hug. She holds him while they both ponder his initial question? "What else could it be?" Her cuckoo clock chimes midnight. "It's time to go."

"It will most likely be too dark to show you my paint job." Hector's not sure she understands. "Cocker and I painted the Tabernacle. He's not too good, a little shaky, so I would go back when he wasn't there and touch up his work."

Outside, they are joined by the adults of Rubicon quietly walking east, across the wash, past The Kitchen, across AZ 85 to the Tabernacle, a procession of mute people gathering to share their secret with an outsider. Even the neighborhood dogs are silent.

22

THE TABERNACLE

The Tabernacle, Cocker's evangelical church, is the current usage of a crudely constructed vegetable warehouse hastily built in the late-1940s, after a world war challenged religious beliefs to their very core. A place for peace at the intersection of simple America and worldly America. Jesus Christ would be worshipped here in this desert, pushed along in an intimate relationship with the Holy Spirit. At the edge of a Native-American reservation whose people converted to Catholicism centuries earlier when Jesuit missionaries traveled north out of Mexico to convert these primitive people, the Tabernacle would seek to abolish poverty and end suffering while waiting for The Rapture.

When Cocker arrived from southeastern Arizona in 1969 to establish his own congregation as directed by God, he was impatient. The warehouse needed renovations. So, Cocker set up a temporary church a few blocks away in an old cinderblock building covered with adobe. It didn't survive as a church, but it did as a meeting house for wayward souls. Eventually, The Call. But Cocker never abandoned his hope to restore the warehouse to its roots, and a Tohono O'odham woman supported him in his dreams even though she was Catholic. She saw the spirit within him and felt his soul. Sonoran Catholicism: a blend of beliefs that includes the wind.

Rubicon hides in the dark behind the building until no cars are passing, and then one by one they enter the Tabernacle. The few windows have been covered with black construction paper so no one can see in and no light escapes. When the last person enters, CJ closes the door, and they wait. Two end table lamps with recessed 40-watt bulbs cast light across the floor almost as if Why has an ordinance to prevent light from interfering with the telescopes on Kitt Peak over 50 miles to the east.

"Where's Cocker?" asks Alf.

"He'll be here," answers Libby. "He promised. Maybe he went to get our guest." She worries through her words. A breeze drifts in.

They talk among themselves in hushed tones, the way real secrets are passed on. After fifteen minutes, there is a knock at the door. Cocker still has not appeared, and this sharing should not occur without him, cannot occur. CJ unlatches the door, and Crystal's youngest boy escorts Walt Kramer in. CJ closes the door behind the visitor. He motions for Walt to join the others at the front of the building, near the free-standing closet.

"I'm going to go fetch Cocker," says CJ. "He probably fell asleep back at his place. I won't be long.". He cracks the door and slides into the night.

Smitty steps to Walt and shakes his hand. "We do weird things in Rubicon, in case you never noticed. We're moving another sojourner up the line, been looking for a unique location for him. We couldn't just pass him along like the others. Had a hunch you might be interested in this one, in our weird rituals."

Walt holds onto Smitty's hand just a moment longer and responds. "I was snuck into Poland a few years back to retrieve a Solidarity operative. This is right up my alley." He pats Smitty on the back with his free hand and releases the handshake.

"You are a complicated fellow, Kramer, that's for sure. My people couldn't get into that layer of you."

"What's this about Cocker?" asks Walt.

"Don't know for sure. He's just not here. Let's hope CJ can find him, that our resident minister isn't drunk or high."

The door opens suddenly with a jar and two men enter, one shining a flashlight. That man pushes CJ hard into the center of warehouse where he stumbles onto the floor. "Stay down, *Joe.*" The shadows don't disguise the figure who now brandishes a pistol. Lizardo.

The shorter man nods to the taller, younger, fitter man. They use hand signals, barely visible in the darkness. The single streetlight, a frequent target of Cocker's wrath after an evening of drinking, sheds a minimal amount of light on his house. The nod is a go signal. The younger man rams his shoulder into the rear door, which swings open easily. Both men storm the room catching a lookout vulnerable, just

The Why Intersection

buttoning his pants after using the toilet. He surrenders without incident, raising his hands while his slacks slide down to his ankles. The shorter man holsters his weapon, handcuffs the lookout, duct tapes his mouth, and guides the new prisoner to the floor. The shorter man uses additional duct tape around the man's ankles and uses another set of handcuffs to secure him to a radiator. Still, there is no verbal communication. The team enters the bedroom where they find Cocker in a similar condition as the man who was recently bound and gagged. The shorter man puts his finger to his lips, cautioning Cocker to remain quiet while his cuffs and tape are removed.

"Are you okay," whispers Cooley.

Cocker nods.

On their way out, the taller man checks the radiator for its strength. Satisfied, the seaman follows Cooley and Cocker. They run across the deserted desert highway to the Tabernacle. Again, hand signals.

Lizardo flicks his pistol indicating to the Rubiconers to move to the side of the room opposite where a door was painted on the wall just hours earlier. He smirks. "Ignorant losers. Do you think I didn't know? I didn't care about the illegals or babies, but the bail jumpers you hid provided me with a steady income. I got a paycheck for each one. Now, you're going to tell me about the little girl's shooter so I can collect the reward."

"Where's Cocker?" asks Libby.

"Back at his house. I've got a lackey there watching him. He's my ace in the hole. He's not as tough as some of you; he'll talk when I pressure him. Ask *Joe*."

"It's not Cocker you want, it's me." Hector releases Thalia's hand and steps forward. "Prisoner exchange, sort of. No retribution from these people."

"Step back, *Dehiya*, or whatever your name is. If you were important, that Navy officer would never have released you. He's searching for the big fish, too, the guy I want to talk to," Lizardo slows for dramatic effect and turns his head in the direction of Walt. "Step out of the way, Kramer."

Walt moves forward and away from the others. He keeps his eyes on Lizardo's eyes, trying to determine if Lizardo would actually pull the trigger. He determines that he would, but he might hesitate if he knew who his target was. Where did Lizardo get his new information, because he clearly did not possess it earlier? It makes no difference at this moment, but it might down the line.

"You're a bit like a junior high smart ass, Frank. Can I call you *Frank*? You know enough to pretend you're someone, but not enough to realize you aren't. It's no wonder you were fired from the Kansas police force. Too many mistakes by a junior officer makes the rest of the force look bad. It's more than that though; it's you've never been able to tell the good guys from the bad guys. These people have all made mistakes, but most of them were because they were trying to do good. You can't say enough in life about trying to do good." Walt drops his eyes and shuffles two more steps away from the group. His earlier question draws a possible answer, a sensible answer. In response to Walt's movement, Lizardo slides toward the group. "When you lose sight of this, Lizardo, that it's the effort that counts and not just the result, you can forgive yourself a lot of grief. Lot of these people still have a hard time with that too, so you're not alone." Walt pauses. He sees the periphery, sees Jack moving his hand slowly to a side pocket on his chair. "Now might be a good time to put your weapon down, Lizardo, and slide it across the floor to me."

"What the hell are you talking about, Kramer?" Lizardo lifts his pistol to chest level and points it at Walt.

Walt raises both palms indicating to Lizardo to be cool. "Hear me out. You've got the upper hand and can afford to be patient. You've got Cocker." Walt keeps his palms up. "There's only five or six people here who could provide you with the information you think they have, and all of them are in this room, all except Cocker." Walt looks over to Smitty. "One of your group is compromised." He turns back to Lizardo. "Regardless, Lizardo, this is a bad ploy because you can't get away with it. The information you want is inaccessible. To you. To me. You see, that's the secret. This loose collection of losers, as you call them, are loyal. They won't give him up. You could shoot one of us and then ask again, but no one would tell. I'm pretty sure before you got

The Why Intersection

to all of us, you would be dead, because several of us carry." Walt drops his hands. "You can stand up now, CJ. Nice try."

At that moment Cooley and his communications officer open the door at the back of the room, both with weapons drawn. A second later, Cocker bursts through the wall where Hector painted the door earlier in the night. Startled, Lizardo spins and fires. CJ rushes toward his brother, and Lizardo fires again before he is struck by bullets fired by the Guardians. Amid the smoke and confusion, a ghost-like figure slides unnoticed from behind the closet, out Cocker's door, and into the desert darkness.

∾

Desert winds are legendary and have many names. The desert is never still, only more or less windy. Wind is the constant companion, a reality for those who choose to make the desert their home. Earlier, the winds around Why were strong and foreboding, what meteorologists call a convergence when two air masses collide, forcing their power to rise, an updraft that created for a cloudy afternoon in western Arizona. Those winds subsided with the passing of the daylight, and now, only their offspring remains, allowing for a clear night. Far to the east, a lightning storm illuminates the sky on the far side of the Tohono O'odham reservation. What remains in western Arizona is a gentle breeze, but a sad and lonely air movement that carries the desert concert to those with time to hear. The hunters are out, Orion in the sky, and the coyotes and owls searching the terra firma for movement, for prey. On this night, no one in Why has time to marvel at the cosmos or listen to the symphony. What was to be a farewell, a sendoff with closure, has been canceled. Tonight, two Whyans secretly ride the wind out of western Arizona.

∾

Rose and Crystal drive Cocker to the Ajo hospital. Libby won't leave his side. Smitty phones Sheriff Harr in Tucson to see if he could drive out to investigate a "sensitive incident." It will take the sheriff a couple of hours to get to Why, time enough for the Guardians to concoct a believable story, that the conflict was between Lizardo,

Alf, and CJ over the reward PD was offering for information about the shooting that injured the little girl. Captain Cooley's assistant takes Lizardo's lookout to an undisclosed location far from Why. Two bodies lie covered with blankets usually reserved for pilgrims. Jade kneels beside one and weeps. When the crime scene is in order, Smitty sends Jack and Julie back to The Call. "You weren't here." He sits in a plastic chair near the altar with Alf, and the two men finally breathe normally again. At the back of the warehouse, Cooley and Walt Kramer talk in quiet tones.

"How did you know I'd show up?" asks Cooley.

Walt smiles gently. "Because you're good at what you do. Thorough. Because you didn't trust me completely. Because you saw me leave my trailer. I was beginning to be concerned about your timing though. And being Navy . . ." Walt smiles and Cooley nods.

"How'd you figure it was CJ?"

"I wasn't a hundred percent sure, but he seemed willing to remain on the floor while Lizardo threatened the group. His behavior indicated self-guilt. Jack would have spit in Lizardo's eye. Smitty would have at least gotten up and joined the group. Alf would either have jumped back up and started a fight or been shot in the process. I was hoping it wasn't Julie, but it could have been, but when I looked over at her, there was no guilt, just anger. None of them knew the whole story."

"Hector and Thalia?" ask Cooley.

Kramer smiles wryly and shakes his head, as if the answer is obvious. "The two individuals I was seeking from the beginning." He pauses. "Obviously, I let my emotions run amok."

Cooley looks closely at Walt Kramer before extending his hand. "I've got to file a report, Kramer. I hate paperwork. Close this case."

"Done." Walt nods. "You'd have made a good Army soldier, Cooley." It's a backhanded compliment.

The two outsiders shake Smitty's hand and leave, walking back to the RV park together.

☙

Smitty ushered Hector and Thalia out immediately after the shooting before he advised the others on what the story would be for the

The Why Intersection

sheriff. He told Thalia she and Hector might not find the grocery in the house where he has stayed off and on for over a year, Smitty's house, but he would be watching them. "Out back among the cactus, beyond the pool. Call to him. Tell him Barkley wants to see him again. It's code." He handed Thalia the keys to a non-descript Ford station wagon and told her to take it. "It's always packed with provisions. Leave your car here. Our little planned sendoff now has to be an escape. Drive through the reservation. Don't go north immediately. If you sense any problem, stop in Sells at Libby's house. They'll help."

While she knelt beside Cocker before the ambulance arrived, Libby whispered to Hector that it was time to release the soul, give it back to the fugitive. "He will be ready now." She pulled Thalia down and hugged her. "Your grandfather understood. Now, it's your turn."

"Where should I go?" asked Thalia.

"Go back home, Thalia," answered Smitty, "where people know you. Write local stories about good people. We have safe houses along the way."

Libby kisses Thalia on her forehead. "Nurture your new man. Protect him. Allow him to get out into the open air again where the wind can muss his hair. We will pray for you. Now go."

At that moment, Thalia looked into the eyes of both Libby and Smitty—and they were the same.

∾

Diego sits in Smitty's car while Hector hugs Thalia. Hector has no words.

"I have to go," says Thalia.

From somewhere, Hector hands her an old coffee can half-filled with dirt. "For Diego. He'll explain in his own time." Hector's eyes fill with tears. "Now go."

23

ESSE EST PERCEPI, AUGUST 1987

"Phoenix got the story all wrong," says Crystal. "Thalia should have written it up."

"They reported it just as we told them," laughs Jack. "Just good reporting."

"I see where Hector was back at the warehouse this morning. Cleaning up, painting, fixing the hole in the wall, patching the bullet holes. Do you think he can move into our neighborhood now?" Julie stands behind the bar with her Bible open. The wind is up, and the rains will come hard later in the afternoon.

Smitty folds the newspaper and lays it on the table. "I asked him, but he said he would be leaving soon, heading back up to the reservation when the elders come for him. He said he didn't want to turn into a loser like the rest of us."

"He never said that," says Julie.

"Smitty's kidding, darlin'," laughs Jack. "Cocker will be pleased, but also sad over losing his only congregant."

"Jade's taking this pretty hard," says Crystal. Julie extends her hand across the bar and covers Crystal's hand. Crystal shakes her head softly. "Can you believe it was CJ?"

"I knew it all along," says Jack.

"I call bullshit on you, my old friend." Alf sits up and stretches his neck. "I'm gonna let you all in on a secret. It stays here. Maybe some time I'll tell Cocker and Libby, but no one else is to know." He looks to the four people in the bar. Three days have passed since the shooting. "CJ was a good guy; one of us. It hurts something terrible, and at his funeral I'll cry. I've been pondering what it would have taken for him to tell that asshole Lizardo about our affairs, and it hit me. Lizardo must have discovered about the murder of the snitch in the union."

Crystal blurts out, "What?"

"Relax, union girl. What's done is done. Can't be changed. The snitch was working for us when we found out. PD ordered it. It was

The Why Intersection

Carlos who fired the shot into the scab's house that injured the little girl. Did it to discredit the union but wasn't trying to hurt the girl. I was going to kill him if I could find him, but CJ found him first. We buried him up by the mine." Alf pauses for a sip of coffee. The others wait. "We may never find out how Lizardo discovered this, but somehow, he did. PD had offered that huge reward, and it had never been claimed. Lizardo was angling for that. My guess is he couldn't connect the dots and thought I fired into the house."

"Shit!" says Crystal softly but with feeling. "I always thought it was you."

"It's a nice theory, Alf. Blackmail. I can live with that," says Jack.

"What will you do now, Alf?" asks Crystal. "Will you ask for the reward?"

Alf laughs out loud. "You think PD would ever agree to giving me that money? And there'd be way too many questions, like where did Carlos disappear to." He shakes his head. "Either go back to my wife and kids or bring them back here. Been too long without them."

"More coffee, Julie, please," says Smitty. He returns to the paper.

Jack watches Julie fill three cups on the table. He looks to the empty chair. "We got an empty chair, hon."

Julie stops and stands straight up. She tilts her head, stands like a statue for a moment, but only for a moment before returning to her station behind the bar. She sets the coffee pot back in its stand and picks up her Bible. "I think it might just be best to move the chair to one of the other tables. Your table already has enough bullshitters for now."

Smitty smiles. "Cuss jar."

It goes quiet in the bar for a time, each pretending to occupy his or her time, but all of them thinking of the events at the Tabernacle in all its interpretations. A half-hour passes while only Smitty talks, commenting on various newspaper articles. "There was a false missile warning from Elmendorf in Anchorage." He smiles knowingly to himself. "It says here world population will surpass five billion this year. Maybe Cocker's been right about this all along. Too many people to expect all of us to get along." He turns the page. "Hey, Julie, there's a new *Star Trek* TV series coming on in September. Called 'The Next

249

Generation.' No William Shatner though." Nobody responds to his musings with more than an un-huh or hmmm.

Around noon Libby and Cocker enter through the side door. Libby had called earlier to tell them the Ajo hospital, the old Phelps Dodge company hospital, was releasing Cocker. She wasn't sure what he would want to do, losing his brother and all. He took a bullet in the upper arm, not life-threatening, but inconvenient for several weeks. Left arm. Libby helps him into his seat at the table and then goes to the bar where she sits next to Crystal.

The men reach across the table to shake his hand. They wait.

Julie watches. Cocker holds his head down slightly, his left arm pinned against his chest, his right hand softly on the table. She calls out, "Cock," and raises a bottle of beer.

He looks up and shakes his head. "Thanks, Julie, but maybe a cup of coffee would be better," he answers in his raspy voice.

Julie grabs Cocker's special cup from the shelf, an over-sized mug with a map of Texas on it, fills it, and walks it over to the table. She sets it down and then leans over and hugs Cocker from behind. "I'm so sorry about your brother," she whispers in his ear. Cocker reaches up with his right arm and returns Julie's embrace.

"Says here," reads Smitty, "President Reagan wants to meet with Gorbachev later and continue talking about arms reduction. Both countries will need to upgrade their computers."

"Better late than never," says Jack. "Doubt if much will ever come of it though."

At the bar Crystal turns to Libby. "Do you think Hector ever had that soul?"

Libby asks Julie for a shot of mescal from her private stash before answering. She sips it for a few minutes, each time studying the glass for enlightenment. "More likely a channeler, but I really don't know. There are things in Nature for which we have no explanation. We accept and move on, believing in the wisdom of I'itoi . . . God."

༄

Hector looks at his watch. One-thirty. Lunch time. He sets down his hammer, steps off the ladder, wipes his brow, and walks over to a table to get his sack lunch. The wind rattles the Tabernacle, a sign today's monsoon rain will be right on time. He steps outside to get a bit of sunshine, to study the clouds which are gathering over the Tohono O'odham reservation to the southeast over Baboquivari. Wet summer, a majestic time in the desert. A violent time. He feels no callings, just a sense of freedom and independence. He moves back inside, inside to a cooler spot. He sits on the floor and opens his sack. Oddly, there is a note in a plastic baggie that holds an apple.

"I came here, was directed here, by my grandfather from 25 years in the past. You were directed here, or carried here, by the wind. Each of the Guardians came here for an unexplained mission. Libby's right. We will never be able to explain this. It was. It's over. It's time to move on. But know that you will carry a part of me now with you wherever you go from here. And I you. You are a beautiful man, Hector Dehiya, and I will remember you." It is signed, *"T."*

∾

In St. Louis Thalia veers off I-44 onto I-70 for the leg to Indianapolis. Her passenger has said little, choosing to sleep or simply watch the scenery, over 1800 miles of solo driving for Thalia, stopping twice to sleep at houses in Roswell, New Mexico, and Rolla, Missouri. Just past Terre Haute, they will stop again, cook on a camp stove, and sleep in cheap sleeping bags just inches apart at a KOA campground. Another station. Thalia plans on another day-and-a-half of driving to get to Bay City, Michigan. She will not go over the speed limit, will not pull into Bay City after dark, and will not surprise her family. In Saginaw she will call and let her mother know.

"It's Tammy Frazier back home. I like Thalia, but it's not my name. It's the name Hector will remember me by." She rubs the back of her tired neck and moves her head from side to side. "I'm going to fall asleep like a baby tonight."

Her passenger nods his head slightly and bites the inside of his lip. Finally, he speaks a complete sentence, more than just a simple yes or no. "I'm looking forward to meeting your family." Thalia continues to look straight down the highway, but she smiles. "It will take some time, I imagine, and I hope they will be patient with me. I won't be able to tell them about my life, the hidden life, but there are some things."

"I understand. I can help you with that," says Thalia. They go quiet again. "How shall I introduce you? I mean, what do you want to be called?"

"I've been thinking about that. A lot. I think something common like John—John Folgers. He finally looks at Thalia. They both smile. "And I want you to tell me about your grandfather. He was the one who directed me to Why."

Thalia nods as if a missing piece of a puzzle has been found and waits for a moment. For the entire drive, her passenger has cradled the coffee can. Now, she asks, "What's that for? What does it mean?"

"Just dirt, I guess. Hector had it at the house in Why sitting on the kitchen counter. On the morning of that last day, he filled it with this desert dirt. I asked him why, but he just shook his head and indicated he didn't really know." John lifts the can to eye level. It's a red Folger's can. He points to the name, his name now. "He said a priest gave him this can back on his reservation. The desert is all about dust, swirling dust moving on the wind from place to place. Who's to say this Rubicon dust didn't start on his reservation or from Colorado?"

"What will you do with it now?" asks Thalia.

"I don't know. Maybe, when I get settled, I'll plant a cactus in it." John smiles.

"Your stay in my town will be temporary. After a while, after your credentials come and you've established a short backstory, you'll move to the Upper Peninsula and become a Yooper. I hope you like snow. The town of Kingsford is a bit different from Why."

Bellena Kramer feels her husband's relief. There is no more itch. It's done. She's glad. She sits with him and their daughter on the bench she purchased over a year ago overlooking a simple rock in the corner of St. Mary Cemetery a few miles south of Buena Vista, Colorado. The creek's flow at the end of the summer makes only a low babble.

"The rock stays," says Walt.

"I assumed it would," says Bellena.

The Why Intersection

Walt turns to his wife, takes her hand and smiles. He leans over and kisses Babette Princecella on the forehead. "I found out where the river is, the one Barkley referred to. I'm talking with Smithfield the day I left, telling him I couldn't figure that part out. You know, 'Cross over the river.' He looks down at the ground and tells me we're standing on it, but at that moment it was dry. Rubicon Wash. 'You see,' he said, 'this is what separates Rubicon from Why. Those people over there,' and he waved his hand over towards Why, 'don't believe. We do. Unless you commit, unless you cross this here wash, you can't live here. I can't explain it to you, Kramer,' he says, 'you just have to accept what happens here in my desert or you don't. If you don't, you're not a Rubiconer.'"

Princecella yawns. Bellena hands her to her father, stands and walks to the river, where she squats and lets her fingers touch the current. When she turns back to the cemetery, she sees Walt sitting on the ground next to his son's memory stone. He's talking gently to his daughter as she sits on his thigh, listening intently.

"*Esse est percepi*," he says. "To be is to be perceived." Princecella reaches over and takes hold of the necklace her father wears, the silver chain with a filed off copper key.

24

LATE SUMMER, 1987

A screen door bangs shut somewhere on the far side of Why, in the last neighborhood on the western edge of the Sonoran Desert. Dog barks and children's shrieks pierce the summer air at twilight, an evanescent time of day where hide and seek is still the favorite game. It is 1987 and time is catching up with this isolated town just as it will with every rural community in America. Cocker is late for his tee time at Waddell Smithfield's Golf and Gun Club. While he can't swing a club yet, he rides in the carts with Smitty and Jack and talks about overpopulation and The Rapture. For the moment, Cocker has given up drinking, but Jack believes it won't last. Libby has bet twenty dollars that it will, at least until Christmas. Julie prepares lesson plans for the neighborhood children when school begins in a few weeks. She will use a Howard Zinn book to teach history, her new act of rebellion against the State. Ruby, Crystal, and Jade are no longer picketing. The Union was decertified, and all legal charges were dropped; it had all been done by Phelps Dodge to intimidate the workers and picketers. The cowbell remains hanging from behind the bar, however.

Smitty hires a company out of South Tucson to build another two holes for his golf course. He writes a letter to Captain Cooley thanking him for sharing information over the previous year, information beyond generic computer failures. They are both convinced that the secret of the tragedy at Yamantov is secure—but for different reasons. Cooley responds that the tip about Dan that put Walt Kramer on the move that led Cooley on this investigation was ridiculous in retrospect. Smitty rewrites his will, leaving Rubicon to the Notajo Gang who are now grocers too. Still, Smitty has no plans for retiring to that greenest 19th Hole soon. He will continue to evaluate America's missile defense computers for The Government.

"All those other characters who muddy up the waters," as Miss Fisher taught to her junior high students when teaching *Of Mice and Men*, have moved on. They were directed to Why for a reason, but

The Why Intersection

now they are on their next journeys, each with a mutilated key given as an unexplained token by Waddell Smithfield, sent to him by a man who had a jar full of them. While some have left Rubicon, the wind will bring others, "just as it does in all fairy tales." The safe house at the Why Station will remain open for weary pilgrims in need of a respite. The dusty neighborhood in a harsh desert at the intersection of Arizona highways 85 and 86 makes no apologies for its existence.

THE END

www.ingramcontent.com/pod-product-compliance
Lightning Source LLC
LaVergne TN
LVHW010157070526
838199LV00062B/4400